THE EFFECTIVE
REFERENCE LIBRARIAN

LIBRARY AND INFORMATION SCIENCE

CONSULTING EDITORS: *Harold Borko and G. Edward Evans*
GRADUATE SCHOOL OF LIBRARY SCIENCE
UNIVERSITY OF CALIFORNIA, LOS ANGELES

Thomas H. Mott, Jr., Susan Artandi, and Leny Struminger
Introduction to PL/I Programming for Library and Information Science

Karen Sparck Jones and Martin Kay
Linguistics and Information Science

Manfred Kochen (Ed.)
Information for Action: From Knowledge to Wisdom

Harold Borko and Charles L. Bernier
Abstracting Concepts and Methods

G. Edward Evans
Management Techniques for Librarians

James Cabeceiras
The Multimedia Library: Materials Selection and Use

F. W. Lancaster
Toward Paperless Information Systems

H. S. Heaps
Information Retrieval: Computational and Theoretical Aspects

Harold Borko and Charles L. Bernier
Indexing Concepts and Methods

Gerald Jahoda and Judith Schiek Braunagel
The Librarian and Reference Queries: A Systematic Approach

Charles H. Busha and Stephen P. Harter
Research Methods in Librarianship: Techniques and Interpretation

Diana M. Thomas, Ann T. Hinckley, and Elizabeth R. Eisenbach
The Effective Reference Librarian

THE EFFECTIVE
REFERENCE LIBRARIAN

Diana M. Thomas
Ann T. Hinckley
Elizabeth R. Eisenbach
University of California, Los Angeles
Los Angeles, California

ACADEMIC PRESS

A Subsidiary of Harcourt Brace Jovanovich, Publishers

New York   London   Toronto   Sydney   San Francisco

ACADEMIC PRESS, INC.
111 Fifth Avenue, New York, New York 10003

United Kingdom Edition published by
ACADEMIC PRESS, INC. (LONDON) LTD.
24/28 Oval Road, London NW1 7DX

Library of Congress Cataloging in Publication Data

Thomas, Diana M.
    The effective reference librarian.

    (Library and information science)
    Includes bibliographies and index.
    1. Reference services (Libraries) I. Hinckley,
Ann T. II. Eisenbach, Elizabeth R. III. Title.
IV. Series.
Z711.T48   025.5'2   81-1037
ISBN 0-12-688720-9

PRINTED IN THE UNITED STATES OF AMERICA

81 82 83 84   9 8 7 6 5 4 3 2 1

Contents

Preface   *ix*

Introduction   **1**

CHAPTER 1
Reference Functions   **7**

Introduction   7
Reference/Directional Assistance   8
Instruction in the Use of the Library   10
Special Counseling Services   12
Compilation of Bibliographies for Library Users   15
Maintenance and Development of Special Indexes and Files   19
Interlibrary Loan   21
Split Positions   23
Troubleshooter   24
Public Relations Functions   25
References and Suggested Readings   25

CHAPTER 2
Resources for Reference Work   **27**

Introduction   27
A Reference Collection Policy   28
Reference Books and Principles of Their Selection   28
Nonbook Reference Resources   30
Selection Aids for Special Areas   32
The Stack Collection   38
References and Suggested Readings   38

CHAPTER 3
Evaluating Reference Sources   **41**

The Publishing of Reference Books and Serials   41
How to Examine a Reference Work   50

The Reviewing of Reference Sources   52
References and Suggested Readings   63

CHAPTER 4
Selection Aids for Reference Collections   **65**

Introduction   65
Selecting Books and Serials for the Basic Reference Collection   65
Current Awareness   82
Special Problems   90
References and Suggested Readings   93

CHAPTER 5
Desk Technique and the Library User   **95**

Introduction   95
The Reference Transaction   98
Special Concerns   126
References and Suggested Readings   134

CHAPTER 6
Administration   **137**

Importance of Administration   137
Importance of Personal Attributes   139
Management Systems   141
Responsibility and Authority   144
Organization   147
Goals and Objectives   151
Budget Preparation and Funding Mechanisms   158
Utilization of Staff from Other Sources   161
Personnel   162
References and Suggested Readings   169

CHAPTER 7
Current and Continuing Issues   **173**

Introduction   173
Philosophies of Reference Service: The Institutional View   174
The Librarian's Position   182
Social Responsibilities   189
Censorship   191
Technical Services Issues Critical for Public Services   192

APPENDIX
Responsibilities and Ethics: The Profession's View   **195**

Statement on Professional Ethics, 1975   195
A Commitment to Information Services: Developmental Guidelines   197
Library Bill of Rights   202
Resolution on Challenged Materials: An Interpretation of the
    Library Bill of Rights   203

Name and Title Index   *205*
Subject Index   *211*

Preface

This book is designed to introduce the library school student and the new librarian to the context and complexity of actual reference work. The skills to be cultivated by reference librarians are so numerous and varied that reference courses easily become fragmented and emphasize only isolated aspects of reference service. It has been over thirty years since the American Library Association published Margaret Hutchins' *Introduction to Reference Work,* and we have felt the lack of a current text that would reveal the multiple aspects of reference work. Here we describe how the reference department and its staff function in a variety of contexts, and discuss underlying considerations of which prospective reference librarians should be aware. We have tried to make our presentations clear and straightforward but not simplistic. Suggested readings and notes have been included at the ends of chapters where appropriate. Individual instructors can easily devise questions emphasizing aspects tailored to their classroom contexts.

Chapter 1 provides an overview of today's reference services, suggesting the rich possibilities for applying basic professional skills. The next three chapters treat the resources for reference work from a different perspective. Rather than list sources used to answer questions, we consider the identification, evaluation, and maintenance of reference materials. We hope the discussion of reference book publishing will be especially valuable. Chapter 5 covers the activities of the librarian at the desk. Methods of responding to patrons and their questions are discussed, as are other desk responsibilities, including safety, security, and difficult situations involving patrons or colleagues. Chapter 6 alerts the beginning reference librarian to the political and fiscal realities of providing information to library users. Administrative considerations and managerial styles are described, and some advice is proffered. The final chapter provides a framework for discussion of broad questions important not only to reference work, but also to librarianship as a whole.

From our combined six decades of experience, ranging from being the sole professional for a small collection through responsibilities in large and sophisticated libraries, we recognize reference librarianship as both demanding and rewarding, and we hope we have conveyed our pleasure and pride in our work.

Introduction

Reference work has an immediate appeal for the beginning library school student. For students faced with discouraging displays of new terminology and concepts in courses such as cataloging or information science, course work in the reference class at least offers the relief of studying some relatively familiar materials. Then there is the excitement of the hunt or search, which adds to the problem-oriented assignments the quality of a game. This combination occasionally results in premature and ill-advised decisions by some students that reference work is for them, and they want to plan their courses at library school accordingly. While reference instructors welcome the resulting dedication to classwork, this pleasure is usually coupled with a certain uneasiness. It is not difficult to teach the proper use of an encyclopedia or index, or even the necessary steps in successful search strategy, but mastery of these basic processes is little assurance that the student is adequately prepared or suited for reference work. A good librarian has a complex combination of personality traits and learned skills, and little of the former can be taught in the library science classroom.

It is easy to list and recite all of the personal characteristics of the successful reference librarian, although one runs the risk of having it sound a little like the Scout creed: A good reference librarian is tactful, intelligent, imaginative, ingenious, helpful, empathic, curious, persistent, energetic, sensitive, polite, and assured. Endowed with the gift of being able to both listen and question (at times, almost simultaneously) and possessed of a phenomenal memory, marvelous feet, and a perpetual smile, this paragon always is ready to meet the public without losing balance or a sense of humor.

The reasonable reader readily sees that most of these traits should be acquired and fostered early in life. Yet reference instructors teach students who legally qualify as adults. Although it is a little late to change bad habits, the conscientious teacher subtly tries to instill both a sense of awareness and a sense of importance of these attributes. New techniques are constantly explored, and a few, like the use of the videocamera, are helpful in emphasizing the necessity of satisfactory interpersonal communication. The true meaning of the cliché "A picture is worth more than ten thousand words," is never more evident than when students first see themselves on camera after simulating reference interviews in the classroom. Failures in body language and nonverbal communication are conveyed instantly, and usually no comments are necessary.

But for the most part, teachers' efforts are toward encouraging and strengthening performance in academic areas and skills that can be learned in the library school's program. The authors of this work have had experience behind both reference desks and classroom lecterns and have felt strongly the lack of an adequate text on the training and education of the reference librarian. Bibliographical guides to reference books are numerous; current guides to administering a reference department are nonexistent. This book will attempt to discuss fully some of the major segments of work in a reference department with emphasis on reference functions, administrative techniques, and professional responsibility. It is designed to be useful to both instructor and student, to serve as an incentive to classroom discussions, and it is hoped, to fill some of the lacunae that now exist in the literature of librarianship.

The academic areas and skills also need to be analyzed and understood by both instructors and students. What do students need to *know* for an entry-level position in reference work? What do reference departments look for in their professional personnel? On which courses in library school other than the ones set aside and marked "reference" should students concentrate? Are there classes in other schools and departments that would be useful?

Here the ground is firmer. There are many competencies that the prospective reference librarian can acquire; some things *can* be taught, and the student is being poorly advised if these skills are not emphasized. The list again is long but not unmanageable. Within the library school, students should be urged to concentrate on their cataloging courses, and, if time permits, to pursue advanced studies in this field. It is inconceivable that a librarian can function effectively in a reference department without a strong foundation in cataloging and in the variety of classification schemes. Directly or indirectly, bibliographical questions usually comprise the greatest number of reference queries that pass the desk on a single day. Interpreting the card catalog to users is a reference function but is impossible without understanding both its rationale and idiosyncrasies. Interlibrary loan is based on bibliographical checking, and more hours may be spent in front of catalog drawers and in checking bibliographies than behind the desk. Library schools may teach cataloging and reference as separate courses but, by the time a student graduates, these two functions should have merged. Providing access to the library's resources is the reference librarian's job, and this access is afforded primarily by the library's catalog.

Reference librarians select books as well as interpret their contents. In public libraries, they frequently perform a reader's advisory service. The selection of reference books will be covered in detail in three chapters of this book, but it should be emphasized here that courses in book selection and reading interests should not be slighted by students ambitious for a reference position. Familiarity with publishers and with national and trade bibliographies is easily gained; the authors certainly hope that all librarians enjoy reading and will share their enthusiasms and tastes with readers.

Ideally, reference librarians also will be good bibliographers. Most library schools offer special bibliography courses which are invaluable because of the emphasis on specialized reference tools found in large reference departments. They help provide the library school student with some ''subject'' competence and an overview of a field of study. And when faced with the task of compiling a bibliography, the librarian with such a background should approach such an assignment with confidence. There are those who accuse librarians of only consuming bibliographies; with adequate preparation, they also should be able to lead the field in compiling them.

Interpersonal communication does not stop with the patron; reference librarians must work with colleagues both within their department and in other sections of the library. Concurrently, they may both supervise and be supervised. Management and personnel skills increasingly are recognized as a competence with a legitimate place in the library school curriculum. Such courses also afford the opportunity of at least superficially touching upon problem areas of personality by providing an appropriate forum for discussion of the difficulties faced when working with others.

Finally, no reference librarian can afford to ignore any opportunity of gaining familiarity with computers. Increasingly, advertisements for reference positions are ending with the following words: online experience desirable. Today, it is difficult to conceive of a library school that neglects to offer its students a chance to experiment with databases and gain at least a nodding acquaintance with programming and a computer language.

And what of the reference courses themselves? Surely, the student must start with a good working knowledge of the reference sources. This must be taught in the classroom and generally forms the core of most reference courses. As much as some students would prefer spending all of their time talking about search strategy, problem patrons, and the reference process, they are going to find that employers will insist that they be able to use effectively the major reference tools at the time they are hired. It is true that new works constantly are being published, but librarians should be able to handle efficiently the analysis that these new works require if they have been properly trained in the basic skills of evaluating reference sources. There is no reason why reference techniques cannot be integrated into discussions of the reference works; one should not be separated from the other.

The major areas of knowledge that the prospective reference librarian can acquire in library school have been described briefly, but these are only some of the learned skills needed behind the desk. A good general education is essential; excellent reference techniques should be accompanied by an interest in the information sought by the user and by some ability to evaluate it. An increasing number of general reference departments are demanding a subject background, and the single master's degree in library science may be considered insufficient preparation for reference work in an academic library. But with or without the second advanced degree, all librarians working in public service positions should keep current in world affairs and special areas of interest in their library.

A neglected area is competence in foreign languages. Any librarian who is fluent in Spanish will have an edge in applying for a public service position in most public libraries today. The Spanish-speaking population in the United States is large and rapidly growing; it looks as if this country may have a permanent bilingual ethnic minority. To be able to provide library service to this population in their own language is an obvious advantage for any (prospective) librarian. No large library restricts its reference tools or service to the English language. Bibliographical proficiency in even the more exotic tongues is considered a reasonable demand by such libraries. It is unfortunate that with the need for foreign language skills increasing, many colleges and universities are lessening or eliminating language requirements. Many library school students are suffering from the parochialism of this trend in education and must compensate for it at the graduate level.

Those interested in personal interaction should note that psychology departments and education and management schools have a remarkable array of courses covering this area, as well as having members of their faculties specially trained in these areas. Perhaps the time will come when library school faculties also will be expected to have this kind of teaching competence. Also in the areas of communication, commitment to full reference service means that librarians not only must be able to provide information service, but also must be able to instruct patrons in the use of the library and to prepare appropriate bibliographical aids. So, teaching aptitude and writing ability must be added to the impressive array of credentials held by the ideal reference librarian.

By now it is apparent that reference librarians need a wide combination of talents and skills to be successful on the job. Today, it also must be recognized that a high level of public accountability and responsibility is expected. Since they interpret the library's resources to users and act as an intermediary between these users and the rest of the library staff, the reference librarians' role in establishing the library's image and standing in the community cannot be overestimated. Therefore, their training must take into account complete acceptance of the importance of this unique contribution. If it fails to do so, then education for reference librarianship fails, and this is not acceptable or supportable in our present society.

Anyone who works with people must be prepared for the unexpected. Perhaps that is why a career as a reference librarian offers so much diversity and excitement. At the same time, it also is a demanding and difficult profession. The authors hope that this textbook will shed enough light on the predictable elements of reference librarianship so that students will be able to understand and withstand the heat that inevitably will be generated if they decide to work in this environment. Then, they should be better-equipped to anticipate problems, turning them into challenges rather than burdens, and have the time and enthusiasm to look for creative remedies and new solutions. This requires a successful mixture of competence and imagination, which, the authors feel, is the combination that, without exception, can be found in every effective reference librarian.

CHAPTER 1

Reference Functions

INTRODUCTION

Because libraries exist in order to provide their clientele with books and other information sources, they also must provide various services in order to make these materials accessible. Public service personnel are therefore among the busiest members of a library's staff. Until such time as our cataloging and indexing systems require no explanations, and until libraries succeed in acquiring all desired materials in advance of need, the library's clientele will require knowledgeable, sympathetic assistance. Indeed, given human nature, it is likely that individuals will still find librarians necessary to explain the use of even a perfect information resource and delivery system.

Of the various public service functions of a library, an astonishing array is performed by reference librarians. Because they are in the "front lines," reference librarians frequently determine whether a library is successful in serving its clientele. It is therefore crucial that they represent the library with distinction.

Reference librarians must also expect to serve in the development and utilization of information networks which extend beyond the confines of their own institutions. Because of rising costs and the increasing numbers of information sources, more libraries are acquiring less of the available materials. Consequently, information networks have evolved that embody the concept of resource sharing. Books and photocopies of articles are obtained by libraries through interlibrary loan networks, and the matching of an information need with a remote information resource increasingly is being done by the information and referral centers. Metropolitan library networks, regional library consortia, and multi-university systems all are developing increasingly sophisticated union lists and communication mechanisms, and they are beginning to use each other's resources more than ever before. Bibliographic utilities, such as those developed by Ohio College Library Center (OCLC), the Research Libraries Information Network (RLIN), and the Washington Library Network (WLN) have revolutionized reference and interlibrary loan work, in addition to providing shared cataloging capabilities. Never has so much information been available to so many, and perhaps in recognition of the increased resources, independent learners are proliferating.

Even reference librarians who do not work at a library which is a member of a formal network can obtain desired information by writing or telephoning the nearest center (or library that is a network member). Librarians have always responded generously to a request for assistance from a colleague, so long as the requesting librarian has been careful to give precise information as to what is needed and what has already been checked without result.

Because of this expanded universe in which a reference librarian operates, there is virtually no limitation on the demands for varied types of assistance, just as there is no limit to the number and type of reference tools which a librarian may use to assist with a particular problem. Computers, reference books, periodicals, the telephone, correspondence, and consultation with experts all are means relied upon by reference librarians responding to the needs of library users. In addition, ingenuity, sound knowledge of reference techniques and sources of information, as well as emotional stamina and the desire to help are personal qualities which must be brought to bear on each of the reference functions discussed hereafter.

REFERENCE/DIRECTIONAL ASSISTANCE

The basic function provided by anyone who serves as a reference librarian is to give informational and directional assistance to the users of the library. Directional questions can be minimized (but never eliminated) by the use of attractive graphics, informational sheets, and audiovisual aids. Whether a library has a separate station or desk for reference service depends on funding, administrative organization, and available space. Many libraries offer reference assistance from one main station that serves as the circulation and the reference desk. In a small library this arrangement is not only frugal but also efficient. It is impressive to have the librarian in a small local library say, ''I'm sorry, the library's only copy of that book was checked out two days ago, but your name will be third on the waiting list!'' Having one skillful librarian providing all services can be more dazzling than having a computerized system of access. There are always program limitations for computerized systems, whereas the librarian can exercise unprogrammed inventiveness in handling particular problems. Conversely, use of a computer can expedite good service by freeing the librarian to do other necessary work.

Separate Service Desks

Aspiring reference librarians should be prepared to serve at any one (or a combination of) service desks, because the organization and arrangement of libraries vary as greatly as do the inquiries received for information. Where the volume of use of a library is large enough, separate reference desks for different subject disciplines and children's collections are frequently warranted. Under these circumstances, it is desirable to provide general directional assistance near the entrance to the library, perhaps at the loan desk or at the library's catalog. These information stations often function as screening devices as well as referral centers and may be manned by students, nonlibrarians, or librarians. Sometimes a small core collection of reference materials is maintained at these points in order to answer simple "look-up" questions. Some reference service desks maintain very extensive core collections and utilize computer terminals to access the library's automated acquisition and cataloging systems. Online, interactive searching of commercially available databases may also be done at the reference desk, although terminals used for these more complex searches, which require a carefully planned search strategy, are generally located away from the distracting activity of the reference desk.

TELEPHONE ASSISTANCE

If there are sufficient funds, telephone assistance is usually available at one or all of the service desks described in the foregoing. To protect the walk-in clientele from the annoying interruption of ringing telephones, telephone service is sometimes provided at a separate station, away from public service desks. Some libraries have a policy of not answering the telephone if any person is waiting for service; others have a policy of asking the caller to "please wait"; and still others have tape-recorded messages explaining that phone service is offered only between certain hours or that the librarians are busy. It is hoped that no library permits telephone calls to interrupt the reference process initiated by a person who has come to request service at the reference desk. Simple courtesy requires that a person be given precedence over a ringing telephone. If a library cannot manage to provide telephone service and to assist walk-in patrons, it is better not to attempt to give telephone assistance.

CORRESPONDENCE

Most libraries receive a fair number of correspondence inquiries and attempt to respond to them as time permits. Many inquiries refer specifically to local history and special collections for which a particular library may be the single best source. In such an instance, even though one may not have the staff resources to provide research services, a reference librarian should attempt to respond briefly, confirming or denying that certain needed materials are in the collection and perhaps to suggest means by which the correspondent can obtain the desired specific information (e.g., by suggesting the purchase of a photocopy, the hiring of a "research assistant" from a local educational institution, or perhaps a visit to a library in the correspondent's own vicinity to consult particular sources or to initiate an interlibrary loan request). On the other hand, a librarian should not feel obliged to spend time on frivolous or irrational requests. Common sense suggests that it is usually unproductive (and even foolish) to respond and thereby to encourage further inquiries from "cranks." If the courtesy of some reply seems desirable, a form letter stating that the library cannot answer such inquiries may best serve the purpose.

When one receives an inquiry from another librarian, it is a matter of professional courtesy to do all that time permits in making a response. However, it is equally important that as a librarian, one never writes to another library asking for assistance without first having investigated all possible sources in one's own library. A cardinal rule for making a reference inquiry or for initiating an interlibrary loan request is always to provide a published source of reference for the elusive citation and to indicate the sources already checked. Unfortunately, inexperienced librarians frequently shortchange their clientele by not using all of the resources in their own collection in an intelligent, thorough manner. Sloppy reference work and lack of verification effort inevitably result in damaging a librarian's credibility with other librarians from whom assistance may be sought. When this occurs, the careless librarian's requests may be returned after only a cursory check indicates that the requested information is "nil as cited."

INSTRUCTION IN THE USE OF THE LIBRARY

Library users are introduced to the specifics and vagaries of each library in a variety of ways and instructional levels. Signs, library guides, leaflets on how to find a book or a periodical, tape/slide shows, video displays, and audio tour units are some of the most frequently used methods to acquaint a newcomer with the art of using a library. With the advent of computer-based reference tools, many librarians are also finding that demonstrations of these automated systems provide tantalizing bait to lure the nonlibrary user to instructional sessions. Reference librarians are constantly searching for more effective means of providing such instruction so that their time can be spent assisting users who have less routine needs.

GENERAL ORIENTATION/TOURS

The most elementary form of instruction which reference librarians should be prepared to offer is at the general orientation level. Simple explanations of the physical organization of the library, the content of the card catalog and other bibliographic records, hours of service, and where to go for assistance are topics repeatedly covered by reference librarians. Sometimes the information is conveyed by some of the aids mentioned above, but the librarian also must expect to provide the same information verbally. If one works in the library of an educational institution, tours at the beginning of each school session are customary. Special orientation programs may be arranged for all new students, and self-paced instruction programs with learning exercises are often useful.

COMPILATION OF LIBRARY GUIDES AND FINDING AIDS

Traditionally, reference librarians have developed and provided library guides which are intended to provide a general introduction and orientation to the use of the library. This type of general guide should be distinguished from the more specific ones developed in support of bibliographic instruction. Sometimes there are self-guided tours which describe the library services and indicate locations of particular tools. The forms they take may be leaflets, workbooks perhaps intended to accompany audio units, or narration developed to accompany tape/slide shows or video displays. Often such guides are developed as a single sheet or small leaflet to explain the use of library resources such as the card catalog, the *Monthly Catalog of United States Government Publications,* or periodical indexes. Listings, often produced from the library's computerized serials or acquisitions files, may be developed to identify titles received by the library in certain languages and/or subject fields.

Most reference librarians would agree, however, that unless these aids are attractively presented and the reference librarian on duty presents a cold, formidable appearance (akin to *La Belle Dame sans Merci*), library users prefer to ask rather than to read about the library's services. Prominently displayed slide shows and audio units keyed to the use of a particular tool on display seem to offer the only real competition to the reference librarian in providing general guidance on the use of the library. But unless such devices are simple to operate, they may defeat their purpose.

Another variation of a finding aid, perhaps seen less often in this era of budget constraints, is the annotation of various bibliographies to show which of the cited items is owned by the library. The checking and noting of call numbers for the books indexed in the *Essay and General Literature Index* and for the sources of Walker's *Twentieth-Century Short Story Explication* is a service much appreciated by library users. Unless the library is very small, however, such checking is rarely done by the professional staff.

CLASSROOM INSTRUCTION/BIBLIOGRAPHIC LECTURES

In academic institutions reference librarians must often be prepared to give specific lectures on the bibliography of a particular discipline and to teach courses devoted to research methodology and the use of library resources. Some-times the classes or lectures are offered by an academic department within the institution, and librarians participate as lecturers. The library may or may not receive reimbursement for the librarians' time in these instances, but increasing numbers of colleges and universities are developing formal programs of biblio-graphic instruction in which the library is compensated for the instructional work of its staff. Indeed, many libraries themselves are offering such courses of instruction, although the administration of such programs is expensive and must be weighed against other service obligations.

The level of detail for this type of instruction is considerably greater than for general orientation programs and can range from specific, one-shot sessions on how to handle interlibrary loan requests, or bibliographical sources for material on the dance, to a full-length course on the sources of information for the social sciences. Various teaching aids, including CAI (Computer Assisted Instruction), can be employed here.

ORIENTATION AND TRAINING OF LIBRARY STAFF

One usually thinks of a reference librarian's instructional duties as being focused solely on library users, but in a library where there is more than one staff member, one soon discovers that in-house training of staff (not just reference staff) is often a function of the reference librarian. Ordinarily the training of staff revolves around specific library procedures, but the location and use of various reference tools are sometimes the subject of special tours and briefings. The composition of the card catalog and the filing rules which govern it are also frequest subjects of in-house training sessions.

In training reference librarians, "team teaching" at the reference desk is desirable. Further, evidence is accumulating to show that videotaping the refer-ence desk operation (in an unobtrusive way) helps reference librarians see how—as well as how *not* to do it (Mucci, 1976). There is probably no better or more entertaining way of improving desk techniques than by providing staff with the opportunity to see blunders which they occasionally commit as well as the laudable *savoir faire* with which they dispatch some reference questions.

SPECIAL COUNSELING SERVICES

Similar to library instruction efforts are the special counseling services which libraries can provide. Sometimes the services are set up in an impromptu way to meet some emergency need. Information on how to apply for financial or legal assistance after fire, flood, or earthquake may be provided. More often, how-ever, counseling services are of an on-going nature in response to regularly expressed or observed needs of the library's clientele. While it is admittedly difficult to distinguish some of these counseling services from what many consider to be standard reference service, the emphasis given them in many libraries prompts the following separate discussions.

READER'S ADVISORY SERVICE

When library users do not know what they want to read, a reference librarian must be prepared to suggest specific titles and subject headings which will coincide with a user's particular interests. Naturally, this service can be better performed if the librarian has catholic interests and is widely read. It is a delectable opportunity to introduce a patron to the writings of a favorite author, such as M. F. K. Fisher, whose works, one hopes, will delight the patron both for their gastronomical *tours de force* as well as for the unforgettable anecdotes. If one encounters a young patron who is an animal lover, such books as Ernest Thompson Seton's *Wild Animals I Have Known,* or Kipling's *The Jungle Books,* or (for a fact-oriented, older reader) Konrad Lorenz' *On Aggression,* may enthrall the patron and cause his or her addiction to the librarian's recommendations. Whether a patron is seeking fact or fiction, assisting them to find material of interest is tremendously satisfying. The sources which one can use to stay *au courant* as a reader's advisor are discussed in a later chapter, but nothing can take the place of constant reading in all varieties of fact and fiction on the part of the reference librarian. One's personal response to a particular book, conveyed with warmth and enthusiasm, is likely to produce high levels of user satisfaction and to generate scores of devoted library patrons.

I & R (INFORMATION AND REFERRAL)

Reference service has always had a leg in the camp of social welfare, simply because reference librarians must have the social conscience of welfare workers if they are to provide patient guidance and assistance for those seeking to use library resources. In the last few years, however, public libraries have begun to offer in a more active way, some of the information and referral services previously provided in communities by various social service agencies. What this means is that reference librarians go beyond the point of identifying a *source* to meet an individual's need; they actively make a *referral* to an appropriate agency. The information aspect of the function usually is subordinate to the responsibility of insuring that the patron knows exactly where to go and what to do to get whatever personal assistance is necessary. Much of the work is done by telephone, and the reference librarian may even make an appointment for the patron with an individual in the appropriate agency. For example, an unwed woman who fears she is pregnant may have appointments made for her at a medical clinic, followed by appointments with an attorney in a legal assistance society, and counselors in abortion clinics or maternity homes. In a very few libraries, specific personal counseling may be given, although that is obviously "foreign to the training, work, and expectations of most library professionals" (Childers, 1979, p. 2037).

To publicize these services, librarians have begun outreach programs in order to encourage their community clientele to use the constantly updated files of local resources. Standard advertising mechanisms, such as spots on radio and television, signs in buses and on billboards, and widely disseminated leaflets are used if money is available. Many libraries have built I & R services into their budgets on a fairly generous scale, perhaps reasoning that the library's increased prominence in giving essential community assistance will result in larger budget allocations. Nevertheless, I & R services can be very costly in themselves because of the continual need to develop and maintain information files and to compile and update directories. Such files and directories may be computer-produced in order to streamline the process of updating the information, and they may be accessed in an online interactive mode in order to expedite the retrieval of the most current information. Additional telephone lines are another cost which will probably be necessary, and, of course, more staff to handle telephone inquiries and extensive counseling may also be required.

Happily, except for the debatable personal counseling aspect of I & R, a reference librarian's training is ideal for these duties, and a new librarian should master the techniques and sources very quickly. Good reference service has always required that a librarian refer a patron to other libraries or avenues of assistance, if the user's needs cannot be met by the library's local resources.

TERM PAPER CLINICS

In academic libraries serving undergraduates, term paper clinics frequently are established. Students are encouraged to come to group or individual sessions where a librarian provides advice on research methodology, format, and bibliographical style. Sometimes the librarian prepares a special guide to be handed out to students who come to the clinics or to be distributed at the reference desk. In some colleges and universities, such term paper counseling is provided in conjunction with particular classes and in cooperation with particular instructors. The reference librarian may provide continual counseling to individual students as the preparation of their assigned papers progresses, and the students' levels of desperation reach their zenith.

THESIS ADVISING

The next step in academic counseling is to establish a thesis advisory service. In this instance the librarian must work very closely with the graduate division of the university and with the various academic departments which require theses and dissertations. In some institutions, physical and format standards may be determined by the librarian to meet archival requirements. The same reference librarian may work with the student in resolving research and bibliographical style problems for the duration of the thesis project.

SPECIAL SUBJECT COUNSELING

If a library has strength in special collections such as patents or genealogical materials, it may behoove the reference librarian to offer special workshops or counseling sessions in their use. If such sessions are advertised in local news-papers, they usually are heavily attended. Instructional guides, tailored to the use of particular reference works, can be handed out freely or used in conjunction with these group instruction activities.

COMPILATION OF BIBLIOGRAPHIES FOR LIBRARY USERS

While many libraries manage to provide lists of references on certain currently important subjects which can be consulted or given away to interested users, most libraries lack the funds to compile specific subject bibliographies to meet the needs of individual users. Special libraries that exist to serve a select clientele are a notable exception, and their librarians are accustomed to producing bibliographies on demand which will assist their business, industrial, medical, or other specialized clientele. These bibliographies are still compiled manually in most American libraries, even though technological advances and the existence of cataloging databases and computerized versions of printed indexes and abstracts are rapidly changing the picture.

Although computer-produced bibliographies can usually be produced more efficiently than those compiled by hand (and are discussed specifically in the following section), the use of the computer is not always possible, feasible, or desirable. A reference librarian may lack the funds to obtain a computer-produced bibliography, or, the subject of the needed bibliography may not be adequately covered by existing databases, or, the subject may be such that the simple photocopying of a few pages from an index under a single heading would be the most cost-effective way of producing a needed list of references. For any of these reasons, a reference librarian may find that a careful, manually conducted search of appropriate sources is required. As with any bibliographic research, it is important to note the sources from which each reference came. In the event of any incorrect citations, one can then return to the "scene of the crime" and discover whether the error was in the source or in one's fatigued perception of it.

When references have been assembled, the bibliography may be formally typed in a classified arrangement, an alphabetized list, or it may be presented as a stack of carefully sorted index cards. Instead of the bibliographic listing, it may even be presented as a collection of books and journals with relevant pages marked. Should this be the case, the reference librarian is performing a "documents delivery" service as well as compiling a bibliography.

COMPUTER-PRODUCED BIBLIOGRAPHIES

Because library users are generally attracted by the idea that computers (and reference librarians) save them work, inquiries about computer-produced bibliographies as well as numerical databases can be expected by every reference librarian. Not only are numbers of the most frequently used indexes, abstracts, and directories produced by computer, but also some important bibliographies such as the *International Bibliography of Research in Marriage and the Family* (and its supplements), and thesauri such as *Thesaurus Linguae Graecae*. If the data stored in the computer is updated regularly and more often than a printed version, database publishers frequently provide (for a fee) direct access to the computer's files through telecommunications lines. Thus a librarian, or anyone else with a computer terminal and telephone connections, can "dial-up" a computer's information files and obtain the most current information from the databank. This presupposes, of course, that the library has entered into the necessary contract with the commercial vendor or database supplier who has the desired databases "mounted" and accessible by special passwords in return for a specific sum of money, usually assessed on a "per hour" use rate.

If a library expects constant use of a particular database from a supplier or vendor (perhaps a cataloging database such as OCLC), there may be a "leased" or "dedicated" line devoted solely to the access of a particular database in return for a stipulated annual fee plus a "per citation" or "record" assessment for information retrieved and printed. There is no limit to the variations in charging schemes, and librarians should be alert to the advantages of group contracts when considering acquiring the right of access to these automated sources for their libraries.

The primary advantage of computer-based literature searching is that one can, within the limits of each database and search system, have the computer identify, sort, match, and eliminate particular references with great speed—and then have the desired citations organized and printed out in a specified format. Another advantage is that some computerized versions of indexes and abstracting services, such as Medline and Psychological Abstracts, give a greater number of subject and other "access points" to a bibliographic citation than do their printed counterparts.

Every vendor such as System Development Corporation, Lockheed Missiles and Space Company, and Bibliographic Retrieval Services, as well as the database publishers such as the New York Times Information Bank and the National Library of Medicine has its own search system by means of which one gives orders to the computer in order to retrieve the desired data. Some systems provide access to the same indexing or abstracting databases but vary in the approaches that can be used in a search, and it behooves a good "search" librarian to be aware of these differences. Most subjects require careful formulation of a computer search strategy, and one vendor's system may be better than another for retrieving a bibliography of relevant citations on a certain subject from a particular database. If the search features are equal, cost may be the deciding factor. (Different vendors have different rates.) Sometimes the search language or the way a particular automated information file has been structured will not permit precise retrieval of relevant citations (e.g., to retrieve information on oil prices in Europe, one may very well have to list each European country separately). The reference librarian must be prepared to judge how successful a search may be and so counsel the prospective user. Some individuals are satisfied with a 50% "hit" rate because they feel they can more quickly weed out the "garbage" than they could compile the needed bibliography by hand; other individuals are irate if 5% of the retrieved references are not relevant. There is no way to predict precisely the outcome of a computer search, so reference librarians must advise their clientele of possible disappointment and encourage them to investigate all of the printed sources in preparation for, or instead of, a computer search.

Retrieval of Data—Online and Offline

Once a reference librarian has decided that a computer search is an appropriate means for compiling a bibliography for a user and the search system has been selected (if there is a choice), the only consideration is how much time to spend conducting the search in an "online" mode. Online searches are conducted while one maintains a telephone connection to the computer and can give immediate commands to modify, refine, or discontinue the search. This is a more expensive process, but it permits one to negotiate with the computer and to call up references immediately for examination in either video or printed form. Search parameters which are defined in "interactive" negotiation include the number of years or months of the file being searched, various specific topics, names, combinations of concepts and words, exclusion of phrases or words, and so on. If the number of retrieved citations is large, however, or if one does not have a printer attached to the terminal, a command for offline prints usually is given after the initial sample of retrieved citations has proved to be satisfactory.

Offline searches, usually processed at night and batched according to database, are more efficiently performed when one already has formulated the search strategy and commands in an online mode. If one has to formulate a search offline, the search strategy cannot be assessed until the first results have been printed offline and sent to the librarian. Then additional time elapses while the "profile" is modified to improve the accuracy of the retrieval process. Although compilation of retrospective bibliographies *online* has all but replaced the *offline* batch process (except for SDI services discussed in the following section and for the printing of large numbers of citations which would be too costly to print online), a few databases are accessible only in the offline mode.

SDI (Selective Dissemination of Information)

SDI searches are formulated to meet a current-awareness need, and they are an excellent example of good use of the offline mode of data retrieval. Thus, if one has already had an online search to produce a large retrospective bibliography on pregnancy as a factor in high school dropouts, the librarian can instruct the computer (with some systems) to perform the same search each month when new data have been added to the file. The profiles for such search requests are stored by the computer, and the requests are then batched and run offline at appropriate, regular intervals, with the results mailed to the subscribing library or sometimes directly to the individual. Depending on how often a user wants updated information and how often it is added to the file, it may be economically more advantageous to run the same search online every six months, rather than storing the profile in the computer and paying for the storage plus a monthly printout.

SEARCHER QUALIFICATIONS

Reference librarians who are trained and experienced in the use of the printed versions of automated files are also recognized as being exceedingly adept in adapting to the use of online databases. Familiarity with the nature of an index (e.g., does it have a particular structured subject arrangement such as the Library of Congress subject authority file; or does it permit only free text searching on selected keywords from the title, abstract, or article; or both?) and skill in conducting a careful interrogation to determine the user's precise needs give a reference librarian the essential qualifications for conducting computer-based reference work. To add this dimension of service to a library's operation, funding must be secured for sufficient online practice time and training workshops. Potential search librarians can then be trained to master the mechanics of the terminal, the different search languages, and the peculiarities of each automated file.

Although the use of databases seemed to be very mysterious and deserving of exceptional treatment only a few years ago, librarians and their clientele now have recognized that automated information retrieval is a logical extension of good reference service and is not usefully categorized or glamorized as a separate function. Library users who are captivated by the idea of an automated search can be easily steered to all of the relevant sources for their information needs—not just to a computer search service—if the automated tools are recognized as part of the regular reference repertoire of a librarian. It is doubtful that a commercial search service would refer a prospective client to all of the relevant printed sources freely available in a library, and for this reason it is important that such services be offered through a library.

In the future, the number of library users who can themselves conduct an online, interactive search will increase, but reference librarians should be prepared to be the "intermediaries" and to perform "delegated" searches for the majority of libraries' clientele. The intricacies for each system and database's software (i.e., the search language and access mechanisms used to instruct the computer) require frequent use in order to maintain proficiency. Most library users would rather not have to concern themselves with learning complex search languages in order to retrieve desired information any more than they wish to master our cataloging rules. It is also difficult for the average library user (and alas, even the librarian) to keep abreast of the new information tools in a particular field. Reference librarians, therefore, can be assured of an essential role in the use of complex, computerized tools and must keep up with the development of new files and changes in search languages. Today, it is no longer sufficient to be aware of only new printed sources.

MAINTENANCE AND DEVELOPMENT OF SPECIAL INDEXES AND FILES

Traditionally, reference librarians have developed and maintained in-house files and indexes to meet local needs. The various categories of special files and indexes, discussed in the following, usually have been designed in a printed medium, but, of course, with the advent of computer technology these files and indexes can be developed and maintained in an automated version. If the file is large, instead of typing the information on 3 × 5-inch index cards, it may be more economical to have the same data converted to a machine-readable file. This data then can be manipulated and retrieved according to the access keys (e.g., subject headings, names, numbers, and so on) set up in the computer program.

REFERENCE/INFORMATION FILES

When a reference librarian spends any length of time on a question for which there is no obvious source to provide an answer, it is often a good idea to make an information note or card on the subject. If specific subject headings are established for such information (i.e., an authority file), considerable time can be saved the next time the question is asked. The key to the successful utilization of such a file is to communicate the availability of it to all members of the reference staff and to remind them to maintain familiarity with the contents. Elusive quotations, the names of the architects who designed and built the library and other local buildings, and the existence of a bibliography on a certain subject in an issue of a journal are examples of items which can be usefully incorporated into an information file. One must be sure that such information cards, or pages in the reference manual, are dated, include the source of the information, and provide the name or initials of the librarian who contributed the data. It then becomes an easier matter to determine if the information may be out-of-date and in need of revision. Conscientious maintenance of such a file is not as time-consuming as repetitious searches on the same recurrent question.

Of course, reference librarians often benefit by developing their own files of information. The names and phone numbers of irreplaceable "human resources," the citation to an article on evaluating reference services, or a transliteration table for an unfamiliar non-Roman alphabet are all examples of information kept by reference librarians for their own use. Obviously, even such a personal file is only as useful as the system devised by which the information can be retrieved. Unsystematic storing of notes and file cards can keep a would-be reference librarian unproductively busy.

Indexing of Local Newspapers/In-House Publications/Institutional Archives

Reference librarians are frequently responsible for compiling indexes to local publications and documents which are not indexed in any of the standard services. Indexes to the local newspapers, of interest to general, trade, or special communities, are a boon to the library's users. The library's own publications and documents recording the activities of important institutions such as municipal governments, corporations, or the university where the library is located, represent another category of material which often requires indexing by reference librarians. These special indexes must be regularly updated, carefully utilizing subject and name authority files, and always anticipating that the index should be of sufficiently good quality that it could be reproduced in, for example, a photo offset process, or manipulated and reproduced in varying forms by a computer.

Should the library be part of an information network, indexing assignments can be shared among the participating libraries with beneficial effect. It obviously makes no sense for every library in a region to put its librarians to work indexing the same publications. Instead, once the level of indexing is agreed upon and authority files established, librarians can pool their efforts and provide invaluable access to local documents and publications in a cost-effective manner.

Such indexes are a valuable link in the whole chain of national information resources—another reason to be sure that the indexing system and the authority file conform to those used on a national scale.

CLIPPING FILES

Libraries with responsibilities for providing detailed, specialized information frequently subscribe to specific newspapers and journals in duplicate in order to clip articles and illustrations of interest for particular subject files. Libraries with microform subscriptions frequently clip paper copies after the microform is received, and commercial clipping services are also used if funds are available, and if they can supply the clippings with the desired regularity. Reference librarians who work for motion picture companies, public libraries, and performing and visual arts libraries are among those for whom specialized clipping files are often a necessity. A library may have clearly defined policies as to which subject illustrations will be clipped, or the library may leave it to the discretion of the reference librarian. A librarian who is well-acquainted with the library's clientele will have a sharp instinct for preserving needed materials. Recipes, garden tips, beauty formulas, articles on art works, furniture, houses, local personages, and so on, are all useful contents of clipping files.

UPDATING OF DIRECTORIES

Because many of the names and addresses given in various directories of persons, companies, institutions, and elusive agencies quickly become out-of-date, one of the most common reference functions is to annotate directories with updated information. Elections are perhaps the single most common cause of obsolete information, and they also engender numerous inquiries, such as ''Who is my new councilman and where are his offices?''

Again, if the library is part of an information network, the updating of such directories can be shared among the participants or done at the network headquarters. Sharing of responsibility for this function is not as common, however, because librarians usually can save time in the long run for themselves and their patrons by updating in-house all frequently consulted directories.

INTERLIBRARY LOAN

One of the most useful responsibilities which can be assigned to a new reference librarian is that of interlibrary loan. Whether one works on either borrowing or lending requests, the intricacies of accurate bibliographic identification can be learned more quickly than with any other assignment. There is no limit to the number and variety of bibliographic inaccuracies which can be found in interlibrary loan requests; and, consequently, librarians who enjoy bibliographic mysteries never will be bored with the challenges of interlibrary loan transactions. A patron may submit a beautifully legible request for a book with a distinctive author and title, accompanied by a reference to the journal article from which the citation was gleaned. Only after some time spent checking all of the library catalogs (and perhaps the OCLC or RLIN databases) for the elusive book, might it occur to a new reference librarian that the requested work may be an article or a paper—not a book. Checks of relevant periodical indexes or abstracting services may verify the fact; if not, the reference librarian will probably have to seek out the patron's original source to determine if the citation was copied by the patron as it was given.

Another advantage for the new reference librarian to be found in interlibrary load work is that the resources of one's own library are learned with great rapidity. The librarian must master the use of the verification and location tools and also confirm that the library really does *not* own a requested title. It is a real triumph for a librarian to discover that the library does indeed own a book which a user thought was lacking. However, there is less cause for rejoicing and more need for a conference with the cataloging unit if the user missed the book because of inadequate cataloging. For economic reasons, alas, some librarians do not separately catalog certain monographic series. A requested book, therefore, such as Howard Lawrence Hurwitz's *Theodore Roosevelt and Labor in New York State, 1880–1900,* may not be listed in the catalog under Hurwitz's name. Instead, it may only be listed as number 500 of the *Columbia University Studies in History, Economics, and Public Law* series. Such additional but essential information as a series note may not be discovered until a check of the *National Union Catalog* or an online cataloging database reveals it.

The borrowing of material on interlibrary loan is a logical extension of reference service, because, at the same public service desk, the user can be assisted in identifying a needed work and can request it on interlibrary loan (ILL) if the library does not own it. In many libraries, however, the borrowing function is carried on in an independent library unit or as part of a nonreference operation. The lending of materials on interlibrary loan is frequently handled in loan or circulation divisions of a library, and for this reason, there are fewer reference librarians with lending responsibilities. If requests for loans are regularly received from libraries with inadequate bibliographical tools, however, the services of a librarian are often needed to verify the requested title. This assumes that the lending library can devote time to assisting smaller libraries, and it also assumes that the requesting librarian did as much bibliographic checking as was possible. Nothing is more annoying to a lending librarian than to receive a request for a title, which when verified, turns out to be in a series subscribed to by the requesting library! (Nothing should be more humiliating to a borrowing librarian than to have overlooked a needed book in one's own library.)

In libraries where lending and borrowing operations are combined in one unit, the choice of an institution from which to request material on ILL is facilitated. The knowledge of libraries to which one's own institution regularly lends permits judicious selection of libraries to which one may direct both ordinary and exceptional ILL requests. Of course, the development of the ILL module of the OCLC database means that a librarian can feed the request to the computer with instructions to send it to as many as four libraries in a sequence until the request is filled. Other cataloging databases (e.g., RLIN) plan to develop an ILL module also, and the competition should prove to be advantageous for libraries and their patrons.

SPLIT POSITIONS

Some of the most challenging and rewarding reference positions are those in which the reference librarian spends half of the time in reference work and the other half in an assignment not necessarily associated with public service. In libraries with only one librarian, obviously the librarian does *all* of the professional tasks and probably (if the truth be told) also a good portion of the clerical ones.

ACQUISITIONS/CATALOGING

Learning to be a proficient cataloger or acquisitions librarian not only increases one's skills, but also broadens the perspective by which each job is viewed. A cataloger who also works as a reference librarian is much more aware of the difficulties which people have in using the catalog and is more likely to make all the necessary subject and added entries; conversely, as a reference librarian, the cataloger usually has more detailed knowledge of cataloging rules and can find difficult entries more readily. Similarly, acquisitions librarians who double as reference librarians are usually more aware of what the library is acquiring, what has just arrived, and what the library will not buy.

Of course, these half-time assignments are sometimes very specialized, and a reference librarian may do half-time cataloging or acquisitions only for the reference unit. Or, the librarian may be a subject specialist who does reference work, cataloging, and/or acquisitions—only in some special subject or language.

DOCUMENTS

Because government documents are so specialized, it is common for a librarian to work solely with them. Their acquisition, processing, and housing is a major task which must precede the reference service offered. In a smaller library, the general reference librarian may handle documents as an additional assignment, just as another general reference librarian may be additionally responsible for selecting all of the library's books and journals in the social sciences or another discipline. Within the sphere of documents, there are internal specializations covering federal, state, local, foreign, and international agencies. Every reference librarian should take pains to become familiar with his or her library's treatment of official documents.

SERIALS

Because much of reference work is concerned with the identification of periodical citations and monographic series, a split assignment between reference and serials can be beneficial. When the periodical and newspaper indexes are located within a periodicals reading room, reference assistance must be provided there. In such a setting, a reference librarian can refer users more readily to particular issues of periodicals (not yet indexed) that contain coverage of certain subjects, or to selected periodicals which are in the desired language.

As a serials/reference librarian, one can learn the intricacies of dealing with subscription services, serials record-keeping and invoicing, and continuations cataloging. One frequently has an opportunity to learn about microform materials and equipment, too, since so many serials are available in microform. Working in periodicals is a distinct advantage to librarians who are interested in keeping up with current events.

TROUBLESHOOTER

One function of a reference librarian, not legitimatized by inclusion in the curriculum of a library school, is the role of a troubleshooter. When a library user comes to the reference desk in frustration and desperation—perhaps in a rage or in tears, it is often an unforgettable (and sometimes unpleasant) opportunity to test one's problem-solving abilities and diplomatic talents. Sometimes the users' problems are the result of ignorance or unwillingness to make the necessary effort on their own. Reference librarians will inevitably encounter some very difficult people, but they should not cater to them at the expense of others. If demands for special treatment and attention prevent the reference librarian from attending to the needs of others, the problem patrons should be referred to a higher authority. One should avoid giving less effort to the resolution of a problem presented by a calm, well-mannered individual than to those presented by loud, demanding, and persistent pests.

Library users ordinarily are unable to get "behind the scenes" to find what they need, which may be in the process of being cataloged, readied for the bindery, or being repaired. A conscientious reference librarian should be ready to serve as an intermediary between users and nonpublic service departments, and occasionally the librarian may be required to resolve a misunderstanding between a user and another service unit. In these instances, it is important to avoid putting one's colleagues in another unit on the defensive or deprecating another unit to a patron. The library's overall image, as well as that of the individual librarian, is enhanced more by a tactful handling of an in-house problem without airing the dirty linen in public.

This function may not seem of the highest professional calling, but if the goals of the library and the reference librarian really are to provide needed assistance, one must expect that ''troubleshooting'' will be a regular, time-consuming task. If problems caused by certain procedures or snags seem to proliferate, the reference librarian should work to improve the policies and the procedures. In troubleshooting, it is important to treat the cause as well as the symptom of the problem.

PUBLIC RELATIONS FUNCTIONS

Related to instructional responsibilities, but having an entity of their own, are the public relations efforts which are required of reference librarians. Directional signs and special signs in honor of donors, valuable collections, and noteworthy events must often be designed and mounted by reference librarians. Library exhibits and their catalogs, special library publications, and cultural events sponsored by the library are all major efforts to which reference librarians may be asked to devote considerable time. Lastly, goodwill tours for civic groups, members of the board of directors, or for individuals of importance to the library are rather commonplace. These promotional tours usually are distinguished from their instructional counterparts by the emphasis given to the fine services or the funding needs of the library.

Because public relations efforts seem to consume time in proportion to the library's budget, some larger libraries assign these duties as regular responsibilities to particular members of the staff. More often, public relations duties are simply ''fitted in'' as the needs and occasions demand.

REFERENCES AND SUGGESTED READINGS

Blanchard, J. 'Where's the washroom' and other reference questions I've been asked. *RQ*, 1978 *17*(Spring), 204–206.

Childers, T. The future of reference and information service in the public library. *Library Quarterly*, 1978, *48*(October), 463–475.

Childers, T. Trends in public library I & R services. *Library Journal*, 1979, *104*(October 1), 2035–2039.

Clark, D. Helping librarians to help their users. *Unesco Bulletin for Libraries*, 1978, *32*(November), 363–374.

Easton, C. Sex and violence in the library: Scream a little louder, please. *American Libraries,* 1977, *8*(October), 484-488.

Eisenbach, E. Bibliographic instruction from the other side of the desk. *RQ,* 1978, *17*(Summer), 312-316.

Elchesen, D. R. Cost-effectiveness comparison of manual and on-line retrospective bibliographic searching. *Journal of the American Society for Information Science,* 1978, *29*(March), 56-66.

Griffin, H. L. Dial your problems away: Reference service by telephone to libraries large or small. *Illinois Libraries,* 1978, *60*(April), 347-350.

Job, S. Cooperative reference and the small academic library. *RQ,* 1978, *17*(Summer), 325-327.

Jones, C. S. (Ed.). *Public library information and referral service.* Syracuse, N.Y.: Gaylord Professional Publications, 1978.

Kusack, J. M. On-line reference service in public libraries. *RQ,* 1979, *18*(Summer), 331-334.

Mershon, L. K. A model automated resource file for an information and referal center. *Special Libraries,* 1980, *71*(August), 335-344.

Miller, S. W. Library use instruction in selected American colleges. University of Illinois, Graduate School of Library Science, *Occasional Papers,* 1978, *134*(August).

Morgan, C. D. Cooperative reference: Hazards, rewards, prospects. *RQ,* 1979, *18*(Summer), 355-368. [Includes papers on "Interlibrary Reference Communication" by Carl Orgren, "Quality Control," by Andrea C. Honebrink, "Computerized Cooperative Reference" by Susan Snow, and "A View from the Top" by George H. Caldwell.]

Mucci, J. Videotape self-evaluation in public libraries: Experiments in evaluating public service. *RQ,* 1976, *16*(Fall), 33-37.

Reino, C. A conversation with Hendrik Edelman. Cornell University Libraries, *Bulletin,* 1973, *182*(March-April), 4-7.

Wagers, R. American reference theory and the information dogma. *Journal of Library History,* 1978, *13*(Summer), 265-281.

Williams, G. Interlibrary loan service in the United States. In K. Barr & M. Line (Eds.), *Essays on information and libraries: Festschrift for Donald Urquhart.* London: C. Bingley; Hamden, Conn.: Linnet Books, 1975, pp. 195-206.

Wilson, P. Librarians as teachers: The study of an organization fiction." *Library Quarterly,* 1979, *49*(April) 146-162.

CHAPTER 2

Resources for Reference Work

INTRODUCTION

Users rarely are curious about methods and resources employed by reference librarians in answering questions. They would be surprised but perhaps still indifferent if they became aware of how much time is spent in becoming familiar with available resources and in perfecting reference skills. Awareness, however, brings out a strong response in library school students. "Panic" is frequently an appropriate word and particularly applicable when the thousands of books in dozens of languages that fill the shelves of a large reference department are first noticed.

This trepidation is somewhat quieted when students discover the abundance of bibliographical guides that list and describe reference works. Unfortunately, many of these works are obsolete or superseded by the time the guides make their appearance. In addition, most guides are selective and only a few give a complete picture of the wealth of material available to a reference collection. Also, it is not sufficient just to know how to use the existing resources in the department; it is necessary to become knowledgeable in the selection of new and additional titles.

The principles involved in the selection of reference materials have not received adequate attention in reference textbooks or in the professional literature. The authors hope that their book will supply the guidance that has been lacking in this area. This chapter will present an overview of the resources used in reference work, while Chapters 3 and 4 will discuss in detail the methods and tools used by librarians in selecting reference books and serials. In all three chapters, annotations are provided for identified selection aids. As the work is not designed to be another bibliographical guide, only sources that have value in the selection process are considered. Inevitably, some will be useful also as working tools for answering a patron's question, but this feature is not part of the criteria for inclusion.

A REFERENCE COLLECTION POLICY

A written collection development policy establishing guidelines on the scope and size of the reference collection is beneficial. These written policies are not always formal documents; in many cases they are in the form of a card file or an in-house manual which describes the policy for different categories of material. Such policies help to define objectives and set standards for both acquiring new material and weeding obsolete tools. They may include information about the subject scope of the collection, its optimum size and specific criteria for including and excluding publications. Responsibility for selection will also be indicated.

A written policy can be first aid for the librarian faced with the irate patron wanting to know why certain books are in the collection and others are not. It also is useful for the new librarian in becoming oriented to the department and in understanding the relationship of the department and its collection to the entire collection of the institution. When procedures are spelled out and priorities set, goals are clarified. This means better reference librarians will be trained and, inevitably, better reference service will result.

REFERENCE BOOKS AND PRINCIPLES OF THEIR SELECTION

Books and reference serials in traditional format comprise the largest percentage of the resources used in reference work. Depending on the size and functions of the department, a satisfactory collection can range anywhere from a few hundred titles to many thousands. *Reference Books for Small and Medium Sized Libraries* (see annotation, Chapter 4) lists 1048 titles considered essential in even a small collection. The *Library of Congress Main Reading Room Reference Collection Subject Catalog* (see annotation, Chapter 4) includes 11,000 monographs and 3000 serials.

For students who already have taken a book selection course, the methodology for selection will be familiar. The same care must go into selecting a work of reference as any other book in the library. In fact, greater care should be taken because greater expense can be involved. Prices of reference sources are staggering, and budgets are shrinking.

A reference book is defined by the *ALA Glossary of Library Terms* (ALA, 1943) as "a book designed by its arrangement to be consulted for definite items of information rather than to be read consecutively." The emphasis on arrangement and effective access to the information are two of the factors that add to the expense of these works along with the inflationary spiral also evident in the cost of living. Current figures show the average price of a reference book to be well over thirty dollars, and large research libraries who purchase foreign bibliographical tools and expensive multivolumed sets may find their average cost per book running over $100. A glance through the latest catalogs of R. R. Bowker Company and Gale Research Company (two of the largest reference book publishers in the United States) reveals few single titles quoted at under twenty dollars, and prices of $50 and up are listed for many of their books. G. K. Hall and Company reproduces library catalogs of research institutions in book form, and some of these sets may cost many thousands of dollars.

Many reference tools are serial in format, and these reference serials often are considered the most important part of the collection. It certainly is difficult to imagine a department functioning without its quota of indexes and abstracts or almanacs and yearbooks. As a healthy part of the budget goes into maintaining subscriptions, initial selection must be particularly careful. Publishers compete with each other and produce similar tools. In addition, reference books can date rapidly and supplements, cumulations, and new editions are cost factors that must be taken into account. Handling also poses headaches; unless the library is large and has a separate serials department, the problems and cost of checking, claiming, and bindery preparation may belong to the reference department. Today, no general reference department buys everything that falls under its scope; few special libraries completely cover their field.

Once students realize that they will be working with a limited number of reference tools, four factors become apparent: (1) A greater emphasis must be placed on learning all of the resources in the library. Reference work has never been confined to reference books, but now it is even more important to know strengths and weaknesses of the stack collection. (2) More time must be spent in becoming familiar with existing reference resources so that they can be exploited fully. (3) Materials should be added only on the basis of clearly defined needs. Adequate study of users and types of questions assumes a greater significance. (4) The selection process should not be a hasty one. New editions of encyclopedias, supplements to earlier works, and annuals will not be purchased automatically but after consideration of the value and substance of the additions and changes. Decisions on new acquisitions ideally will be made after careful examination of the works to ensure they are necessary, of high quality, and do not duplicate material already held in the collection. When the book is not available for examination, the next step is to look for information and reviews that assess the strengths and weaknesses of the work under consideration.

Always remember that principles of successful book selection remain constant and will include a knowledge of user needs, familiarity with existing resources and selection aids, a good critical eye, and a realistic assessment of budgetary problems. Unfortunately, the latter is assuming a new dimension and importance as taxpayers' revolts spread throughout the country. This means, among other things, that librarians in charge of selecting books can no longer afford the luxury of making a mistake.

NONBOOK REFERENCE RESOURCES

CATALOGS AND INDEXES TO COLLECTIONS IN THE LIBRARY

While the book collection within the reference department may be considered its principal resource, questions are frequently answered and services provided by a multitude of nonbook resources.

Of course, the major nonbook resource is the library catalog and its supplements (regardless of format). It would be impossible to conceive of providing reference service without resorting to its use. Not only is the existence and location of a particular book revealed, but the catalog is also the best place to begin a literature search as it will direct you to the information sources on a subject, e.g., bibliographies, indexes, encyclopedias, and so on (see Chapter 4, Fig. 4-2). However, the importance of the catalog has been stressed so repeatedly in cataloging and reference instruction that it should not need reiteration. Nobody can become a competent librarian who is not aware that it is impossible to give proper reference service without understanding the catalog.

In a large library, the reference librarian may have to become familiar with two catalogs—the main catalog that includes the holdings for the entire system, and a special catalog housed in the reference department listing only the holdings and locations of material within that section. The larger and more complex the library, the greater advantage there is to having this separate catalog.

Very few reference departments shelve all of their books in regular classified order. The most heavily used tools and/or those that require the greatest control are generally shelved behind the reference desk. The most popular biographical dictionaries and indexes frequently are placed on special tables for the convenience of the user. Access to this material is speeded up if the location is noted in the catalog. As material is shifted around the department or sent to the stacks, the catalog will require updating. It is easier for both the user and the librarian if there is a small catalog available with this information.

The shelf list of the reference department is usually housed behind the desk, and holdings and locations are noted here first. In addition, because of its classified arrangement, a shelf list is useful for browsing as one quickly can see what the department has in a given field. The shelf list is useful for selection as duplications can be avoided more easily and gaps revealed more readily.

INFORMATION FILES AND PAMPHLETS

Reference desks are service-oriented centers of activity. At first glance, one may only be conscious of the people stationed behind the desk and those waiting in front. A closer look is needed to become aware of the files as well as the books in close reach of those people behind the desk. Depending on the nature of the library and its users, one can predict the type of books and other materials that fill the shelves and files. In addition to the books kept there because they are the most frequently consulted by both librarian and user or because tighter control over their circulation is necessary, one expects to find local maps and bus schedules, give-away materials providing information on the use of the library, reading lists, archives of the institution such as annual reports, newsletters, master plans, statistics, and so on. If space permits, pamphlet and picture files also may be housed. Files of frequently asked questions and their answers, current directory-type information, forms for special library services (i.e., inter-library loan, computerized reference services, and so on), instructions to the reference staff, homemade indexes to special collections all help fill any available space.

Heavy use of current directory-type of information occurs when libraries provide ''information and referral'' services. This kind of help requires constant updating of names and addresses; frequently librarians only can do this by regular and careful reading of local newspapers and spending a considerable amount of time on the telephone.

Each reference department will determine the kind and quantity of such materials kept within reach of the librarian, and, obviously, it will be determined by user demand as well as space limitations. But these resources can be as important to the operation of reference service as the books themselves.

As mentioned earlier, many libraries produce their own indexes to special materials or special indexes to their collections. These are invaluable because they are compiled on the basis of a clearly felt need, and guides to some of these lists and indexes have been published. A good example is Sally Dumaux' *Index Omnibus* (Los Angeles: Southern California Answering Network, 1974), compiled for the Los Angeles Public Library. This guide to the internally produced indexes reveals that each was created to provide for reference needs in separate subject departments. Included are such special indexes as California in Fiction, Bandits and Sheriffs, Los Angeles Street Names Index, Television Reviews Scrapbook, interlibrary loan verification file, and debate indexes. The list in all of its variety goes on.

A more general guide is *Library Bibliographies and Indexes* (Detroit: Gale Research Company, 1975) edited by Paul Wasserman and Esther Herman, as it is a subject guide to resource material available in libraries and information centers all over the United States and Canada. It identifies and locates 1500 of the lists and indexes that librarians have been compiling for their institutions.

Increasingly, there is a trend toward putting current, and especially, directory-type information in the computer and making it available online. This automation of information files will mean that, within a few years, terminals will become standard equipment at a reference desk or at a site strategically located within the department. Reference librarians should welcome automated files and consider them an additional resource for providing the best possible service to users.

THE TELEPHONE

After a long day of responding to the telephone ring at a reference desk, many librarians would welcome any attempt to interrupt this service. The problem of telephone service versus personal service is discussed in other sections of this book.

But it is well to be reminded that the telephone is a resource for reference work as well as a hindrance. Dial ''information'' for the latest phone number, consult a subject specialist for help on a difficult question, or call other librarians to find out what sources they use for unsolved problems. The telephone is the connection to other people who may be the only ''resource'' that can help in providing adequate reference service.

TELEPHONE DIRECTORIES AND COLLEGE CATALOGS

An extensive collection of telephone directories from all over the world is maintained in any large reference department, and most academic libraries, regardless of size, house a current collection of college catalogs. The big investments in these tools are in the space they require and the staff time required to keep them in order. While both telephone directories and college catalogs now are published in microform, these microform collections unfortunately are expensive. As there is no question that they constitute a group of information sources that are heavily used and necessary to acquire, it becomes a trade-off for the librarian who will have to decide whether the greatest squeeze is coming from the budget or tightness of space.

SELECTION AIDS FOR SPECIAL AREAS

MEDIA

Today, a complete definition of the term ''media'' includes films, filmstrips, maps and globes, multimedia kits, programmed instruction materials, recordings on discs and tapes, slides and transparencies, video and computer tapes, and even reproductions of works of art including the plastic arts. Except perhaps for maps, these are not standard materials usually found in a general reference department. However, school libraries have become ''media centers,'' public libraries circulate films and records as freely as they do books, and media materials are being used more heavily in academic libraries.

So even if a department handles only a few maps and the only multimedia materials are those that deal with library orientation, libraries still are expected to provide reference service in this area. This means librarians must become familiar with all varieties of equipment directories, media indexes, and reviews, discographies, filmographies, and so on.

In recent years, quite a few guides for selecting media reference sources have been published, but they must be used with a few warnings. First, most of the ones covering films include only "educational" films, and it is necessary to look elsewhere for guidance on theatrical releases. Second, reference materials in these areas change format and coverage with a discouraging degree of frequency, so the information given in guides quickly becomes outdated.

Valuable for its currency is *Audiovisual Market Place: A Multimedia Guide* (New York: Bowker, Annual), a guide to manufacturers, distributors, associations, and so on, but also including periodicals and reference sources. Margaret Chisholm's *Media Indexes and Review Sources* (College Park, Md., University of Maryland, 1972) identifies and describes the major indexing and review services for nonprint material. *Index to Instructional Media Catalogs* (New York: Bowker, 1974) lists about 600 catalogs of suppliers of specific instructional materials. James L. Limbacher's *A Reference Guide to Audio Visual Information* (New York: Bowker, 1972) is one of the few books to include information on the theatrical motion picture. About 400 reference books and some 100 periodicals are annotated. In addition, an assortment of miscellaneous information includes a glossary, a directory of publishers, and information for a "ready reference file."

An excellent work is Margaret I. Rufsvold's *Guides to Educational Media* (Chicago: American Library Association, 1977). Good annotations and detailed information are provided for 245 educational media catalogs, indexes, and reviewing services. Films, filmstrips, multimedia kits, programmed instruction materials, recordings, slides, transparencies, and videotapes are covered. An index, including references to names and subjects mentioned in the annotations but which are not main entry titles, adds to the value of this guide.

Additional sources that may prove of service include Mary Robinson Sive's *Selecting Instructional Media* (Littleton, Colo.: Libraries Unlimited, 1978), Dorothy T. Taggart's *A Guide to Sources in Educational Media and Technology* (Metuchen, N.J.: Scarecrow, 1975), and *Guide to Reference Books for School Media Centers* by Christine L. Wynar (Littleton, Colo.: Libraries Unlimited, 1973). Coverage is equally useful for the public and academic library.

When long-playing records and tape cassettes came on the market, listening habits were changed all over the country, and this, in turn, had its effect on the library. Audio centers, now found in most public libraries, are becoming increasingly popular in college libraries and may be administered by the reference department. Even if that were not the case, the need for bibliographical control over recordings and tapes is obvious to anyone who has ever tried to buy a record.

So far, reference tools are inadequate. There is no satisfactory listing of all new or available records. Attempts to analyze their contents have been minimal, and librarians find themselves dependent on commercial tools such as Schwann catalogs and *Phonolog*. Specialized discographies do exist and as many of them are in periodicals, it is all the more important that bibliographies of discographies have made their appearance. Two significant ones are

Gray, Michael, ed. *Bibliography of Discographies*, Vol. 1.—Classical Music, 1925–1975. New York: Bowker, 1977.

A listing of basic information on more than 3000 discographies of classical music published in American, European, and Russian journals between 1925 and 1975. General discographies of the composer or performer are listed first, followed by discographies of the work by medium or form, and, finally, discographies of specific works or types of works. There is one combined index of compilers, authors, series titles, and selected monographic titles.

Plans are to make this a five-volume set, and jazz, popular music, ethnic music, and general discographies will be covered in later volumes.

Cooper, David. *International Bibliography of Discographies: Classical Music and Jazz and Blues, 1962–1972*. Littleton, Colo.: Libraries Unlimited, 1975.

Part of a series, *Keys to Music Bibliography*, No. 2, this bibliography of discographies lists almost 2000 entries in 21 languages from 37 countries. Restricted to Western classical music, jazz, and blues, it is arranged by type of music with a special section on national discographies, catalogs, and review sources. One index includes authors, titles, series, and subjects.

As yet there are no comprehensive bibliographies of filmographies.

MICROFORM

Microform is a good example of a technology that has created new problems for libraries while solving some old ones. While it was designed to save space and money, additional problems of selecting and housing expensive machines have been created.

In the beginning, there was no standardization of format or terminology. There was microfilm on reels and then microfiche on cards; both are film transparencies of the original material. There was also microprint, which is an opaque photographic reduction. Finally, some sensible soul decided on the adoption of "microform" as the generic term to include all methods of photoreduction, whether transparent or opaque.

This solved the predicament of what to call "it," but little else. Progress toward standardization of format has been slow. Many commercial firms have entered the market each with their own reader. The United States government began publishing its technical reports on microfiche, and gradually this is becoming the standard format.

Special concerns affect a reference department. While ordinarily not the most desirable form for reference material, microform is satisfactory for less frequently used tools. More and more, catalog supplements and current union lists for serials for particular regions are being produced by the computer and put on microfiches. This means machines have to be purchased and maintained, and space has to be found for them. There also is the growing tendency to publish in dual media editions. For example, *Newsbank,* a current information service on urban affairs, publishes its text on microfiche and provides a reader, but the indexes are printed in hard copy. The user is supposed to consult the index, then reach out and select the indicated fiche and insert it into the reader. But just as most reference departments are limited in space for books, they have even greater difficulty in providing adequate space for readers. So, in a large library, it may be necessary to house all fiches and readers together in a separate department while the printed indexes remain in the reference room. Finally, most users need instruction in the use of microform materials, which consumes a chunk of the librarian's time.

While the quality of existing readers is improving, nobody really enjoys reading in a microform format. And there are still technical problems to be solved. However, microform is here to stay. Libraries do not want backfiles of newspapers filling up ever-diminishing stack space. Out-of-print material as well as bulky formats such as technical reports, telephone directories, and college catalogs are being reproduced in microform. Updating services for bibliographic tools such as the annual *British Books in Print* are available on microfiche and are regularly consulted by librarians and users.

In addition to problems in selecting equipment, the standard selection process for materials continues and the librarian needs good current bibliographical tools. For books and serials on microform (including reference books), use the annual *Guide to Microforms in Print,* 1968–   (now incorporating *International Microforms in Print*) and its companion *Subject Guide to Microforms in Print,* 1962–   . Both are now published by Microform Review (Weston, Conn.) as are a quarterly, *Microform Review,* 1971–   and *Micropublishers Trade List Annual (MTLA),* 1976–   . Use them for ordering information including price and format.

University Microfilms International, a division of Xerox, makes available its list of books that can be purchased either on microfilm or in paper copy. The Library of Congress provides lists of newspapers on microform in two volumes, one for the United States and one for foreign countries. It also is responsible for the *National Register of Microform Masters*, 1965–   , an annual catalog that identifies microform masters (those used only for the purpose of making copies).

Today, catalog supplements and current lists of serial holdings are being produced by computer on microfilm (a process known as Computer Output Microform, or COM). It is obvious that libraries that take advantage of this process also must provide a reader for listings in this format.

Reader's Advisory Work

In many public libraries, it may be the reference librarian's responsibility to provide reader's advisory service for users. This means that it will not be sufficient to be aware of just the information needs and resources of the library, but also necessary to keep up with the current novels, genre fiction, and general nonfiction. The librarian should spend time with patrons to try to determine their interests and match the right books to these interests. When the library cannot supply these books, it is part of the reader's advisory function to suggest new titles.

All of the advice and most of the tools suggested for new reference books apply to selection of fiction and general nonfiction. Read ads, *Publishers Weekly,* examine national and trade bibliographies, know publishers, and read reviews. (For a fuller discussion, see Chapters 3 and 4.)

While studying *Book Review Digest* (see annotation Chapter 3), one sees that the subject index is invaluable for locating books on particular topics. All of Wilson's Standard Catalog Series (including *Fiction Catalog*) have subject and analytical indexes. *Subject Guide to Children's Books in Print* (New York: Bowker, Annual) provides subject access to fiction as well as nonfiction. The lists of "best books" are long, but libraries accepting reader's advisory work as one of their obligations will do well to acquire as many as they can afford.

No tool is a substitute for actually reading the books and allowing time to talk to patrons and noting their tastes and interests. The rewards are immense. When a child is turned on to books and reading, a lifelong "friend" of the library has been made; match the right book to the right adult, and that patron will return again and again to the library and the librarian who provided this service. In the stress on "information" and "education," it is important to remember that libraries also provide "entertainment" and "recreation."

Databases

In the 1970s, databases emerged as important adjuncts to the resources of a reference department, and their growth will be even more spectacular in the next decade. However, the new reference librarian will find that decisions as to their selection properly are made only after careful analysis of their benefits to the library's clientele and their relationship to the printed tools that already are present in the collection. Selection, of course, is only one area to consider when dealing with these technological marvels. In other sections of the book, the reader will find a discussion of problems such as staffing, fees, training, location, and so on.

Cost and the expense of maintaining them online preclude the outright purchase of databases for most libraries. Libraries acquire *access* to these databases through vendors such as Lockheed Missiles and Space Co., Inc., System Development Corporation, or Bibliographic Retrieval Services. Functioning as a middleman, each vendor has price lists and descriptions of services that are available in both printed and machine-readable format.

While most of the databases used by libraries have been bibliographic (almost all major indexing and abstracting services are available online), there has been an astonishing growth in nonbibliographic (especially numeric) machine-readable data available for research in the sciences and social sciences. At last, bibliographic tools are appearing that include information about these kinds of data.

For the reference librarian desiring information on commercially or publicly available databases, good assistance comes from:

Computer-Readable Data Bases: A Directory and Data Sourcebook. Washington, D.C.: American Society for Information Science, 1979.

A comprehensive directory of machine-readable databases, the 1979 edition lists more than 500 databases worldwide. Each listing includes the name and producer of the base, coverage, year of origin, number of items in the base, availability in either batch or online mode, and price. Multiple indexes and a list of outmoded databases add to its usefulness. Not all databases listed are bibliographic; some contain factographic and numeric information.

The Directory of Online Databases. Santa Monica, Calif.: Cuadra Associates, 1979–

This directory is particularly valuable because of the inclusion of descriptions of nonbibliographic databases. Six types of databases are described: bibliographic, referral, numeric statistical, databases of chemical or physical properties of substances, combination numeric–textual, and full-text. The reference includes over 275 descriptions uniformly formatted. There are multiple indexes. Updates are quarterly with a complete reissue every six months.

Information Market Place: An International Directory of Information Products and Services, 1978–   . New York: Bowker, Annual.

Useful for its lists of database publishers, machine-readable databases, and print products, this directory includes information on online vendors, government and international agencies, conferences, periodicals and newsletters. An additional listing of databases and print products arranged by subject is an added feature.

In such a rapidly developing field as online services, the birth and death rate of reference and selection tools is impressive but dismaying to those trying to stay abreast of new titles. For a good state-of-the-art report, see Nitecki (1980).

Note: United States Census information is now available in machine-readable format. Part 2 of the quarterly *Catalog of United States Census Publications* provides access to these data files. (For a fuller discussion, see the section on "Statistical Sources" in Chapter 4.)

THE STACK COLLECTION

Not all reference questions are answered by materials in the reference department. Remember that the entire library, and especially the stack collection, must be used in order to provide complete information service. The smaller the reference collection, the greater is the need for the reference librarian to become acquainted with the stacks. Any work of nonfiction is a potential reference source provided there is some kind of decent access through either a table of contents, the basic arrangement, or an index. It is especially important that reference librarians have a sound knowledge of the classification scheme for the collection so that they can browse the shelves and perhaps find the one book that will help the user.

When searching through *Publishers Weekly* and other tools for indications of new reference books, take the time to note what is being published in the various fields. If the library is an academic institution, a knowledge of the course offerings of the various departments and schools will provide some insight as to the materials being acquired for the stacks.

Finally, the stack collection holds many old editions of reference books. No reference department is large enough to keep all editions within reach. Very few new editions completely supersede earlier ones. So the old encyclopedia or biographical dictionary that was sent to the stacks a few years earlier might just have the particular piece of information that is needed.

REFERENCES AND SUGGESTED READINGS

American Library Association. *ALA glossary of library terms*. Chicago: American Library Association, 1943.

Barzun, J. Bedside reading: A reference book. *Wilson Library Bulletin*, 1964, *39*(November), 246–247.

Bonk, W. J. & Magrill, R. M. The Selector and Non-Book Materials. In their *Building library collections* (5th ed.). Metuchen, N.J.: Scarecrow, 1979, pp. 125–156.

Chisholm, M. Selection and evaluation tools for audio and visual materials. In her *Reader in media, technology and libraries*. Englewood, Colo.: Microcard Editions Books, 1975, pp. 370–384.

Coleman, K. L., & Dickinson, P. Drafting a reference collection policy. *College & Research Libraries*, 1977, *38*(May), 227–233.

Evans, G. E. Collection development policies. In his *Developing library collections*. Littleton, Colo.: Libraries Unlimited, 1979, pp. 122–136.

Fetros, J. G. Information files of old chestnuts and chestnut nags. *Wilson Library Bulletin*, 1973, *48*(December), 329–331.

Hernon, P. The use of microforms in academic reference collections and services. *Microform Review*, 1977, *6*(January), 15–18.

Lynden, F. C. Sources of information on the costs of library materials. *Library Acquisitions: Practice and Theory*, 1977, *1*(April), 105–116.

Matley, M. B. Building your phone book collection—a gold mine of low-cost information. *Wilson Library Bulletin*, 1973, *48*(December), 318–323.

Nitecki, D. A. Online services. *RQ*, 1980, *19*(Summer), 319–322.

Perkins, D. L. (Ed.). *Guidelines for collection development*. Chicago: American Library Association, 1979.

Perry, M. The college catalog collection. *RQ*, 1971, *10*(Spring), 240–247.

Plosker, G. R., & Summit, R. K. Management of vendor services: How to choose an online vendor. *Special Libraries*, 1980, *71*(August), 354–357. Reprinted from *Library Management Bulletin*, 1980, *3*(Spring), 2–5.

Siebert, G. A. The reference catalog. *RQ*, 1969, *8*(Summer), 262–263.

Wall, C. E. The making of a reference book. *RSR*, 1973, *1*(January–March), 5–7.

CHAPTER 3

Evaluating Reference Sources

THE PUBLISHING OF REFERENCE BOOKS AND SERIALS

As areas of knowledge advance and overlap, there is a need for materials that define and summarize these developments as well as identify the people responsible for them. As sources in these fields multiply, a corresponding need for bibliographic tools to list and describe them also grows.

As a result, reference book publishing is a rapidly expanding field. The increase in demand for the reference sources also coincides with the spread of reference services in all libraries during the twentieth century. Books have been acquired, cataloged and classified, stored and circulated for hundreds of years. Sophisticated reference work involving interaction of the librarians, the user, and the information source came much later. The library school student today faces a different philosophy of reference service than those early pioneers taught by Melvil Dewey at New York State Library and Columbia University. Now, the prospective librarian, in order to perform competently in a reference department, must be able to select and master a vast number of information sources. A good beginning is to become acquainted with the variety of publishing houses whose imprints can be found on a majority of the frequently used reference works. A lack of familiarity with this area is a contributing factor to errors many librarians commit in the selection process.

MAJOR PUBLISHERS

The easiest way to acquire a quick overview of reference books published in the United States and their publishers is by studying Bowker's *Publishers Trade List Annual* (*PTLA*) (see annotation, Chapter 4). The index in the front alphabetically lists the publishers included in the six-volume work. An additional listing of publishers by subject field was added a few years ago. A careful examination of *PTLA* shows that reference books are published by (1) trade publishers who, with few exceptions, publish reference tools exclusively; (2)

trade publishers whose list includes some reference titles along with works of fiction and other works of nonfiction; (3) university presses; and (4) library associations. Other groups who publish reference material but may not be found in *PTLA* are governments, learned societies and scholarly organizations, and subscription book publishers. Most publications in these latter groups are not sold through ordinary channels of the book trade.

The following is a selective list of the major publishers concentrating on reference books and serials. The selection, based on a study of reference syllabi from various library schools, as well as publishers' catalogs, should give some idea of what to expect from these houses. Get on the mailing list for their announcements and catalogs; most of them supply standing orders and subscriptions and will send out books on thirty-day approval.

ABC–Clio, Inc., Box 4397, Riviera Campus, Santa Barbara, Calif. 93103.

Founded in the fifties, the American Bibliographical Center–Clio Press is best known for its effort to establish bibliographical control over the periodical literature in history and related fields. The Center is responsible for *Historical Abstracts, America: History and Life, ABC POL SCI,* and *ARTbibliographies.* Clio Press is its book publishing arm and its catalog reveals textbooks and monographs as well as reference works and specialized bibliographies. The European Bibliographical Center–Clio Press, in Oxford, England, handles sales and subscriptions outside the United States and Canada.

The Center was among the first to apply computer technology to the production of its indexes and bibliographies. It also publishes *Bibliographic News,* a free newsletter informing subscribers of the Center's full range of bibliographic activities.

R. R. Bowker Company, 1180 Avenue of the Americas, New York, N.Y. 10036.

Almost exclusively a publisher of reference material, the history of this house goes back over a hundred years when *Publishers Weekly* and *Publishers Trade List Annual* had their beginnings. While formally established in 1872, Bowker's roots can be traced to 1854 when Frederick Leypoldt, a German immigrant, opened a bookstore in Philadelphia. He was responsible for the first issue of *Publishers Weekly* and then associated himself with Richard Rogers Bowker. These two men, along with Melvil Dewey, were responsible for founding *Library Journal* and the American Library Association. Leypoldt died in 1884, six years after he sold *Publishers Weekly* to Bowker. The firm became incorporated in 1914 as the R. R. Bowker Company with Bowker as the head until his death in 1933. In 1967, R. R. Bowker Company became a unit of Xerox Corporation.

Today, Bowker is not only responsible for keeping the library world informed about new books through its chain of trade bibliographies (see section on National and Trade Bibliography, Chapter 4), but also helps with the bibliographic control over serials (see section on General Guides to Serials, Chapter 4). Special organizations like the American Film Institute and the American Association for the Advancement of Science use Bowker as a distributor for their publications. European booksellers like Eyre & Spottisford, Chelsea House, and George Allen & Unwin (Great Britain), and other publishers from France, Italy, and Spain also release material through Bowker.

A glance at a Bowker catalog shows that the two other areas of interest are librarianship and the booktrade. In addition to its comprehensive annual catalog, monthly annotated lists of new books appear in a small pamphlet called *Portfolio*.

F. W. Faxon Company, Inc., 15 Southwest Park, Westwood, Mass. 02090.

The beginnings of this company date from 1881, and its publications always reflected an interest in libraries and periodicals. Its oldest periodical, *Bulletin of Bibliography*, 1897–   , regularly featured a section titled "Births, Deaths, and Magazines Notes," useful for information about new and deceased periodicals. Faxon also publishes many indexes to composite works or anthologies that are used heavily in both public and academic libraries. Initiated in 1907 as the "Useful Reference Series of Library Books," some of the best known in the series are *Index to Handicrafts, Index to Illustrations, Index to Fairy Tales, Index to Women, Index to One-Act Plays,* and *Index to Full Length Plays*.

Gale Research Company, Book Tower, Detroit, Mich. 48226.

Founded in 1954, Gale publishes primarily for the reference department of a library. Its first title and possibly the most heavily used is the *Encyclopedia of Associations*. Some of the others are *Contemporary Authors, Research Centers Directory, Book Review Index, Statistics Sources,* and *Directory of Special Libraries and Information Centers*.

Gale has also initiated several series of bibliographical guides. One, known as the *Gale Information Guides,* covers a variety of subject fields. Another, called *Management Information Guides,* is concerned with aspects of business and industry.

Gale Research Company is also well-known for its reprints and as a distributor for Europa, one of Great Britain's leading publishers of directories and yearbooks. In addition to being advertised in a large annual catalog, Gale titles announced for the first time are described in a monthly publication *New Book News*.

G. K. Hall & Company, 70 Lincoln St., Boston, Mass. 02111.

Organized in 1942 and now owned by ITT, G. K. Hall is the principal supplier of book catalogs of outstanding library collections. Microform technology has been used to reproduce library card catalogs and then print them in a standard book format. Over 300 titles are listed and annotated in an annual catalog, making it a useful bibliographical tool in its own right. All fields of knowledge are covered and some of the collections represented are those of the New York Public Library, the library of the Metropolitan Museum of Art, the School of Oriental and African Studies of London University, and the Bancroft Library of the University of California. Because special research libraries usually do extensive cataloging, many of these book catalogs contain analytics for composite works and periodicals. So these catalogs serve as an extension to a general library catalog. Indexes to special periodical collections such as the *Ryerson Index to Art Periodicals* and the Pan American Union's *Index to Latin American Periodical Literature* are also part of the G. K. Hall publishing program.

G. K. Hall also publishes a series called *Bibliographic Guides* consisting of annual subject bibliographies based on the acquisitions of the Library of Congress and the New York Public Library. This series provides an interesting example of how the computer and MARC tapes can manipulate data from one or two sources to create many separate bibliographical tools. These guides are especially useful for the library whose interests are specialized, but librarians in a general reference department operating on a limited budget should be aware that they are paying principally for a convenience tool.

Other publications of G. K. Hall include reference guides in literature, film directors and genre, and area studies. An annual *Index to Reviews of Bibliographical Publications* may prove a useful addition with the first volume covering reviews for 1976.

Libraries Unlimited, Inc., Box 263, Littleton, Colo. 80160.

Founded in 1964, Libraries Unlimited specializes in library science works as well as reference materials for school, public, university, and special libraries. Perhaps best known to reference librarians for its *American Reference Books Annual* (ARBA) (see following annotation), it also has developed bibliographical guides on many subjects.

Marquis Who's Who, Inc., 200 East Ohio St., Chicago, Ill. 60611.

While acquired by ITT as a wholly owned subsidiary in 1969, the A. N. Marquis Company had its start in 1898 by Albert Nelson Marquis, also responsible for the publishing of telephone directories. Its first publication was *Who's Who in America, 1899–1900* and since has followed with *Who Was Who in America, Who's Who of American Women, Who's Who in the World,* and a whole group of specialized biographical dictionaries. It recently absorbed Academic Media and now puts out such reference works as *Yearbook of Higher Education, Annual Register of Grant Support,* and *Standard Education Almanac* under the imprint of Marquis Academic Media Publications.

Students should not confuse Marquis' ''Who's Who'' series with the British counterparts, *Who's Who* and *Who Was Who,* published by Black in London.

Pierian Press, Box 1808, Ann Arbor, Mich. 48106.

The most recent in this list of publishers of reference materials, Pierian Press was established in 1968. Known for its serial publications such as *Consumer's Index to Product Evaluations, Index to Free Periodicals, Media Review Digest,* reference librarians are also beginning to rely on two quarterly review sources it publishes, *Reference Services Review* and *Serials Review* (see following annotations). Pierian Press also is responsible for cumulated indexes to the *Monthly Catalog of U.S. Government Publications, Poole's Index to Periodical Literature,* and *Public Affairs Information Service.*

A recent addition to bibliographical control, *Best Buys in Print,* 1978-   , provides access to remaindered books, special remaindered imported books at low prices, as well as providing prepublication discount data.

Rowman & Littlefield, 81 Adams Dr., Totowa, N.J. 07512.

Rowman and Littlefield is the library division of Littlefield, Adams & Company. The latter was founded in 1949 and began as a publisher of a line of paperbacks for college courses. In 1950, Rowman and Littlefield became part of the company as a publisher of reference works, scholarly books, and reprints, mainly of British origin. It is probably best known for its quinquennial cumulations of Library of Congress catalogs, its series of bibliographies of bibliographies based on Theodore Besterman's fourth edition of *A World Bibliography of Bibliographies,* and a group of international biographical dictionaries.

K. G. Saur Publishing, Inc., 175 Fifth Ave., New York, N.Y. 10010.

The firm of K. G. Saur Publishing, Inc. was established in 1977 by Klaus G. Saur, also founder of Verlag Dokumentation, Munich. Saur handles all orders for books and journal subscriptions of Verlag Dokumentation and is achieving prominence for its reference book publishing on an international level. It is responsible for such major works as the *Bibliography of German Language Publications 1911-1965* and the *Marburger Index,* which is photographic documentation of art in Germany, and is publishing the new 360-volume *British Library Catalogue of Printed Books to 1975* (incorporating the old *British Museum Catalogue*). Saur also is well-known for its contributions to the literature of librarianship and handles IFLA (International Federation of Library Associations) publications.

Scarecrow Press, Inc., 52 Liberty St., Metuchen, N.J. 08840.

Established in 1950 and now merged with Grolier Inc., Scarecrow Press operates under two additional imprints—"Scarecrow Reprint" and "Scarecrow Mini-Print." Its aim is "to publish scholarly works in limited editions at a reasonable price," and its list emphasizes professional tools for librarians as well as bibliographies and other reference tools. A "reasonable price" has meant a sacrifice in aesthetic appeal. Margins usually are not justified and the books, while sturdily bound and printed on durable paper, are not physically attractive. However, their list includes many titles and series that get heavy use in reference departments. Some of the better-known series are *Author Bibliography Series, American Imprints Series,* and *The Historical and Cultural Dictionary*

Series of Latin America. Bibliographies on topics of current interest such as drug abuse, energy, and homosexuality are published regularly.

The Shoe String Press, Inc., Box 4327, 995 Sherman Ave., Hamden, Conn. 06514.

Founded in 1952, Shoe String Press now publishes its "scholarly work" under its Archon Imprint, and professional library literature carries the name of Linnet Books. Another firm that feels a lower price tag on a book is more important than its physical appearance, Shoe String Press still is concerned with conservation and prints its books on acid-free paper. The catalog of Shoe String Press shows an emphasis in the fields of language and literature and history. Reference librarians make heavy use of their many literary checklists as well as their indexes to literary, drama, and poetry explication and criticism. Some of their better-known series are *Drama Explication Series, Guides to Subject Literature Series,* and *Plots and Characters Series.* Many of their releases are titles originally published in Great Britain.

The H. W. Wilson Company, 950 University Ave., Bronx, N.Y. 10452.

H. W. Wilson is one of the oldest and best known of publishers of reference materials in the United States. Founded in 1898, it is responsible for pioneer work in the indexing of periodicals. Familiar to all librarians and many users are *Reader's Guide to Periodical Literature, Applied Science and Technology Index, Business Periodicals Index, Art Index, Biological and Agricultural Index, Education Index, Humanities Index, Index to Legal Periodicals, Library Literature,* and *Social Sciences Index.* Wilson also indexes book reviews (*Book Review Digest* and *Current Book Review Citations*), essays (*Essay and General Literature Index*), plays, short stories, bibliographies and so on. Until recently, science was not well-covered by Wilson, but in 1978 it began a new monthly periodical indexing service, *General Science Periodical Index.* Music remains one of the few fields that Wilson has not indexed. For new books, *Cumulative Book Index* (*CBI*) (see annotation Chapter 4) is indispensable, and the Standard Catalog Series discussed in the next chapter is used for book selection in public and school libraries.

Many Wilson serial publications are sold on the service basis with a subscriber charged only for the amount of service used. The charge is based on two factors: (1) number of entries required each year for the indexing, and (2) the number of subscribers to the index who also subscribe to the periodical. A basic rate is then determined and, by this method, the subscribers to each periodical are the ones who support the indexing of it. There is, however, a minimum charge. This method results in a reduction in price for large libraries because small ones help pay publication costs; at the same time, small libraries are not subject to a flat rate which would prohibit them from subscribing to these reference serials.

Since 1914, H. W. Wilson has been responsible for a monthly publication

Wilson Library Bulletin, a popular periodical for all librarians, which regularly reviews reference books, alternative periodicals, selected government publications, and so on, as well as focusing on library news of interest.

The catalog of H. W. Wilson publications is published annually in September to coordinate with the beginning of the educational year and the fall buying season. A quarterly newsletter *The Lighthouse* offers news and notes of the H. W. Wilson Company and is available free of charge.

Note: In addition, catalogs of publishers such as American Library Publishing Company (formerly Chicorel Library Publishing Corp.), Facts on File, Inc., Greenwood Press, Kraus International Organization Limited, and Neal-Schuman Publishers, Inc., should be checked for their contribution to reference book and reprint publishing.

OTHER TRADE PUBLISHERS

Many other prominent United States publishers include reference books on their list even though their principal output may be in other areas. For example, Charles Scribner's Sons has a reference department that is responsible for such well-known tools as the *Dictionary of American Biography, Dictionary of American History, Dictionary of Scientific Biography,* and the *Dictionary of the History of Ideas.* They also distribute foreign language dictionaries that are published abroad. McGraw-Hill is responsible for major reference sources of which *McGraw-Hill Encyclopedia of Science and Technology, Encyclopedia of World Art,* and *Encyclopedia of World Biography* are good examples. St. Martin's Press and Frederick Ungar Publishing Company, Inc. are two additional names that are noted for their reference titles as well as their general lists.

It would not be feasible or even particularly useful to attempt a comprehensive list of these publishers. Look at the imprint of a reference work that is heavily used and respected, and then study the catalog of that publishing house. Conversely, students can start by scanning backlists of major publishing companies in order to identify and then to examine their reference publications. Then, when a new tool is advertised, they will have some idea of what to expect in coverage and quality.

UNIVERSITY PRESSES

All universities publish some reference material—even if it is only a bibliography in a highly specialized field, and most university presses are listed in *Publishers Trade List Annual.* Chicago, Columbia, Cambridge, Harvard, and Oxford are well-known for their reference publications, and one usually can be assured of a high degree of scholarship in these works.

SOCIETIES AND ASSOCIATIONS

Organizations such as the American Chemical Society, the American Library Association, the Bibliographical Society of America, the Modern Language Association (MLA), the National Council of Teachers of English (NCTE), and many other similar groups publish some outstanding bibliographical tools. American Chemical Society's *Chemical Abstracts* and the *MLA International Bibliography* are just two examples.

SUBSCRIPTION BOOKS PUBLISHING

"Subscription books" are not sold through the regular booktrade channels (i.e., bookstores) but through the mail or door-to-door. Usually, most subscription books are encyclopedias, but some dictionaries and books in special areas are still sold in this fashion. This is not a new practice, but it flourished in the eighteenth century when it was necessary to have a certain number of subscriptions (with partial payment in advance) before a publisher felt they could afford to initiate an expensive publishing undertaking.

Four principal publishers of this type exist in the United States today. The most prominent is certainly Encyclopaedia Britannica, Inc. Its long history goes back to the first edition of the *Encyclopaedia Britannica* that came out in three volumes between 1768 and 1771 in Edinburgh, Scotland. Now one of the largest reference book publishers in the world, it acquired in the 1960s the F. E. Compton Company (*Compton's Encyclopedia*), G. & C. Merriam (Merriam-Webster's dictionaries), and Frederick A. Praeger, Inc. In the same decade the Encyclopaedia Britannica Educational Corporation was formed to develop educational films and other instructional materials. Its international operations began to expand, and today Britannica is publishing encyclopedias in French (*Encyclopaedia Universalis*), Spanish (*Enciclopedia Barsa*), and a Japanese language *Britannica International Encyclopaedia*.

Field Enterprises Educational Corporation was established in 1944 by Marshall Field III, and while its operations were not as extensive as Encyclopaedia Britannica, Inc., its principal output, the *World Book Encyclopedia,* continues to maintain an enormous degree of popularity in the home and in libraries. It appears in international editions, braille, and large-type editions. Field Enterprises, also interested in children's reading, developed *Childcraft* and the *How and Why Library*. Today, World Book and Childcraft, Inc. is a separate corporation and is owned by another American-based concern, Scott and Fetzer.

Grolier Incorporated was originally started in 1895 but has undergone frequent reorganizations and mergers with other related firms. Its most famous purchase was the oldest of American encyclopedias, the *Encyclopedia Americana.* Two other encyclopedias, *Encyclopedia International* and the *New Book of Knowl-*

edge, have helped Grolier maintain its prominence in the subscription books publishing field.

Crowell-Collier Publishing Company was founded in 1877 but is now part of Macmillan, Inc. The latter, of course, distributes most of its books through bookstores but maintains a reference and subscription book division to distribute such encyclopedias as *Collier's Encyclopedia, Merit Students Encyclopedia, International Encyclopedia of the Social Sciences, Encyclopedia of Philosophy,* and the *Encyclopedia of Education.*

Over the years there have been many criticisms and lawsuits over "unscrupulous" sales practices by some subscription book publishers. Today, there are regulations controlling their sale, and abuses have been curtailed. Multivolume sets such as *Academic American Encyclopedia* are beginning to make their appearance in bookstores. Librarians should feel a responsibility toward their patrons seeking advice on a home purchase of a reference set and encourage them to examine and compare the sets the library owns as well as study the guides that have been designed to help them make a wise decision.

Special Publishers

In addition to the above, students should make note of the many houses that specialize in particular types of reference materials. Chilton Book Company is probably the largest publisher of repair guides for automobiles and motorcycles, and there is no end to the clamor for these tools at a reference desk. Hammond, Incorporated and Rand McNally and Company are household words in map and atlas publishing. Congressional Quarterly, Inc. and Congressional Index Service are the principal private publishers of reference materials for government documents. In the reprint field, Burt Franklin, Johnson Reprint Corporation, and Kraus–Thomson Organization, Ltd. are prominent names. The list is long!

Note: The federal government is a major publisher of a variety of reference material including catalogs and indexes to its own publications. For a fuller discussion, see Chapter 4.

Problems in the Publishing of Reference Material

The rapid growth in reference book publishing in recent years indicates that it is a lucrative area for the publisher. However, reference books are expensive to publish. Currency, accuracy, and comprehensiveness are qualities essential to the typical reference work; all three of these attributes add to its cost. While publishers are in business to make a profit like any other concern, most publishers of reference material are interested in turning out quality and excellence in their product. A few publishers may not be as scrupulous. Not every "new edition'' deserves that title. With the coming of the computer, indexes and bibliographies have proliferated. Supplements are frequently skimpy and add little to the basic volume or set. Reprints occasionally neglect to advertise that fact, and the inexperienced librarian may discover too late that a fair amount of money has been spent for a book that is really thirty years old.

Another problem presents itself with multivolume sets. These are frequently contracted for prior to publication, and they appear a volume at a time, sometimes out-of-sequence. In addition, the time lag between volumes may be unpredictable. The librarian finally is faced with a set where the first and last volume have copyright dates and information that span many years. A classic example is *The Encyclopedia of Library and Information Science* (New York: Marcel Dekker). Publishing began in 1968, and the set was not completed until 1981. An interim index appeared at the end of Volume 6. Meanwhile, the profession had gone through some dramatic changes. For example, MILC (Midwest Interlibrary Loan Center) became CRL (Center for Research Libraries)—too late for the information to be included in the ''C'' volume. It began to look as if our professional encyclopedia would suffer the same fate as France's *Catalogue Général* of the Bibliothèque Nationale, which is finally being completed after eighty years of irregular publishing activity.

An awareness of the vagaries of publishing and the need for careful consideration of every purchase are even more important in the time of diminished book budgets and a tight job market. Just as there is no substitute for experience at a reference desk in order to understand the reference interviewing process, there is also no substitute for personal examination of a reference book in order to understand its value in a collection.

HOW TO EXAMINE A REFERENCE WORK

Most books about reference books give advice on how to study these tools; all of it is sound. Authority, scope, level of audience, arrangements, and so on are useful precepts to follow when looking at these books for the first time. This equally is true whether the examination is to determine their utility in a collection or the best method of using them efficiently.

''Authority'' frequently is difficult for the student to evaluate. How does one know whether the publisher is reliable or whether the author is an expert? The recommendations of subject specialists may help; so will experience. Students are faced with a paradox in reference courses because they must begin to judge and evaluate tools without prior experience or use.

Not all compilers of reference works clearly indicate the scope or the limitations that have been imposed on a work; this is particularly frustrating for the student and librarian. Another common omission is a statement of the level of the intended audience.

In the beginning, do not try to evaluate beyond present competence. Pick up the book and browse a little to try to determine the kinds of information it contains and whether there is a familiar or interesting area to examine in greater detail. Then go back and pursue a more methodical examination. Certain pages and sections will provide the necessary clues to its contents and arrangement:

(1) Title page. Standard information usually discussed in the second week of a cataloging course, the title page should include a minimum of author, title, place of publication, and publisher. A subtitle may reveal something about the scope, and an edition statement may be included especially if it is not the first edition.

(2) Verso of title page. Often referred to as the copyright page, it frequently tells a great deal about the history of a work because this is where complete copyright information should be found, and, if it is a recent book, also the cataloging-in-publication (CIP) data. If the latter is included, subject tracings and notes on bibliographies and illustrations reveal important clues as to the character of the book in hand. Be sure to look for any indication that the book first was printed abroad. British books have a way of undergoing slight title changes when they fall into the hands of an American publisher and vice versa. Geoffrey Glaister's *Glossary of the Book* (London: Allen & Unwin, 1960) became *An Encyclopedia of the Book* (Cleveland: World, 1960) when it crossed the Atlantic. Clarence Major's *Dictionary of Afro-American Slang* (New York: International Publishers, 1970) became *Black Slang* by the time it arrived in England (London: Routledge & Kegan Paul, 1971).

One thing to avoid is inadvertently buying the same book twice; it usually happens to librarians at some point in their career, and it will make them feel foolish and wary of publishers. Both reactions probably are necessary developments in the evolution of a competent book selector.

(3) Table of Contents. An examination of the table of contents is the quickest way of determining the scope and arrangement of a work. Some authors are more generous than others in the amount of detail offered, but it should be noted if the volume includes supplementary material or appendices. Often, a small supplementary index will appear at the end of the work following the main index. The table of contents indicates when there is more than one place to look for information in a volume. If the work purports to be a new edition, perhaps this supplement is the only part of the work that is new and the major section remains unchanged. This awareness may influence a decision to purchase a "new edition."

(4) Preface, Introduction, and so on. There is such a variety in length and data in introductions and prefatory matter that it is difficult to offer formulas for examining them. But the information can be interesting as well as enlightening.

In addition to offering details of little attraction for the average reader such as credits to everyone who helped create the work, a history of the various editions can be included and frequently provides clues in using the book. And they can be clues! One has to read the introduction to Theodore Besterman's *A World Bibliography of Bibliographies* carefully to find out what an asterisk before a title means or the significance of brackets around a number. At the same time, he offers a fascinating account of the history of "bibliography of bibliographies," and this enrichment modifies one's impatience at having to dig for information that should be clearly visible.

(5) Indexes. The importance of an index to a work or set has been belabored sufficiently in all reference textbooks so it should not be necessary to do any further preaching. But remember to note the number and kinds of indexes if there is more than one. Sometimes, the final index may serve only the supplement and not the entire work. A good example is the *Historical Atlas* by William Shepherd (New York: Harper & Row, 1973). Now in its 9th edition, each edition adds a few maps, but instead of one cumulative index, the new maps are located through a small supplementary one.

THE REVIEWING OF REFERENCE SOURCES

INTRODUCTION

When it is not possible to examine a reference book personally, a librarian turns to reviews. In many cases, this is desirable even when a copy is available. Some reviewers are subject specialists and complement a librarian's skill in analyzing types of reference tools with their knowledge of the field. At the very least, reviews may speed up a decision as to the value of a work by providing information on its history and a comparison with similar tools.

Reviews of reference works can be found in many sources but especially in the professional literature. At the present time, there are nine established book-reviewing media; they include annuals, book review journals, and library journals that have regular departments covering reference material. In addition, specialized library journals like *Notes,* the journal of the Music Library Association, *ARLIS,* a publication of the art librarians of North America, or the *Bulletin* of the Geography and Map Division of the Special Libraries Association regularly review information sources in their respective fields. Most academic journals review all types of materials within their subject scope. Librarians soon become familiar with the sources for reviews and recognize and depend on those that are reliable.

If there is difficulty in locating a review, the best solution is to turn to the book review indexes.

INDEXES TO REVIEWS

Book Review Digest, 1905–   . New York: Wilson. Monthly except February
and July with quarterly and annual cumulations. A 70-year cumulated index,
1905–1975.

Book Review Digest indexes and excerpts reviews (appearing in approximately
83 periodicals) of books that are published in the United States and Canada. But,
in order to qualify for inclusion, any work of nonfiction must have received at
least two reviews. This restriction explains why one cannot always locate a
review in this digest. An exception to the rule is made for *Reference and Subscription Books Reviews* (see the following annotation). A review by this source
automatically guarantees inclusion in *Book Review Digest.*

Despite the limitations on coverage, the excerpts from reviews as well as a
subject index make this work unique and, frequently, invaluable. There is also a
title index while main entry is under author of the book reviewed.

Book Review Index, 1965–   . Detroit: Gale Research Company. Bimonthly.
Annual and decennial cumulations.

Now indexing over 290 periodicals, *Book Review Index* offers a greater diversity in coverage than *Book Review Digest.* However, it lacks the latter's files
back to the beginning of the century, and it does not include any excerpts from
reviews. *BRI* indexes all reviews appearing in every issue of the periodicals
examined. These include those in the humanities, fine arts, social sciences,
sciences, as well as general interest magazines. Entry is under author of book
reviewed.

Current Book Review Citations, 1976–   . New York: Wilson. Monthly
except August. Annual cumulations.

Indexing book reviews appearing in more than 1200 periodicals, *Current
Book Review Citations* provides comprehensive coverage not available in its
Wilson companion, *Book Review Digest.* However, no excerpts from reviews
are included. All major fields are encompassed. Entry is under author of book
reviewed.

Index to Book Reviews in the Humanities, 1960–   . Detroit: Philip Thomson.
Annual.

Appearing only annually, this index is not as valuable as it could be for current
book selection. However, it does index periodicals not included in the Wilson or
Gale publications, and coverage of some foreign language material adds to its
usefulness in an academic library. The definition of "humanities" has varied,
and archaeology and a great deal of history are excluded. Entry is under author of
the book reviewed.

Index to Reviews of Bibliographical Publications, 1976–   . Boston: G. K. Hall. Annual.

Covers reviews from journals in the fields of English and American language literature and related areas such as history, theater, psychology, and religion. In addition to bibliographical publications, selected reference works such as *American Book Prices Current* and *American Book Trade Directory,* which are important to researchers in the above subject fields, also are reviewed. Entry is under author of the book reviewed.

Internationale Bibliographie der Rezensionen Wissenschaftlicher Literatur, 1971–   . Osnabruck, Germany: F. Dietrich Verlag. Semiannual.

International coverage makes this an important review medium for the research library with a substantial amount of foreign language material. Thousands of periodicals are covered although *IBR* does not claim to include all reviews in these sources. Main entry is under author of the book reviewed. Additional listings by reviewer subject and title may be helpful for the user. Prefatory matter is in English as well as German and French, so librarians and patrons should have no difficulty in handling this work even with a limited knowledge of foreign languages. Useful for reviews of English language works not indexed in other sources. It is a continuation of *Bibliographie der Rezensionen,* 1900–1943.

National Library Service Cumulative Book Review Index, 1905–1974. Princeton, N.J.: National Library Service, 1975. 6 volumes.

A cumulated author and title index to *Book Review Digest,* 1905–1974 and to reviews in *Library Journal,* 1907–1974; *Saturday Review,* 1924–1974; and *Choice,* 1964–1974. Rapidity of access to these reviews has to be weighed against an expensive price tag and the limited demand for dated reviews.

Note: Carrollton Press has entered the field of cumulative book-review indexing with its 15-volume *Combined Retrospective Index to Book Reviews in Scholarly Journals,* 1886–1974 and a 10-volume (in progress) *Combined Retrospective Index to Book Reviews in Humanities Journals, 1902–1974.* Convenient for the reference librarian with a specific work in mind as access is by author, not subject.

New York Times Book Review Index, 1896–1970. New York: Times and Arno Press, 1977. Annual supplements. Decennial cumulations planned.

The *New York Times* has reissued its entire series of book reviews starting with the first issue of October 10, 1896. A five-volume index has been published to cover the 124-volume set. Everything printed in the book review sections has been included in the index, except for advertisements and queries to the editor.

Vol. 1: Author index; Vol. 2: Title index; Vol. 3: Byline index; Vol. 4: Subject index; Vol. 5: Category index. Volume 5 will be of greatest interest to those who look for reviews of reference materials, because one of the "categories" is

"Reference Works," and the arrangement is chronological by year. The first year is 1897, and the first of the seven reference reviews indexed for that year is *Harper's Dictionary of Classical Literature and Antiquities*. This chronological arrangement will appeal to those who are interested in the historical development of reference book publishing.

This index can be used with the bound volumes of book reviews or with the microfilm edition of the *Times*. It is expensive and libraries subscribing to the *New York Times Index* may question the need for it if money is running short.

Reference Sources, 1977–   . Ann Arbor, Mich.: Pierian Press. Annual. Successor to *Reference Book Review Index,* 1970–1972, 1973–1975, and *Subject Guide to Reference Books,* 1970–1975.

The only index that covers reference material exclusively. Over 270 periodicals are scanned for reviews. The 1979 cumulated annual volume *Reference Sources* listed over 3500 titles with citations to over 5000 reviews. This included all reviews in *American Reference Books Annual, Choice, Library Journal,* and *Reference and Subscription Books Reviews.* The majority of the works covered are English language materials published in the United States. Arrangement is by verified main entry with three subject indexes: (1) general subject; (2) classified subject (DDC); and (3) alphabetical by Library of Congress subject headings. Complete bibliographical information, citation to reviews, and an occasional brief annotation are given.

Note: Not included in the above list but of interest to the special librarian are indexes to reviews in special fields, e.g., *Index to Scientific Reviews,* 1975–   . (Philadelphia: Institute for Scientific Information); *Technical Book Review Index,* 1917–   . (New York: Special Libraries Association); and *Index to Book Reviews in Historical Periodicals,* 1972–   . (Metuchen, N.J.: Scarecrow Press).

THE REVIEWING MEDIA

American Reference Books Annual (ARBA), 1970–   . Littleton, Colo.: Libraries Unlimited.

In the short time since it began publication, *ARBA* has become an indispensable source for reviews of reference books and is useful for all libraries. It provides reviews for all new reference books and serials published in the United States each year with the limitation that a "book" must have a minimum length of 48 pages. New editions of older works also are included with frequent comparisons to the earlier editions. Foreign imprints with an exclusive distributor in the United States are selectively covered but generally restricted to material in the English language. Other categories where the reviewing is selective include government publications and reprints.

ARBA attempts to cover books published in January through December in each volume, but if imprints reach the editorial office too late for inclusion, reviews will be found in the volume for the succeeding year.

Following a section on general reference works, arrangement is by subject with appropriate subdivisions. There are separate sections for categories such as librarianship and library resources, ethnic studies, and communications. Detailed subject descriptors are used with specific author and title access provided through an index. A cumulative index covering the first five years, 1970-74, has been published in a separate volume.

Most reviews are signed and contributors are identified at the beginning of each volume; many are subject specialists. Unsigned reviews are prepared by members of the editorial staff, but if the reviews are critical, they are always signed. An excellent feature is the inclusion of references to reviews published in such periodicals as *Choice, Library Journal,* and *Wilson Library Bulletin.* Prices and full bibliographic information are given.

ARBA 's comprehensive coverage for United States trade publications is unique; all other reviewing media are selective. Quality in reviewing can be variable, but *ARBA* has a good record for providing critical comments when indicated and does not hesitate to make comparisons with similar tools. Reviews are the right length; they supply all the important information without burdening the reader with unnecessary detail. The chief weakness is the lack of provision for supplements during the year.

When a more selective approach is wanted, librarians can consult Libraries Unlimited *Best Reference Books: Titles of Lasting Value, 1970-76,* a selection of 818 major reference titles chosen from *ARBA.*

Note: Libraries Unlimited's biennial publication, *Government Reference Books,* 1968/69–   provides the coverage for government reference material lacking in *ARBA.*

Choice, 1964–   . Middletown, Conn.: Association of College and Research Libraries. Monthly. Annual cumulated index. Decennial cumulation, 1964-74. 9 volumes.

Designed for the undergraduate library, *Choice* each month reviews between 600 and 700 new books and editions from the United States and Canadian publishers and some publishers abroad that have a North American distributor. Around 50 of these reviews are for reference books. Arrangement is alphabetical by subject with subject headings corresponding to "names" of academic departments. Reference books have a section of their own. Preceding the main section are lengthy bibliographical essays, other selective reference reviews, and a regular department called "Periodicals for College Libraries," a selective annotated listing that supplements *Classified List of Periodicals for the College Library* by Evan Farber (see annotation, Chapter 4). Mr. Farber also helps prepare this list for *Choice.*

Books are evaluated by college faculty members involved in undergraduate education. Reviews are unsigned, but there is an alphabetical list of consultants at the end of each issue preceding the author and title indexes. Prices and full bibliographic information are included.

The quality of reviewing in *Choice* is superior with concise (about 200 words), informative, and, if necessary, critical reviews. New titles are compared to earlier ones in the field; new editions receive a careful analysis. Although specifically aimed at junior and four-year colleges, the coverage has application for the larger public library and research institution. The chief weakness in this source is the time lag between date of publication of the book and the appearance of its review. Editing by the staff follows the examination by the reviewer, and the delay is usually three to six months and at times even longer.

The first 10 years of *Choice* has been cumulated into a nine-volume set with over 3000 reviews of reference works included. Eight volumes are subject-arranged and the ninth is the index volume. An author and title index cites the review both in the original issue of *Choice* as well as the one in the classified cumulation. A subject index refers the reader only to the cumulation. The index volume may be purchased separately.

College and Research Libraries, 1939–   . Chicago: Amercian Library Association, Association of College and Research Libraries. Bimonthly.

As the official journal of the Association of College and Research Libraries, the articles in *College and Research Libraries* naturally are oriented to the academic library. This is also true of the coverage in the book review section.

"Selected Reference Books" appears semiannually (January and July) and is now edited by Eugene P. Sheehy, who also edited *Guide to Reference Books* (see annotation, Chapter 4). An earlier editor in both instances was Constance Winchell. Despite the byline, the list is actually a project of the reference department of the Columbia University Libraries, and annotations are signed with initials of individual staff members. Full bibliographic information is given, and, when appropriate, code numbers are used to refer to titles in Sheehy's *Guide*. Highly selective, fewer than 75 books are reviewed annually. However, the reviews are important for the coverage of foreign language and other material supporting graduate work. At the end of the reviews a final section called "New Editions, Supplements, Etc." briefly describes new editions of standard works, continuations, and supplements.

Note: Foreign language reference tools (other than dictionaries and encyclopedias) are usually acquired only by academic libraries catering to research needs. Locating reviews for these works is more difficult than for English language material. Indexes such as *Index to Book Reviews in the Humanities* and *Internationale Bibliographie der Rezensionen Wissenschaftlicher Literatur* will be of help. Academic journals in special fields review important reference sources within their subject scope, and a few may be found in the general reviewing sections of some library periodicals. *Library Literature* (New York: Wilson) also may index some of these reviews.

Reference librarians in research institutions must be aware of the academic needs of the departments and the reference material needed to support the collection. These libraries have acquisitions departments who regularly receive catalogs of foreign publishers and subscribe to foreign bibliographical tools that will alert all librarians about new publications. The reference department also will subscribe to the ones needed for reference work.

Library Journal, 1876–   . New York: Bowker. Semimonthly.

Library Journal began publication in the same year that the American Library Association was organized. Three men, R. R. Bowker, Frederick Leypoldt, and Melvil Dewey, were prominent in both the founding of the Association and the periodical. Published continuously since that year, *Library Journal* included regular notes on reference works and bibliographies very early in its history. A formal section for adult book reviews (including reference books) finally was established in 1940 and, while there have been several changes in name, the service has continued without interruption.

Reference books are regularly reviewed in a section under that name in the department called ''The Book Review,'' and occasionally others can be found in the department named ''Professional Reading.'' In addition, each year the April 15 issue features ''Reference Sources,'' an annotated list of the outstanding reference sources of the preceding year selected by the Outstanding Reference Books Committee of ALA's Reference and Adult Services Division. This committee began functioning in 1958 and, to date, around 1500 outstanding titles have been named and recommended for the small and medium-sized library. This same list also appears in *Booklist,* a publication of the American Library Association. In 1978, the April 15 issue also began carrying a new list called ''New Reference Books.''

Library Journal reviews a large number of both fiction and nonfiction books each year. Concise signed reviews (by librarians) emphasize summary and description rather than comparison and analysis. There have been some complaints about the lack of critical comment, but the quantity of coverage plus a minimal time lag between publication and review make this an important source for the librarian. Complete bibliographic information including price is given.

Since 1967, all of the reviews for the year (about 6000) are cumulated into an annual bound volume called *The Library Journal Book Review.* Arranged under 24 broad subject areas, two sections are devoted to reference material—one called ''Reference'' and the other ''Recently Revised Reference Works.'' An examination will show that reviews of special reference books also may appear under the appropriate subject.

For serial selection, be sure to check Bill Katz's department called

"Magazines," which supplements his editions of *Magazines for Libraries* (see annotation, Chapter 4). Indexing services, alternative publications, and reference serials are reviewed in addition to a variety of general interest and academic publications.

RQ, 1960–   . Chicago: American Library Association, Reference and Adult Service Division. Quarterly.

As the only journal solely devoted to reference work as well as reference sources, *RQ* should be read from cover to cover by students interested in becoming reference librarians. As the official journal of the Reference and Adult Services Division of the American Library Association, "the purpose of *RQ* is to disseminate materials of interest to reference librarians, bibliographers, adult services librarians, and others interested in user-oriented library service." The scope includes service for all age levels and types of libraries.

The regular reviewing section is called "In Review" and covers reference books but few serials or subscription titles. Reviews are signed and brief (about 150 to 200 words). Coverage is selective with about 30 to 50 reviews covered in an issue. Occasionally this includes a foreign title. Prices and complete bibliographic information are given.

More important than the reviews are the other articles and columns. In almost every issue, an article examining reference material in a specific subject field can be found; government publications are regularly featured. "Online Services," a regular column about machine-assisted public services by Danuta A. Nitecki, was introduced in the Summer 1980 issue.

A significant annual feature in the Winter issue is "United States of America Bibliographical and Abstracting Services and Related Activities." This compilation is an expansion of the report prepared in reply to the questionnaire sent out by UNESCO and published in its bimonthly periodical *Bibliography, Documentation, Terminology.* These expanded reports have been published in *RQ* or as separates since the first one appeared covering 1961–62. Entries are arranged by form or subject, and the coverage, while not exhaustive, is significant of the wide range of bibliographical activity in this country.

Reference and Subscription Books Reviews, 1930–   . (Formerly titled *Subscription Books Bulletin.*) Now issued as a special department within *Booklist* (Chicago: American Library Association, 1905–   . Semimonthly). Separate bound cumulations published annually.

The most noted of reviewing services for reference books had its beginnings in 1928 when the executive board of the American Library Association created the Subscription Books Committee. The committee was established to promote quality reference books by accumulating information about books sold by subscription as well as reference tools distributed through normal trade channels, and, in 1930, began publishing a quarterly review *Subscription Books Bulletin.* The Committee also was designed to function as a watchdog and to receive reports on questionable sales practices and transmit them to agencies such as the Better Business Bureau and the Federal Trade Commission. In 1956, *Subscription Books Bulletin* merged with *Booklist* to become *Booklist and Subscription Books Bulletin.* "Subscription Books Bulletin" was dropped from the title in 1969 as the reviewing service. Still maintaining its editorial independence, it changed its name to *Reference and Subscription Books Reviews,* with the committee renamed the Reference and Subscription Books Review Committee. Consumer articles as well as reviews continued to be published. About the same time, a separate cumulation of past reviews was first published and today, appears regularly as an annual publication.

There are 50 members on the committee who are appointed by the ALA Executive Board to serve for one- or two-year terms (not to exceed six consecutive years). The members include a cross-section of professional librarians and library school faculty. Any reference book that might be of general interest and all books sold by subscription are eligible for consideration. Technical titles, foreign language works, and interpretive material generally are not accepted. The chairperson selects works that conform to established guidelines, but evaluation of general encyclopedias has been a major function of the committee.

Once a title is accepted for review, a committee member is assigned primary responsibility for the preparation of a draft. This is circulated to the entire committee for evaluation. Members operate upon procedures set forth in a manual published by the committee which cover standards for evaluating accuracy, currency, objectivity, access to the information, physical format, and so on. Every review is revised until different opinions have been resolved. The entire committee is supposed to endorse each review, but the revision is not distributed to each member.

It is obvious that this elaborate mechanism for review creates a great time lag between date of publication and date of review. It also means that a relatively small number of books can be reviewed as the major reviews are exceedingly detailed.

The time lag becomes a serious flaw in the case of expensive multivolume sets and major works that have caught the public interest. It took two years for a review of *Webster's Third International Dictionary of the English Language* to appear and an equal delay for the *Encyclopedia of Philosophy.* The *International Encyclopedia of Social Sciences* was reviewed more than a year after publication and a time lag of more than five years for the *Encyclopedia International.*

While librarians appreciate the amount of factual information included in these reviews, many of them make dull reading. Flaws are emphasized and frequent comparisons made with similar tools, but these are often buried in a mass of minutiae. Perhaps this is the inevitable outcome of a product of a committee rather than an individual. Recommendations for or against purchase generally conclude the reviews with an indication of the type of library that can make the best use of the sources. Full bibliographic information, of course, is given.

Probably in response to the criticism about the limited number of books, the committee has recently enlarged coverage by including shorter reviews and notes in addition to the lengthy reviews of major works. The 11th cumulation covered 139 reviews and 139 notes that originally appeared in *Booklist* between September 1, 1975 and July 15, 1976. However, the notes are not reviewed by the committee but are edited at headquarters.

It might be noted that library school students generally appreciate *RSBR*'s emphasis on detail and comparison when trying to master the complexities of many of the major reference works. Finally, the importance of a review in *RSBR* should not be underestimated. A negative review is bad news for the publisher of a reference work!

Note: In 1980 there was some discussion by the ALA Publishing Services Committee of the Reference and Adult Services Division on separating *Reference and Subscription Books Review* from *Booklist*. A decision was postponed until a market survey could be completed.

RSR (Reference Services Review), 1972–   . Ann Arbor, Mich.: Pierian Press.
    Quarterly.

While *Wilson Library Bulletin* (see annotation below) has the distinction of being the first library journal to inaugurate a regular monthly department reviewing reference books, *RSR* is the first periodical devoted exclusively to reference book reviewing. It emphasizes reviews of recent as well as older reference works of value to general, academic, and special libraries.

Each issue runs at least 80 pages and is divided into departments and special features. Current surveys of reference sources in subject fields such as film, business, botany, political science, and so on provide annotated reviews and bibliographical essays highlighting the state of the art in the particular area. Full bibliographic information with price is included. *RSR* also offers retrospective coverage through review essays on major sources within a narrowly defined subject area. The column "Landmarks of Reference" offers an historical perspective on major reference works.

A noteworthy department, "Reference Serials," first appeared in *RSR* in 1974 but was transferred to the inaugural issue of Pierian Press' *Serials Review* in 1975. It returned to *RSR* in 1979 and continues to feature signed evaluative and comparative reviews of tools such as *Social Sciences Index, Current Index to Journals in Education, Dissertation Abstracts International, Writers and Artists' Yearbook, Federal Register,* and *General Science Index*. Students are advised to pay attention to any review coverage of abstracting services, indexes, serial bibliographies, yearbooks, directories, and other reference serials. They dominate a reference collection, and, as they are issued more than once, will repeatedly dominate a budget.

Other special features of particular interest to the student in a reference class are annotated bibliographies on aspects of reference work such as library instruction and the reference interview. Of even greater use to the reference librarian is the annual review "Bibliography of United States Government Bibliographies," which is an annotated listing arranged by subject. Advertising is accepted, and while few ads for reference material have appeared to date, they do reflect important publishers in the field.

One feature, regrettably dropped in 1979, was the indexing of reviews of reference materials. This column provided quarterly updating of Pierian Press' annual *Reference Sources*. From all indications, this yearly cumulation will continue to make its appearance.

RSR is a young journal and, no doubt, changes in coverage and approach will continue to be noted. However, the editors appear to strive for excellence, and quality in both the reviewing and the writing can be observed. It should become increasingly profitable for students and librarians to become regular readers.

Serials Review, 1975–   . Ann Arbor, Mich.: Pierian Press. Quarterly.

Serials Review has made a promising beginning in alleviating some of the problems created by serials and especially in their selection. It provides bibliographic information and evaluations of periodicals, newspapers, indexes, union lists, and periodical bibliographies. Reference serials, as mentioned above, are covered in the companion reviewing quarterly, *RSR*. *SR* also includes articles on serials budgets, copyright, interlibrary loan, periodical selection and evaluation, and other areas of interest to the reference or serials librarian.

Regular departments feature (1) "Tools of the Serials Trade," which review monographic and serial publications about serials; (2) "Newspapers in Review;" (3) "Review Sources," which focuses on review sources and indexes that are serial in nature, and which should be regularly checked by anyone responsible for selection; and (4) "Cumulative Indexes," which notes and reviews attempts to index serials.

The periodical and newsletter, and government publications reviewing sections are theme-oriented. The indexing of serials in these departments are covered in a supplement called "Indexed Periodicals Supplement."

Serials Review, like *RSR*, is a relatively new periodical and also shows frequent changes in format and coverage. While final evaluation of its worth can wait, *SR*'s efforts to clarify problems in the selection and management of serials should be commended.

Wilson Library Bulletin, 1914–   . New York: Wilson. Monthly.

Wilson Library Bulletin was the first library periodical to establish a regular department devoted exclusively to reviewing reference books. Called "Current Reference Books," it began in 1937 and was first edited by Louis Shores. The present editor is Charles A. Bunge.

Aimed at the small- and medium-sized school, and public and academic library, the reviews are compiled with the cooperation of the Madison (Wisconsin) Public Library. Until the end of 1979, arrangement was alphabetical by subject but standard headings were not used. Subarrangement was difficult to determine, although reviews were serially numbered. With the December 1979 issue, arrangement became alphabetical by author, and reviews have since become lengthier and more detailed. About 20 to 30 titles are discussed in each issue. Regularly issued editions of standard works are not included, nor does space permit in-depth reviews of large multivolume sets.

In addition to the annotation, full bibliographic information, including price, is given. Comments include recommendations for purchase.

"Current Reference Books" is an established part of the reviewing media and important for its long focus on the public library and inclusion of books of interest for home use. There is no cumulation of these monthly reviews.

SUMMARY

Nine prominent reviewing media for reference books and serials have been discussed. In addition, reviews may be located in other periodicals and general reviewing sources like the *New York Times Book Review, New York Review of Books,* and *TLS (Times Literary Supplement).* These are indexed in the standard periodical and review indexes, and the *New York Times Book Review* also publishes its own index. While these sources are very limited in their coverage of reference books, the quality of the reviews occasionally can be extraordinary. Who can forget Kurt Vonnegut's memorable review of the *Random House Dictionary* in the *New York Times Book Review* (October 20, 1966), or the hilarious critique by Marvin Kitman of *Who's Who in America* (June 23, 1968)? Sympathetic readers wept with Dwight MacDonald in his despairing plea for the restoration of the English language after first encountering *Websters Third International Dictionary of the English Language* ("A String Untuned," *New Yorker,* March 10, 1962). Those who followed the coverage the *Times Literary Supplement* gave to the new supplements to the *Oxford English Dictionary* were ready to go into debt to have these volumes by their bedside.

All librarians should read reviews; it is essential if they are going to take part in the selection process in a library and/or do reference work. It is time-consuming but not an unpleasant task, and, with a little bit of luck, occasionally the reward is a witty and brilliant piece of prose.

REFERENCES AND SUGGESTED READINGS

Avant, J. A. Slouching toward criticism. *Library Journal,* 1971, *96*(December 15), 4055–4059.

Bauer, H. Mediocrity better than nothing. *RQ,* 1970, *10*(Winter), 139–140.

Bone, L. E. Choosing the best: A review of the aids for the selection of reference books. *RSR,* 1976, *4*(July–September), 81–83.

Bonk, W. J., & Magrill, R. M. The selector and book selection aids. In their *Building library collections* (5th ed.). Metuchen, N.J.: Scarecrow, 1979, pp. 96–124.

Covey, A. A. *Reviewing of reference books.* Metuchen, N.J.: Scarecrow, 1972.

Crane, K. K. Questions on new editions: Is this revision? *RQ,* 1970, *9*(Spring), 227-231.

Evans, G. E. Producers of library materials. In his *Developing library collections.* Littleton, Colo.: Libraries Unlimited, 1979, pp. 32-66.

Kister, K. Wanted: more professionalism in reference book reviewing. *RQ,* 1979, *19*(Winter), 144-148.

Kurian, G. T. *The directory of American book publishing: From founding fathers to today's conglomerates.* N.Y.: Simon and Shuster, 1975.

Pierson, R. M. Reference and subscription books review committee. *American Libraries,* 1980, *11*(January), 32.

Ream, D. An evaluation of four book review journals. *RQ,* 1979, *19*(Winter), 149-153.

Shores, L. Reference book reviewing. *RSR,* 1973, *1*(October-December), 3-6.

Wagner, S. FTC rules against Grolier on unfair practices. *Publishers Weekly,* 1978, *213*(April 17), 24, 26.

White, C. M. How to avoid duplicated information. *RQ,* 1970, *10*(Winter), 127-137.

Whitmore, H. E. Reference book reviewing. *RQ,* 1970, *9*(Spring), 221-226.

Wood, F. W. Reviewing book review indexes. *RSR,* 1980, *8*(April-June), 47-52.

Young, A. P. The pursuit of mediocrity. *RQ,* 1970, *10*(Winter), 138-139.

CHAPTER 4

Selection Aids for Reference Collections

INTRODUCTION

In this chapter, bibliographical tools that aid in the selection of books and serials for reference collections will be examined and evaluated. As has been previously stated, the purpose of this text is not to discuss the working tools that are used to answer questions. While some of the titles included can serve that function, the emphasis always will lie on their value in the selection process.

In the first sections that follow, bibliographical tools that aid in the selection of retrospective reference material will be singled out. In most cases, these aids will stress English language material published in the United States. Then, a discussion follows on the various ways librarians become alerted to new and forthcoming books and serials. Final sections cover special problem areas such as government publications and foreign language reference material.

SELECTING BOOKS AND SERIALS FOR THE BASIC REFERENCE COLLECTION

GENERAL GUIDES TO REFERENCE BOOKS

Library school students soon become familiar with Eugene Sheehy's *Guide to Reference Books* as it is the primary bibliographical text in most reference courses. Many of them can be observed laboriously copying an annotation on their reference syllabus in the hope that the process will speed up the actual examination of the book itself or make it unnecessary. Few are ready to think about the actual value such a guide has in a reference collection.

The odds are excellent that by the end of a new librarian's first week at a reference desk, a bibliographic guide such as Sheehy will have been consulted in order to find a bibliography or other reference source needed by a user and apparently not in the reference department. A quick look identifies existing tools in all fields; a quick step to the main catalog reveals if the needed book is somewhere in the collection. If it is not in the library, thought should be given to adding it or locating a copy.

A bibliographical guide also is important as a selection aid for the librarian. One does not look here for first aid on the latest thesaurus promoted by full-page ads in *Publishers Weekly* and in Sunday newspaper book review supplements. However, the guide should be consulted to see what it says about existing thesauri; perhaps the new one has little to offer other than a recent publication date and may virtually duplicate an older work. Always keep in mind that book publishing is a business, and reference books are a lucrative outlet. An established guide can help resist the advertising pressures from reference book publishers.

In addition to promoting sales resistance, general bibliographic guides help fill gaps in a collection. The small library with neither the time nor the money to offer sophisticated genealogical reference service, usually refers interested patrons to the largest public library in the area or to the nearest Mormon church office with a library. When a dramatic increase in the number of genealogical questions followed the publication of Alex Haley's *Roots,* this same library undoubtedly felt that some additions to its collection of genealogical reference tools had to be made. Consulting Sheehy proves a wise decision in such a case. The index to the main volume shows that genealogical sources are listed on pages 234–243; a fast count reveals that seven guides are listed and annotated along with over one hundred related reference works.

However, Sheehy's *Guide,* like all books, also must be used with an awareness of what it *cannot* do. Because the guide is a retrospective work, not all titles it lists will still be in print; it may take a bit of searching and a lot of time to locate and/or photocopy that 1911 Shakespeare bibliography. Though a fairly comprehensive source, Sheehy generally offers only a brief annotation. All too frequently the information is only an excerpt from the book's introduction, and the present edition omits any citations to reviews.

Fortunately, there are other guides similar to Sheehy published in other countries. Walford's *Guide to Reference Material* is perhaps the best known and most heavily used; even small libraries purchase it. Walford frequently emphasizes more recent titles and the annotations are fuller. The emphasis on Great Britain complements Sheehy's tendency to include more books published in the United States. Scanning Walford's section on genealogy reveals some duplication with Sheehy but there are richer listings for the Commonwealth countries.

Librarians working in a large reference department should brush up on their French and become familiar with Malclès' works, especially *Les Sources du Travail Bibliographique.* Less parochial than either Walford or Sheehy, the book pays more attention to continental Europe and the Middle and Far East. Annotations and discussions are excellent.

Small reference departments that need help in building a basic collection will welcome more selective lists such as *Reference Books for Small and Medium-Sized Libraries* and *Reference Books in Paperback*. The thousands of titles in the larger guides can be overwhelming when the budget for books is stringent.

But whether working in a small or large reference department, librarians must sharpen their skills at book selection so that they can select wisely. Awareness of the magnitude and type of reference material that has been published can be gained by becoming familiar with these general guides to the reference literature, and that is just the beginning.

The following is a highly selective list of general guides to reference material. Consult Sheehy under "Reference Books" to find others that have been published. Particularly note regional guides like Dorothy Ryder's *Canadian Reference Sources: A Selective Guide* (Ottawa: Canadian Library Association, 1973. 1st supplement, 1976). This is a fine example of a guide with comprehensive coverage of a limited geographical area.

American Library Association. Ad Hoc Reference Books Review Committee. *Reference Books for Small and Medium-Sized Libraries.* Larry Earl Bone, ed. 3rd ed. Chicago, 1979.

Librarians working in the smaller library will appreciate this aid in building or expanding their collection. Brief annotations are included for the 1048 in-print titles considered suitable for public and college libraries. Budgetary constraints are considered in their selection, although some of the inclusions as well as omissions might be questioned. Arrangement is classed with author and title index.

Malclès, Louise-Noelle. *Manuel de bibliographie*. 3rd ed., revised by Andrée Lheritier. Paris: Presses Universitaires de France, 1976.

————. *Les Sources du Travail Bibliographique*. Genève: E. Droz, 1950–58. 3 vols.

Like Sheehy and Walford (see annotations), both of Malclès' works are designed to serve as textbooks as well as annotated guides to reference material. Coverage in *Les Sources du Travail Bibliographique* is comprehensive (ca. 20,000 titles) and international, and includes all types of reference and source materials. Those who read French will find the introductions and discussions in each chapter useful. Heavy emphasis on continental Europe and the Middle East makes this an ideal source to supplement Sheehy and Walford in a large research library. Arrangement is classified with author, subject, and title indexes included for each volume.

The *Manuel de Bibliographie* emphasizes the theory and history of bibliography, and this is apparent in the heavy coverage of bibliographical tools and limited space devoted to general works of reference. However, material published through 1975 is covered, and the inclusion of special bibliographies in the humanities and social sciences adds to its value. Some discussion of automated databases is given. Arrangements is in three parts; "General Bibliography," "Special Bibliography," and "Bibliology." Combined author and title index and separate index of subjects.

Sheehy, Eugene. *Guide to Reference Books*. 9th ed. Chicago: American Library Association, 1976. 1st supplement, 1980.

The history of reference librarianship's most famous work goes back to 1902 when the American Library Association published its *Guide to the Study and Use of Reference Books* by Alice Kroger. From its earliest days, libraries and library schools adopted and used this guide. Two other compilers, Isadore Mudge and Constance Winchell, were responsible for its development over the years into its present format and size. Always aimed at a large general reference collection, many works in foreign languages are included in its scope. However, emphasis remains on books published in the United States.

About 10,000 titles are roughly divided into five classifications: general reference works, the humanities, social sciences, history and area studies, pure and applied sciences. The *Guide* has adopted an alpha–numeric scheme for identifying each item with access through a detailed index.

The first supplement to the ninth edition focuses on the period between fall 1974 and fall 1978, but also includes a number of works omitted from the ninth edition. In general, arrangement of the entries follows that of the main volume, but a new catagory has been added for databases. Also, the growing amount of material on women, blacks, ethnic groups, energy, and cinema is reflected in the increase in entries for the corresponding reference material. Prices are given but their value is only in indicating a possible "range"; it is doubtful whether many will be accurate today.

United States Library of Congress. *The Library of Congress Main Reading Room Reference Collection Subject Catalog*. Compiled by Katherine Ann Gardner. Washington, D.C. 1975.

Approximately 11,000 monographs and 3000 serials are arranged alphabetically by Library of Congress subject headings with coverage to January 1, 1975. Entries are duplicated under all subject headings listed on the LC catalog card. There are no annotations, but entry information includes author, short title, imprint, Dewey number, LC card number, and call number. The catalog is useful because of the multiple subject access, and it provides an overview of the basic reference collection in our nation's leading library.

Walford, Albert. *Guide to Reference Material*. 3rd ed. London: Library Association, 1973–77. 3 vols. (Vol. 1, Science and Technology). 4th edition, 1980.

Like Sheehy and Malclès, Walford is international in scope, although emphasis is on items published in Great Britain. It also is aimed at the student and book selector, is designed as a working tool, and facilitates a bibliographical search.

The three volumes are divided as follows: Vol. 1—Science and Technology; Vol. 2—Social and Historical Sciences and Philosophy and Religion; and Vol. 3—Generalities, Languages, the Arts, and Literature. Each volume has a classed arrangement with an index, all items are annotated, and Vol. 3 contains a cumulated subject index. Volume 1, Science and Technology, of the 4th edition was published in 1980 and continues the format of the 3rd edition. Volumes 2 and 3 will be published in 1982 and 1984, respectively.

Wynar, Bohdan. *Reference Books in Paperback: An Annotated Guide.* 2nd ed. Littleton, Colo.: Libraries Unlimited, 1976.

Designed for the small library and home use, the guide lists 715 titles with annotations and reference to reviews and related works. Grouped by topical catagories with author–title and subject indexes, *Reference Books in Paperback* is a good choice for the budget-minded librarian or patron.

GUIDES TO SPECIAL TYPES OF REFERENCE SOURCES

Regardless of the *subject* emphasis of the reference department, certain *types* of reference sources can be expected to be found in any collection. General and special bibliographies, dictionaries, directories, encyclopedias, and so on have to be available for both the librarian and the user. There are a few published guides to these types of works that will aid in the selection process as well as in reference work. Those specifically designed to be selection tools are frequently revised and can be useful in helping a patron select a reference book for home use. They evaluate, compare, and give prices and references to reviews. Library school students find the detail helpful when working on their assignments.

Atlases

General World Atlases in Print. Compiled by S. Padraig Walsh. New York: Bowker. Frequently revised.

First published in 1966, *General World Atlases in Print* was designed to provide all necessary information for the selection of general world atlases available and published in the United States and Great Britain. For each of the atlases analyzed, the following information is provided: publishing history; editors, cartographers, and contributors; home sale and retail prices; purpose and age suitability; scope, contents, and arrangement; total map pages and types of maps with discussion of scale, projection, and so on; a summary and evaluation; references to other reviews and sources of information. An introductory article offers a general discussion on map evaluation. All atlases are numerically ranked

(25 is the maximum rating). Briefer descriptions are provided for one hundred smaller atlases. Excludes special purpose atlases.

Bibliographies

Besterman, Theodore. *A World Bibliography of Bibliographies*. 4th ed. Lausanne: Societas Bibliographica, 1965–66. 5 vols. Supplement, 1964–74 by Alice M. Toomey. 2 vols.

Age alone precludes consideration of Besterman as a "buying guide" but, in order to develop skill at selecting new material, it is necessary to become familiar with the retrospective sources. Bibliographies are one of the largest group of reference material in a library; the demand appears insatiable and publishers are aware of this. Librarians are being deluged with ads for new bibliographical tools, some of which are unnecessary and many of which are poor.

Besterman has been the classic source for the identification of separately published bibliographies in all fields; the decennial supplement brings coverage through 1974, but entries are limited to material cataloged by the Library of Congress.

In addition, Rowman and Littlefield have issued a series called *The Besterman World Bibliographies*. Titles in different subject fields such as printing, education, Africa, and technology, to name a few, are extracted from the original work and, with varying degrees of revision and additions of new material cataloged by the Library of Congress, are compiled into separate volumes and sold at prices ranging from $10 to $75. To date, over twenty such titles have appeared, but librarians should check the amount of new material in each volume before ordering. An interesting exercise for library school students would be to measure their cost against their value as "convenience" tools. Special libraries that cannot afford the Library of Congress catalogs may find their purchase advantageous; large academic libraries subscribing to the full range of Library of Congress catalogs will weigh more carefully an expenditure of money for convenience and faster access.

Bibliographic Index, 1937–   . New York: H. W. Wilson. 3/yr. Annual cumulations.

Because of its frequency, *Bibliographic Index* is a good source for identifying new bibliographies. It is designed more as a working tool than one for selection as it includes bibliographies appended to periodical articles, as well as those separately published. International in coverage, each bibliography must have at least 50 entries to qualify for inclusion. Prices are not given.

Biographical Dictionaries

Slocum, Robert B. *Biographical Dictionaries and Related Works*. Detroit: Gale Research Co., 1967. 1st supplement, 1972; 2nd supplement, 1978.

International in scope, these three volumes include around 10,000 entries. The introduction defines "related works" as "collective biographies, bio-bibliographies, collections of epitaphs, selected genealogical works, dictionaries of anonyms and pseudonyms, historical and specialized dictionaries, biographical materials in government manuals, bibliographies of biography, biographical indexes, and selected portrait catalogs."

While something less than a buying guide (no prices are given and material is not necessarily in print), Slocum still becomes the first choice for the reference librarian who has exhausted the obvious selection tools.

The work is arranged in three sections: universal biography, national or area biography, and biography by vocation. Indexes are by authors, titles, and subjects.

Dictionaries

Kister, Kenneth F. *Dictionary Buying Guide*. New York: Bowker, 1977.

Designed as a consumer guide to general English language wordbooks in print, the *Dictionary Buying Guide* gives full descriptive, critical, and comparative information for 58 adult dictionaries, 61 school and children's dictionaries, and 225 specialized wordbooks covering acronyms, usage, pronunciation, spelling, etymology, slang, rhymes, and so on. While restricted to the English language, the guide includes dictionaries of foreign terms and phrases. Appendices include a section on recently discontinued dictionaries, a bibliography, and a directory of publishers and distributors.

In the introduction, evaluative criteria are discussed and, for each dictionary, full descriptive information and a critical summary with reference to reviews are included. Prices are given. Valuable for selection in the library as well as in the home, the *Guide* is useful for librarians to consult when working at the desk. Library school students will find that it serves as a study aid when they are trying to master the unit on wordbooks in reference courses.

Large research libraries deal heavily with foreign language reference material and, consequently, they have a greater need for language aids. Librarians in these libraries are expected to be able to handle materials in other languages. It is not so difficult to obtain "bibliographical competence" in Western languages, although the more exotic tongues pose problems for those who suffer from the typical American provincial education. A useful aid is

Walford, A. J. and Screen, J. E. O. *A Guide to Foreign Language Courses and Dictionaries*. London: Library Association, 1977.

Designed for those who want to learn a language quickly, this work also will serve as a selection aid for the librarian. Now in its third edition, it was formerly titled *A Guide to Foreign Language Grammars and Dictionaries*.

Courses and dictionaries are listed and annotated for all Western European languages, as well as Chinese, Modern Greek, Japanese, Arabic, Hungarian, Bulgarian, Russian, Polish, and other Eastern European languages. Twenty-four languages are covered and material is selective, annotated, and graded. No prices are given.

Two bibliographies may prove useful for identifying foreign language wordbooks, although neither is annotated. Taking advantage of Library of Congress catalog cards, Gale Research Company has published the second edition of *Dictionaries, Encyclopedias, and Other Word-Related Books,* edited by Annie Brewer, 1979. It is a classed guide covering wordbooks in all languages since 1966 and cataloged by the Library of Congress. This is also another example of the trend toward taking advantage of Library of Congress and MARC records to compile special bibliographical lists. Librarians must learn to recognize when they are paying primarily for selectivity and superior arrangement rather than for new information. *Fachwörterbücher und Lexika: ein internationales Verzeichnis* [International Bibliography of Dictionaries] 6th ed. (New York: Bowker, 1973. Distributed for Verlag Dokumentation, Munich). This bibliography includes 7000 dictionaries from over 60 countries in 100 languages that cover the broad fields of economics, science, and technology.

Directories

The ALA Glossary of Library Terms (ALA, 1943) defines a directory as "a list of persons or organizations, systematically arranged, usually in alphabetic or classed order, giving address, affiliations, etc., for individuals and address, officers, functions, and similar data for organizations."

Accepting this definition, it should become obvious that there is a problem in keeping this kind of information current, and new editions and supplements have to be purchased if directory information service is to be provided. Even then, with the time lag that exists before manuscript copy can be published and distributed, librarians must rely on other methods for updating. Many reference departments must maintain their own directory files. By careful reading of daily newspapers and news magazines, sources such as almanacs, the *Official Congressional Directory,* and the *Government Manual* can be corrected and kept current. In public libraries that provide extensive "information and referral services," the neighborhood newspaper is invaluable. With the help of federal government funds, some public library networks assume the responsibility of providing the latest "directory" type of information for their region.

For guidance in the selection of new directories, use

The Directory of Directories. 1st ed. Detroit: Gale Research Co., 1980.

Arranged in 15 broad subject categories, over 5000 current directories of all kinds are described. A detailed subject index provides access to entries on a specific subject. There is also a title index. This work cumulates six 1977–78 issues of the *Directory Information Service* and adds 1000 additional listings. The *Directory Information Service, 1977–*   also serves as a periodic supplement and update to the first edition of *The Directory of Directories*.

Another bibliographic source for selection is Bernard Klein's *Guide to American Directories*. 10th ed. (Coral Gables, Fla.: B. Klein Publications, 1978). A classed arrangement covers "accounting" through "women's affairs." A "directory" is interpreted broadly enough to include sources such as the *Cookbook Index* and *Political Handbook and Atlas of the World*. So while over 6000 entries are included in the 10th edition, not all titles will be of interest to the would-be selector.

For international coverage, *International Bibliography of Directories*, 6th ed. (New York: K. G. Saur, 1978) is useful. Frequently revised but highly selective, the bibliography's emphasis is on the United States, Canada, Great Britain, and Western Europe. No annotations are given, but the brief bibliographical description does include price. No explanation of criteria for inclusion or exclusion is offered. Classed arrangement with keyword and geographical indexes.

Further help is provided by *Public Affairs Information Service Bulletin (PAIS), 1915–*   . (New York: PAIS, weekly), which has a regular heading in its weekly edition and cumulations called "Directory of Publishers and Organizations." Prices frequently are given. *Public Affairs Information Service Foreign Language Index, 1968–*   . (New York: PAIS, quarterly) uses the same heading for listings of foreign directories.

Encyclopedias

Neither the librarian nor the consumer has to worry about being alerted to the forthcoming publication of a new encyclopedia. Expensive to produce and facing a highly competitive market, its appearance is preceded by an intensive advertising campaign.

A difference in sales approach occurs when multivolume general English language encyclopedia sets are compared with one-volume works. Most of the former are sold through subscription instead of through bookstores. In the past this has meant a door-to-door sales program preceded by heavy mail advertising. If it is a brand new set, ads will appear in selected general periodicals, such as *Time* and *Newsweek,* as well as those in the book trade and librarianship.

New encyclopedias are heavily reviewed and frequently one can find critical comments in the book sections of general interest periodicals as well as standard book review media such as the *New York Times Book Review* and *Times Literary Supplement*. These, combined with trade reviews, should provide sufficient guidance for the librarian.

One-volume encyclopedias are sold through bookstores and are even more heavily promoted. A good example is the *Random House Encyclopedia*, which was aimed directly at the Christmas 1977 market. Reviews began to appear early in October (*Newsweek,* October 10, 1977), and while many of them were critical, the advertising took effect and Christmas sales were large.

Policies about the replacement of multivolume encyclopedia sets generally are set by the reference department when new printings take place. As "continuous revision" is the typical method for yearly updating, most libraries do not replace all of their sets annually.

Reference librarians in large research libraries face more difficulties in selection because of the number of subject and foreign language encyclopedias needed to complete their collection. Librarians are alerted to these by announcements through the mail, as well as ads and notes in library and booktrade journals. Many of these sets have to be contracted for in advance of publication, and so one cannot turn to reviews for guidance. These encyclopedias may be printed and distributed a volume at a time, and it is impossible to evaluate an encyclopedia without access to the index volume, which would appear only after completion of the set. So, the authority and reputation of the publisher is especially important in these cases. Even then, problems can arise that delay publication.

In most cases, these subject encyclopedias automatically will be purchased on the basis of a clearly defined need and because it may be the only one available in the field. Personal examination and use are the best means of learning to exploit their strengths and avoid their weaknesses. Reviews eventually appear to corroborate these findings or to point out features that may have been overlooked.

For guidance on the purchase of a general encyclopedia for the home or library, Bowker has published an excellent guide:

Kister, Kenneth. *Encyclopedia Buying Guide: A Consumer Guide to General Encyclopedias in Print.* New York: Bowker, 1978.

Detailed profiles are provided for single or multivolume encyclopedias currently available to the American consumer. Both children and adult sets are included. Descriptive information, price, scope, authority, arrangement, access, bibliographies, illustrations, style, format, and special features all are discussed. Summaries of critical opinion are given as well as references to other reviews. While many of the 33 encyclopedias are suitable only for home use, all of the standard English language encyclopedias found in libraries are included. Librarians will find this guide useful for selection and will surely want to make it available to the patron seeking advice on the purchase of an encyclopedia for the home.

Purchasing an Encyclopedia: 12 Points to Consider. Chicago: Reference and Subscription Books Review Committee, American Library Association, 1979.

This useful reprint from "Reference and Subscription Book Reviews," *Booklist,* December 1, 1978–February 1, 1979 provides detailed and critical reviews of 20 English and American encyclopedias. It also suggests criteria to use in evaluating an encyclopedia.

Note: Bowker is now publishing a series of 15 volumes known as *Specialized Encyclopedias and Dictionaries Series: A Consumer Guide to English-Language Word & Fact Books on Specific Subjects.* Kenneth Kister is the compiler, and the first book in the series is called *Art,* which examines approximately 750 titles.

Indexes and Abstracts

The indexing and abstracting tools a library acquires are closely tied to the serials collection, and sometimes it is difficult to tell whether a library has an indexing service because it subscribes to the periodicals, or if it subscribes to the periodicals because the indexing service is available. But the needs of the user and the nature of the library have to be considered no matter where the chain begins.

In addition to periodical indexes, a reference department needs newspaper indexes, indexes to reviews, dissertations, library resources, and indexes to monographic material such as collections of essays, Festschriften, plays, poetry, songs, short stories, and so on. All of these are well-advertised and reviewed and create few problems for the librarian. Catalogs of certain publishers who specialize in this kind of reference material should be scanned. In particular, one should check the catalog of H. W. Wilson for its listing of periodical and other indexes, and F. W. Faxon Co., Inc. and American Library Publishing Co., Inc. (formerly the Chicorel Library Publishing Corp.) for indexes to anthologies and collected works.

Information about indexing and abstracting publications can be found in the *Chicorel Index to Abstracting and Indexing Services: Periodicals in the Humanities and Social Sciences* (New York: Chicorel Library Publishing Corp., 1974); Dolores Owen's *Abstracts and Indexes in Science and Technology* (Metuchen, N.J.: Scarecrow Press, 1974); *Abstracting Services.* 2 vols. (The Hague: FID, 1969); and the first section of *Ulrich's International Periodicals Directory* (see annotation in the following). However, none of these sources evaluates. Look to the reviewing media to help fill this gap. Be sure to remember the regular feature in *Reference Services Review* called "Reference Serials" and Bill Katz's column in *Library Journal.*

Soon all major indexing and abstracting services will be available in machine-readable format as well as in printed form. Selection should depend on consideration of the entire reference collection and its users.

Statistical Sources

A heavy proportion of reference questions is statistical in nature. While this information can be found in many reference sources such as encyclopedias, yearbooks, and almanacs, a reference department cannot rely solely on these tools. In the first place, the amount and variety of information required indicate a need for more comprehensive statistical coverage. In addition, there is always the problem of accuracy and currency. By the time the information reaches an almanac or encyclopedia, the reported figures are several times removed from the agency that originally gathered the data and many months from the time of compilation. Special sources for statistics are described in:

Wasserman, Paul and O'Brien, Jacqueline. *Statistics Sources*. 6th ed. Detroit: Gale Research Company, 1980.

Subtitled a "subject guide to data on industrial, business, social, educational, financial and other topics for the United States and internationally," it includes over 20,000 citations to on-going sources, both published and unpublished.

The main section is arranged alphabetically by subject and there is a title index. Preceding the body of the work is a valuable selected bibliography of key statistical sources including (1) dictionaries; (2) bibliographies and guides; (3) almanacs; (4) United States government monographs and annuals; (5) United States government periodicals; (6) publications of major censuses; (7) statistical abstracts and supplements; (8) annuals and yearbooks; and (9) international sources.

In addition to the above title, Gale Research Company has published four other books covering sources for statistics. All are edited by Joan M. Harvey and are called *Statistics—Africa*, 1978; *Statistics—America*, 1973; *Statistics—Asia and Australasia*, 1974; and *Statistics—Europe*, 1976.

It always should be remembered that the United States Government is the principal and most important gatherer of statistical information in this country. A useful catalog published by the Department of Commerce is the *United States Bureau of Census Catalog of Publications, 1790-1972*. Along with the listing of the many thousands of reports compiled by the agency over the years, information on ordering the printed reports also is included. Current coverage is provided by the quarterly *Catalog of United States Census Publications*, 1946-   , published in two parts. Part II covers data files and special tabulations; this is particularly helpful now that so much statistical information has become available in machine-readable format. The familiar *Statistical Abstract* (Washington, D.C.: Bureau of Census, Annual) found in every reference department always includes a full list of the statistical sources used in compiling their tables. So it, too, qualifies as a selection tool.

SPECIAL BIBLIOGRAPHIC GUIDES OR GUIDES TO THE LITERATURE

One approach to the literature of a subject area is through a special bibliographic guide. The value of such a tool to the student beginning research is exceeded only by the value to the reference librarian lacking subject expertise in that area. A practiced eye quickly picks out the reference structure of the field. This not only enables one to provide better guidance to the user, but also to survey a reference collection with better knowledge of its capabilities. Acquire as many as possible and study them thoroughly!

There is, however, considerable variation in the type and depth of coverage in the hundreds of existing guides. But comprehensive ones covering broad areas such as *Harvard Guide to American History* (Cambridge, Mass., 1974); Robert Rogers' *The Humanities: A Selective Guide to Information Sources* (Littleton, Colo.: Libraries Unlimited, 1979); and Carl White's *Sources of Information in the Social Sciences* (Totowa, N.J.: Bedminster Press, 1973) will generally provide the following information: (1) an introduction to the field with its major divisions and a discussion of recent trends; (2) an approach to research with advice on subject headings and classification schemes; (3) heavily used reference tools; (4) important texts, source materials, and so on; (5) principal journals, including indexing, abstracting, and reviewing publications; (6) organizations including descriptions of their activities and publications; (7) libraries and museums with significant collections; (8) special types of materials used in the field such as government documents, maps, patents, and so on.

There is at least one guide to the literature in almost every subject area, and, in some fields like English literature, there must be at least a dozen. There are also guides that cover just the *reference* material on a subject such as H. Robert Malinowsky's *Science and Engineering Literature: A Guide to Reference Sources*. 2nd ed. (Littleton, Colo.: Libraries Unlimited, 1976), or Ching-chih Chen's *Scientific and Technical Information Sources* (Cambridge, Mass.: MIT Press, 1978). It is surprising to find the number of guides that exist for very narrow fields. A good example is Dean Tudor's *Wine, Beer, and Spirits* (Littleton, Colo.: Libraries Unlimited, 1975), which covers everything one could possibly want to know about the topic except alcoholism itself. Gale Research Company is in the process of publishing *The Gale Information Guide Library*, which will ultimately include over 250 titles covering American Literature, English Literature, American Studies, Art and Architecture, International Relations, Man and the Environment, Philosophy and Religion, and so on.

Note: To locate a guide in Sheehy, look under the subheading ''Guide'' or ''Guides and Manuals'' that follows the introduction of a new subject. The *Library of Congress Subject Headings* generally puts guides under Bibliography-Bibliography-Topic, Reference Books-Bibliography, or under Reference Books-Topic (see Fig. 4.2). Finally, remember that new guides as well as new editions of existing guides are constantly being published. Watch for them!

SELECTIVE LISTS—BOOKS

By their nature, selective lists of books are eclectic and that is their value in building or adding to a collection. Using them judiciously can save a librarian's time because inappropriate, unavailable, or inferior works will be weeded out in advance of selection. However, this never eliminates the need for careful study of the identified tools and/or a thorough check of their reviews.

Below are listed a few major selective lists. In almost every case, the emphasis, will be on books in English, in print, and available in the United States.

General

Public Library Catalog. New York: Wilson. Revised quinquennially. Annual supplements.

An annotated selective guide to nonfiction suitable for medium-sized libraries. All works are in print at time of compilation. The main section is arranged by Dewey Decimal classification with reference works found in the 000–009 classification. Author, title, subject, and analytical indexes are included, as well as a directory of publishers. Also useful for reader's advisory work.

Reader's Adviser: A Layman's Guide to Literature. 12th ed. New York: Bowker, 1974–77. 3 vols.

Vol. 1 British and American Poetry, Fiction, Essays and Criticism, Literary Biography, and Autobiography. Bibliographies and reference works in these areas are also included. Author index, title and subject index.

Vol. 2 British and American Drama; World Literature in Translation. Author and title index.

Vol. 3 The Best in the Reference Literature of the World. This volume is divided into General Reference Books, General Biography and Autobiography, Bibles and Related Texts, World Religions, Philosophy, Psychology, Science, Social Science, History, Communications, Folklore, Travel, and so on. Author and title index.

Reader's Adviser is worth scanning just for the information on reference material in special fields. For example, the section on "Bibles and Related Texts" in Vol. 3 covers 44 pages and everything a librarian needs to know about the various versions, concordances, interpretations, and notable editions can be found there.

Reader's Adviser originated as a series of lessons for classes in book salesmanship during World War I. Today, it is designed for the librarian and student as well as the bookseller and offers valuable advice on various editions (including microform) and reprints of a title. Series information, binding, and prices are given.

Books for College Students

Books for College Libraries: A Core Collection of 40,000 Titles. 2nd ed. Chicago: American Library Association, 1975. 6 vols. Index.

Forty thousand titles represent four-fifths of the 50,000 minimum number of titles that the 1959 ALA standards require for even the smallest four-year academic library. Arranged by modified Library of Congress classification, bibliography is located in the "Z" class. Other reference material can be found in the "A" (General Works) class or with the appropriate subject.

Pirie, James, comp. *Books for Junior College Libraries.* Chicago: American Library Association, 1969.

A selection guide for junior and community college libraries. About 20,000 titles are arranged in classed order with an author index. Reference books are listed in a separate section.

Note: Major universities such as Harvard and Princeton have published catalogs of their undergraduate collections. It may prove useful to check them as well as the above titles.

Books for Children and Young Adults

Children's Catalog; Junior High School Catalog; Senior High School Library Catalog.

Along with *Fiction Catalog* and *Public Library Catalog,* these titles are part of H. W. Wilson's "Standard Catalog Series." All are revised every five years with supplements issued annually. Nonfiction is arranged by Dewey Decimal classification with reference books found in the usual 000–099. All have author, title, subject, and analytical indexes as well as a directory of publishers. Like the *Public Library Catalog,* all are useful in reader's advisory work.

Haviland, Virginia. *Children's Literature: A Guide to Reference Sources.* Washington, D.C.: Library of Congress, 1966. 1st supplement, 1972; 2nd supplement, 1977.

An annotated bibliography of reference books selected on basis of usefulness to adults concerned with service for children through the eighth grade.

Peterson, Carolyn Sue. *Reference Books for Elementary and Junior High School Libraries.* 2nd ed. Metuchen, N.J.: Scarecrow Press, 1975.

An annotated bibliography of reference books arranged by broad subject.

Meacham, Mary. *Information Sources in Children's Literature: A Practical Reference Guide for Children's Librarians, Elementary School Teachers, and Students of Children's Literature.* Westport, Conn.: Greenwood Press, 1978.

Critical annotations for reference books about authors and illustrators, periodical reviewing sources, selection and reference works for specific subject fields, guides that advise on using books with children, and sources on ordering and cataloging. Reproductions of pages from reference tools are included.

Wynar, Christine E. *Guide to Reference Books for School Media Centers.* Littleton, Colo.: Libraries Unlimited, 1973.

A guide that covers reference books for both print and nonprint media useful for students through the twelfth grade and for the professional needs of teachers and librarians. Evaluative annotations are arranged by subject with an author, title, and subject index. Updated by biennial supplements.

GENERAL GUIDES TO SERIALS

It is never too soon to point out that librarians welcome any help they can get with serials. These publications occupy an enormous amount of space in a library, and they can take up the greatest part of the acquisitions budget both in the reference and the general collection. Moreover, their handling and interpretation are time-consuming. First of all, a librarian has to learn of their existence and, while bibliographical control over serials records has improved, it is still easier to find information about a book than a serial. Complications are created when a serial changes its title, or interrupts or ceases publication. Once a subscription is ordered, the serials librarian endures the agonies of claiming the serial, checking it in, keeping track of the title pages and indexes, and knowing when to send it to the bindery. In large libraries, computers are beginning to relieve librarians of much of this handling, but the average small library still keeps manual records.

Serials are expensive and subscription prices are increasing at an alarming rate. There is a growing tendency in libraries both to cancel old subscriptions and to order only essential new titles. As a result there is a pressing need for tools that evaluate these publications.

Reference librarians share these headaches as many reference tools are serial by nature. There is also a symbiotic relationship between the serials holdings of a library and the indexing and abstracting services that form one of the most important groups of tools in a reference department. Studies show that only a small percentage of nonindexed periodicals are used by students or the general public. A different problem obviously is created when a library has the indexes but not the periodicals. Then, it is hoped that the beleaguered librarian will have the necessary union lists so that the desired title can be obtained through interlibrary loan.

There are useful directories and general selection guides for serials, and they are improving all of the time. *Ulrich's International Periodicals Directory* (New York: Bowker, annual) is a standard work to consult. Arranging over 60,000 periodicals from all over the world under 250 subject headings makes it valuable for selection. If a periodical is indexed or abstracted, then that information generally is included along with the usual bibliographical and ordering information. Reference librarians appreciate the list of indexing and abstracting publications at the beginning of the book. Information is also given for publications on microform. *Irregular Serials and Annuals* (New York: Bowker, biennial) is designed as a companion to *Ulrich's* and covers periodicals issued irregularly or less frequently than twice a year. Both are now supplemented by *Ulrich's Quarterly* (New York: Bowker, 1977–   ).

A recent addition and selection aid for serials is Joan K. Marshall's *Serials for Libraries* (New York: Neal–Schuman; Santa Barbara, Calif.: American Bibliographical Center—Clio Press, 1979). An annotated guide to English language annuals, yearbooks, continuations, transactions, proceedings, and directories, its value lies in its information on the non-magazine, non-newspaper type of serial published annually or less frequently. Those planning a budget will appreciate an appendix, ''When to Buy What: A Serials Buying Schedule.''

For more comprehensive coverage of the United States, the *Standard Periodical Directory* (New York: Oxbridge Communications, irregular) is helpful, and it includes the more ephemeral materials like house organs and newsletters.

None of the above titles, however, evaluates serials. The best guide to retrospective periodical selection that gives descriptive and critical annotations is Bill Katz and Berry Gargal Richards' *Magazines for Libraries* (New York: Bowker, 1978). This volume covers more than 6500 titles useful for public, school, and college libraries and is kept current by Bill Katz's column in *Library Journal*. For British periodicals, David Woodworth's *Guide to Current British Journals* (London: Library Association, 1973) gives brief annotations and arranges his titles by subject. Both of the evaluative guides includes ''reference serials.''

SELECTIVE LISTS—SERIALS

Fortunately, annotated lists of recommended journals within a special field exist; some are separately published and others are included within a guide to the literature. Additional assistance can be found in Evan Farber's *List of Periodicals for the College Library* (Westwood, Mass.: F. W. Faxon, 1972), which is updated by his monthly column in *Choice*, or in Marion Scott's *Periodicals for School Libraries* (Chicago: American Library Association, 1973). *American Reference Books Annual* and *Serials Review* provide aid by including reviews of serials under subject divisions.

OUT-OF-PRINT MATERIAL AND REPRINTS

For reference material that no longer is in print, there are several avenues open to the librarian. One is to study booksellers' catalogs, and if the need is sufficient, to advertise or alert special dealers or vendors that handle this type of material. The other is to consider microform or reprints. In either case, be on the mailing list for booksellers' catalogs and the catalogs of reprint houses like Burt

Franklin & Co., Johnson Reprint Corporation, and Kraus-Thomson Organization, Limited. It is important to remember, however, that reprints frequently cost more than a secondhand copy of the work.

The following are a few bibliographical tools that may prove useful in ordering an out-of-print title. Reference books and serials will be included in the listings.

Books on Demand. Ann Arbor, Mich.: University Microfilms International, 1977. 2 vols.

A list of 84,000 books available as "on-demand reprints." These are titles submitted by publishers as being out-of-print and of high interest. The first volume lists by author or title; the second arranges its titles by subject. A 1979 supplement has appeared and further supplements are planned.

Guide to Reprints, 1967–   . Washington, D.C.: Microcard Editions. Annual. 2 vols.

This guide is useful only if you have a specific title in mind as it is arranged by main entry without subject access. Books and periodicals from United States publishers are included in its scope. It is kept up to date by the quarterly *Announced Reprints,* which has expanded its coverage to include books and periodicals announced for reprint in other countries as well as the United States.

International Bibliography of Reprints. New York: Bowker, 1976–78. 2 vols.
  Vol. 1 Books and Serials. In three parts covering 52,000 titles published through 1973. Part 1 is arranged alphabetically by author, part 2 by subject, and part 3 contains indexes for titles and serials.
  Vol. 2 Periodicals and Annuals.

A directory of reprint publishers is included in the set. A quarterly *Bulletin of Reprints* supplements the work.

Note: Many works are reprinted in a series format, so bibliographies of series can be useful for locating out-of-print titles. Keep in mind Bowker's *Books in Series in the United States,* 2nd ed., 1979. Other reprint catalogs include Robert Orton's *Catalog of Reprints in Series,* 21st ed. (Metuchen, N.J.: Scarecrow Press, 1972), as well as the Library of Congress' Monographic Series (see following annotation). Finally the classic Bowker tool, *Books in Print,* regularly reports reprints and works in series.

CURRENT AWARENESS

Librarians become aware of new reference books and serials in exactly the same way they are alerted to other new materials that libraries acquire. They watch for publishers' announcements and catalogs, scan library journals for ads, carefully read journals of the booktrade such as *Publishers Weekly* and its British counterpart, *The Bookseller* (see following annotations), and examine current issues of national and trade bibliographies. This is time-consuming, but there is no substitute and few shortcuts. The willingness to read is the prime requisite for good librarianship.

PREPUBLICATION

Publisher's Ads and Catalogs

It is easy to get on the mailing list for a publisher's catalog or announcement of a new book. Most reference books are published by the booktrade, and this means the publishers are in this business to make a profit. With any encouragement, libraries are deluged with material urging them to purchase new publications. There is a great deal of competition in all book publishing, and ads and blurbs are designed to attract.

Publishers' catalogs generally appear in fall and spring. They not only provide detailed information about new books and those soon to be published, but also continue to list all of their books still in print (frequently called a "backlist"). Ads and blurbs can appear at any time, and these usually are the first indication that a new work soon will be appearing. Generally, there is indication of the expected month of publication, but this is no guarantee of a date. Announcements are planned long in advance, and titles and prices, as well as publication dates, are subject to change.

These same publishers also regularly advertise their new titles in library and booktrade journals. These ads may be grouped together alphabetically in the front of the journal, but they also can be found in the back and scattered throughout the contents. A check of several issues of *Library Journal, RQ,* or *Wilson Library Bulletin* reveals patterns in the layout of this kind of advertising and the type of information provided.

Note: For a full view and comparison of publishers' catalogs, study Bowker's *Publishers Trade List Annual (PTLA),* which binds together and arranges in alphabetical order most of the catalogs of major United States publishers from the preceding season.

Trade Bibliographies—United States and Great Britain

R. R. Bowker's *Forthcoming Books and New Books in Print* and *Subject Guide to Forthcoming Books* (see next section) are invaluable for alerting librarians to new material prior to publication. Both are published bimonthly and *Forthcoming Books* offers information on titles that are expected to be published within the next five months, as well as listing those that have been published in the United States since the last edition of *Books in Print* or *Books in Print Supplement* (see next section). *Subject Guide to Forthcoming Books* covers much the same territory for books not yet published and arranges them alphabetically under Library of Congress subject headings.

For British books, prepublication information is provided by Whitaker's *Books of the Month and Books to Come* (see next section). Announcements in this periodical cover the following two months; all entries are arranged in one alphabet with subject access only through a key word in the title.

NEW BOOKS

Journals of the Book Trade

United States

Publishers Weekly, 1872–   . New York: Bowker. *Weekly Record,* 1974–   . New York: Bowker.

It probably is unnecessary to take the time to recount the uses and wonders of this country's most prominent booktrade journal. In an acquisitions course, students quickly become familiar with it, and in a bibliography course, they learn to recognize its place in the scheme of United States trade bibliography.

Filled with news and gossip about authors, publishers, and new titles, it also provides the latest information on related topics such as copyright, book design, and marketing.

A regular feature of *Publishers Weekly* is "PW Forecasts," which consists of brief, well-written critical annotations of books that will appear in the following two months. Divided into Fiction, Nonfiction, Paperbacks, and Children's Books, it occasionally is useful for an advance notice of a notable reference book.

For reference book selection, *Publishers Weekly* is important because of the articles written about the publication of a major reference work such as the 15th edition of the *Encyclopaedia Britannica* or the stories behind the publishing of a dictionary such as the *American Heritage Dictionary.* Statistics on booktrade publishing are printed every January and include statistics on reference books. The large spring and fall announcement issues alert readers to what to expect in the months to come. Prices usually are included in listings. Special issues cover special subjects; a glance at the cover indicates the features of that particular issue.

The *Weekly Record,* a listing of new United States titles, was part of *Publishers Weekly* until 1974 but is now published separately. Arranged by author, it has limited use for selection of reference material. However, it cumulates monthly into the *American Book Publishing Record (BPR)* (see the following), where the titles are rearranged into Dewey Decimal classification order.

Great Britain

The Bookseller, 1858–   . London: Whitaker. Weekly.

There are many similarities between Britain's principal booktrade journal and *Publishers Weekly.* Both are part of an important chain in trade bibliography that facilitates bibliographic control over new monographs. Both are full of ads and news of the trade that booksellers and librarians find invaluable.

The Bookseller, however, includes its weekly record of new books on the final pages of each issue. Arranged in one alphabet by author, title, and, occasionally, key word, it is not particularly useful for reference book selection. One must wait for the quarterly issue of *Whitaker's Cumulative Book List* for a classed arrangement.

For the librarian selecting British reference books, *Bookseller's* fall and spring announcement issues provide effective help. The size of a telephone directory, these issues not only carry publishers' ads for forthcoming books, but also sections arranged by topic that discuss this new material. One is called ''Reference,'' and this is where details about the new reference books and their publishers are found. A much clearer idea of the publishing scene in Great Britain can be gained by reading these issues.

Note: Small libraries do not subscribe to *Bookseller,* but better reference service can be provided by librarians if they are aware of what is available in the English language throughout the world. Those who work in a small library occasionally should try to visit one that subscribes to the British bibliographical tools and, while there, glance at current bibliographic and selection tools for other foreign countries.

National and Trade Bibliography

Both the United States and Great Britain are fortunate in having excellent bibliographical control over new books. Figure 4.1 reveals the similarities and differences in arrangement, frequency, starting date, and so on of the current national and trade bibliographical tools. The term ''trade bibliography'' refers to material published by the booktrade and made available for sale (generally in bookstores). Trade listings usually exclude federal and other government publications, subscription books, dissertations, small pamphlets, and most elementary and high school textbooks. ''National bibliography,'' an attempt to record all materials published within a country and/or in the country's language(s), includes some of the latter categories but occasionally excludes the more emphemeral trade materials such as cheap paperbacks. Both are necessary for complete control, although the line of distinction between them increasingly becomes blurred. While both can be useful for indicating books newly published, trade bibliographies will have to be consulted for material not yet published. In addition, librarians can count on finding important ordering information such as

Frequency	United States	Great Britain
Weekly	PUBLISHERS WEEKLY, 1872–1974[a] WEEKLY RECORD, 1974–[a]	BOOKSELLER, 1858–[b] BRITISH NATIONAL BIBLIO- GRAPHY, 1950–[d]
Monthly	BOOK PUBLISHING RECORD, 1960–[e] CUMULATIVE BOOK INDEX, 1898–[f] NATIONAL UNION CATALOG, 1947–[a]	BNB Indexes[e] BOOKS OF THE MONTH & BOOKS TO COME, 1970–[b] CBI, 1898– BRITISH BOOKS IN PRINT[g]
Bimonthly	FORTHCOMING BOOKS & NEW BOOKS IN PRINT, 1965–[b] SUBJECT GUIDE TO FORTH- COMING BOOKS, 1967–	
Quarterly	NUC LIBRARY OF CONGRESS BOOKS: SUBJECTS, 1950–	BNB WHITAKERS CUMULATIVE BOOK LIST, 1924–[f]
Semiannual	PAPERBOUND BOOKS IN PRINT, 1955–[c]	BNB
Annual	BPR CBI NUC & LC BOOKS: SUBJECTS PUBLISHERS' TRADE LIST ANNUAL, 1873– BOOKS IN PRINT, 1948–[b] SUBJECT GUIDE TO BOOKS IN PRINT, 1957 BOOKS IN PRINT SUPPLEMENT[c] PAPERBOUND BOOKS IN PRINT	BNB CBI BRITISH BOOKS IN PRINT, 1874–[c] WCBL PAPERBACKS IN PRINT, 1960–[e]
Polyennial Cumulations	BPR (27-year cumulation) NUC LC BOOKS: SUBJECTS	BNB WCBL

[a] arrangement by author only
[b] author–title arrangement
[c] author–subject–title arrangement
[d] classed arrangement with author–title indexes
[e] classed arrangement with author–subject–title indexes
[f] dictionary arrangement
[g] on microfiche

Fig. 4.1. *Comparison of current bibliography for the United States and Great Britain.*

price, ISBN, and so on. For the reference librarian, it is obvious that the lists arranged by a subject or classification scheme will be the most valuable.

The Library of Congress, the depository for copyrighted materials, is responsible for our national bibliography. Entries for these United States imprints appear in the *National Union Catalog* along with those for foreign titles reported by national bibliographies of other countries and contributing United States and Canadian libraries. As the author catalogs are now union lists with hundreds of cooperating libraries contributing bibliographical information, these union catalogs come close to being considered "universal bibliographies." The great set of pre-1956 imprints, popularly known as "Mansell," may well be the richest bibliographical resource in the world. An author catalog, its uses as a working tool are endless, but its limits are obvious for the selector of reference material. Subject control by the Library of Congress is relatively recent, and the array of existing catalogs is so complex that the student is advised to master the publishing history and structure of all of the Library of Congress tools. For current selection, the following will prove valuable.

United States—Current National Bibliography

United States Library of Congress. *National Union Catalog.*

The author catalog is published monthly with quarterly, annual, and quinquennial cumulations. Full catalog information plus price and locations make *NUC* a major resource for librarians in any department. Current coverage on a monthly basis began in 1947. Use for verification, price, and other acquisitions information.

————. *Books: Subject.*

Arranged alphabetically by Library of Congress subject headings, the first quinquennial bears the date of 1950-54. However, coverage actually extends back to 1945. Now a quarterly with annual and quinquennial cumulations, this is the principal Library of Congress catalog for reference book selection. (See Fig. 4.2 for Library of Congress headings and subheadings used for reference books.)

————. *Monographic Series.*

Starting in 1974, a quarterly catalog with annual cumulations. Entries originally listed in *NUC* are now rearranged by series title. Useful because many reference sources are published in series format. Reprints also are frequently found in series.

Note: The Library of Congress regularly publishes lists of new music, records, films and other materials for projection, manuscript collections, and microform masters. Details of these tools are omitted here because few of these materials are purchased for a general reference collection.

United States—Current Trade Bibliography

R. R. Bowker & Co. is the notable publisher of trade bibliographies for the United States. Titles include *Publishers Weekly, Weekly Record, American Book*

Library of Congress. *Subject Headings.* 1975.

Bibliography—Bibliography—topic
Reference books—topic
Reference books—Bibliography (Guides to the
  literature usually found here.)

topic—Abstracts
    —Addresses, essays, and lectures
    —Atlases
    —Audio-visual aids
    —Bibliography
    — —Catalogs
    — —Union lists
    —Bio-bibliography
    —Biography
    —Book reviews
    —Catalogs
    —Chronology
    —Collected works
    —Congresses
    —Criticism and interpretation
    —Dictionaries
    —Dictionaries and encyclopedias

    —Digests
    —Directories
    —Government publications
    —Guide-books
    —Handbooks, manuals, etc.
    —History
    —History and criticism
    —Indexes
    —Law and legislation
    —Maps
    —Outlines, syllabi, etc.
    —Periodicals
    —Sources
    —Statistics
    —Union lists
    —Yearbooks

Fig. 4.2. *Subject headings: How to locate reference books, etc.*

Publishing Record (BPR), Forthcoming Books and New Books in Print, Subject Guide to Forthcoming Books, Paperbound Books in Print, Publishers Trade List Annual (PTLA), Books in Print, Books in Print Supplement, and Subject Guide to Books in Print (see Fig. 4.1 for details).

In addition to the above, special lists are extrapolated from *Books in Print* and are of value in special libraries. A few examples are *Business Books in Print, Children's Books in Print* and *Subject Guide to Children's Books in Print, El-Hi Textbooks in Print, Medical Books in Print,* and *Technical Books in Print.*

For selection of reference books, *Subject Guide to Books in Print* is the most valuable. Arranged by Library of Congress subject headings, the librarian readily can see what is available in the reference field by a publisher in the United States (see Fig. 4.2).

H. W. Wilson and Co. is the other important producer of trade bibliographies. *Cumulative Book Index (CBI)* is a monthly list of English language books wherever published, so it also is useful for identifying and ordering British books. Appearing monthly since 1898, it now cumulates into annual volumes. A dictionary arrangement makes it easy for the reference librarian selecting reference books.

Great Britain—Current National Bibliography

In *British National Bibliography (BNB),* 1950–   (London: The British Library), the British have what is considered by most librarians as the finest example of current national bibliography in the world today. It is published frequently (weekly), cumulations are regular, and access is complete. Basic arrangement is a modified form of the Dewey Decimal classification scheme, and indexes include author, title, and PRECIS subject indexing. As a national bibliography it covers material such as important government publications that are excluded from trade tools. Entry information is full *including* ISBN, BNB number, LC card number, price, and so on. (See Fig. 4.1 for further details.)

The British Library Automated Information Service (BLAISE), an online library housekeeping and information service, created by the British Library, can be used for subject-type searching and so is helpful in the bibliographic checking of new reference tools. Search keys also include ISBN, LC, and BNB numbers.

While the *British Museum Catalogue* (the new edition will be called *British Library Catalogue*) is a magnificent resource for retrospective searching of British and other titles, it is necessary to use BNB for current listings.

Great Britain—Current Trade Bibliography

J. W. Whitaker and Sons qualifies as the Bowker of Great Britain (or vice versa) and is responsible for the *Bookseller, Books of the Month and Books to Come, Whitaker's Cumulative Book List, British Books in Print,* and *Paperbacks in Print.* As Fig. 4.1 shows, there are no separate volumes providing subject access to *British Books in Print.*

Note: The small library in the United States will use *Cumulative Book Index (CBI)* for information on British titles. While not as complete as the Whitaker publications or *British National Bibliography, CBI* usually is adequate for the type of British material a small library orders.

NEW SERIALS

The major ''current awareness'' service for new serials is *New Serial Titles,* 1950–   (Washington, D.C.: Library of Congress. Monthly with cumulations). Two 20-year cumulations, 1950–1970, have been published by Bowker—one for titles and one for subjects.

New Serial Titles identifies and provides locations for new serials from all over the world. ISSN and Dewey number are included in the entry information. A list of title changes and cessations is included at the end of each issue. There are no annotations. Library of Congress also publishes the monthly *New Serial Titles Classed Subject Arrangement,* which rearranges the new serials by Dewey number. Its usefulness is limited as it does not cumulate.

New serial titles and articles about new serials can be found in the following periodicals: *Bulletin of Bibliography, Choice, College and Research Libraries, Library Journal,* UNESCO's *Bulletin of Bibliography, Documentation and Terminology, Serials Review,* and *Wilson Library Bulletin. American Reference*

Books Annual and *Serials Review* are especially useful for their coverage and annotations of reference serials.

Note: Ulrich's Quarterly, mentioned earlier in this chapter, also should be kept in mind for its list of new periodical titles, title changes, and cessations.

SPECIAL PROBLEMS

ACADEMIC AND SCHOLARLY PUBLICATIONS

Theses and dissertations, Festschriften, and proceedings of congresses and conferences are used by students and scholars in pursuit of their research. While some of these materials can be located through standard bibliographical sources, few guides to these special areas exist. Until more of the latter become available, the reference librarian must rely on general guides such as Sheehy, Walford, and so on, or guides to the literature of subject fields.

One important exception is Michael M. Reynolds' *Guide to Theses and Dissertations* (Detroit: Gale Research Company, 1975). This work annotates more than 2000 bibliographies that cover dissertations in libraries in the United States and Great Britain.

FOREIGN LANGUAGE REFERENCE MATERIAL

Foreign language reference tools are the province of the large research or highly specialized library, and no lengthy discussion of their selection will be considered here. General principles for good selection still apply; in addition, the librarian that selects and orders this material needs a working bibliographic knowledge of foreign languages.

Libraries that buy in this area also may subscribe to national and trade bibliographies for Europe, Africa, Asia, and South America. These function as selection tools as well as working tools in the department. If the particular country has a thriving booktrade, there also will be an abundance of publishers' catalogs and blurbs available. Also, UNESCO's bimonthly periodical, *Bibliography, Documentation, Terminology* (1961–   ), has a regular feature called "Bibliographical and Abstracting Services Throughout the World." It is compiled from questionnaires sent to member nations and is invaluable to the reference librarian searching for information on reference tools published in other countries.

The Canadian Library Association publishes a useful handbook called *Books in Other Languages: How to Select and Where to Order Them.* Now in its 3rd edition (1976), it is intended to include all languages spoken in Canada and the United States. Arranged alphabetically by language, both selection aids and suppliers are subarranged alphabetically and are subdivided under appropriate headings when necessary. Brief annotations are included.

GOVERNMENT PUBLICATIONS

The federal government of the United States is the most voluminous publisher in the world. It publishes in almost every subject field, and a great deal of the material is serial in nature. Much of it falls into the category of "reference sources," and many of these tools are indispensable, even to the smallest library. It is difficult to imagine any reference desk without a current copy of the *Official Congressional Directory, Government Manual,* or *Statistical Abstract.*

All three branches of the federal government publish, and thousands of technical reports are issued each year by private concerns under contract to some government agency. In addition, all 50 states publish something, as do most counties and many municipalities. This leaves unaccounted for all of the material issued by international organizations and foreign governments.

The principal source for identifying and selecting all federal government material is, of course, the Superintendent of Document's *Monthly Catalog,* 1895–   . Arranged alphabetically by issuing agency, the catalog includes in the basic information Library of Congress subject headings. Multiple indexes cumulate semiannually. A special semiannual issue lists serials. While most of the literature indicates that coverage in the *Monthly Catalog* is far from exhaustive, it probably is adequate for standard government reference tools. The catalog itself does not cumulate, but its author indexes regularly are cumulated. Pierian Press is responsible for a special cumulated author index covering 1941–1975, while Carrollton Press has published a *Cumulative Subject Index to the Monthly Catalog of U.S. Government Publications, 1900–1971.*

Bibliographical control is inadequate on every level. United States bibliographies cover few government publications; the *National Union Catalog* only lists those that have been cataloged. Periodical indexes cover government periodicals in a highly selective fashion; for example, *Education Index,* a Wilson publication, includes many of the bulletins and reports of the Office of Education. *PAIS (Public Affairs Information Service Bulletin)* includes some state and municipal as well as federal publications in its weekly listings. A newer indexing service, *Index to Government Periodicals, 1974–*   (Chicago: Infordata International, Inc. Quarterly), may prove helpful.

Another officially published bibliographic tool, *The GPO Sales Publications Reference File,* is a catalog of all publications currently offered for sale by the Superintendent of Documents. Issued bimonthly, it is available on microfiche with subject access by key word. At the present time, there is no other general source to indicate that a document is still in print.

Additional help for serial selection can be found in Nancy Patton Van Zant's *Selected U.S. Government Serials: A Guide for Public and Academic Libraries* (Chicago: American Library Association, 1978). Annotating around 600 depository series titles, it is useful for the acquisition of reference sources as well as research reports and periodicals.

For bibliographies, some control is supplied with Carrollton Press' *Cumulative Subject Guide to U.S. Government Bibliographies, 1924-1973* and Pierian Press' *A Bibliography of United States Government Bibliographies* (Vol. 1, 1968-73; Vol. 2, 1974-76). The latter title is regularly updated now and appears in the final issue for the year of *RSR (Reference Services Review)*.

Happily for the reference librarian, some good guides to government reference material have appeared. One of the better ones is Vladimir Palic's *Government Publications: A Guide to Bibliographic Tools*. (Washington, D.C.: Library of Congress, 1975). Over 400 pages with citations for 3000 titles, it covers for the United States publications of the federal, state, and local governments as well as territories under its control. Documents of international governmental organizations and foreign countries are also included. The author is well aware of the limited amount of bibliographical control over government documents in most countries, so he does not confine his list to bibliographies that are officially published. Catalogs, checklists, price lists, accession lists, as well as selected general bibliographies, are considered.

Libraries Unlimited, Inc. has published three selection aids for the reference librarian. For the federal government, there is *Government Reference Books: A Biennial Guide to U.S. Government Publications, 1968/69-* and Sally Wynkoop's *Subject Guide to Government Reference Books* (1972). For representative reference publications issued by various states, consult the annotated list provided by David Parish's *State Government Publications; An Annotated Bibliography* (1974). Finally, *Municipal Government Reference Sources: Publications and Collections* by Peter Hernon, John Richardson, and others (New York: Bowker, 1978) has appeared and should provide some beginnings of control over local documents.

Note: For Great Britain, major government publications regularly are listed in *British National Bibliography*.

STARTING FROM SCRATCH

During the 1960s and early 1970s many new community colleges and similar institutions opened throughout the country. When the first students arrived, both a basic collection of books and an adequate number of reference sources had to be in the library. The American Library Association established standards that required a minimum of 50,000 titles (including reference sources) for even the smallest four-year academic library.

In attempting to determine what reference materials should be on hand when the doors of any new library open, some of the tools previously discussed in this chapter will offer assistance. Bibliographic guides, in particular, should be remembered for their special value in the selection process. Any current national or trade bibliography with subject or classed access can be helpful with new material. For the small and medium-sized public or college library, students should reexamine *Reference Books for Small and Medium-Sized Libraries* and compare its list with the reference tools included in *Public Library Catalog, Books for College Libraries,* or *Books for Junior College Libraries.*

Many years are required to develop a fine reference collection in a large library and to build a few hundred titles into many thousands. User needs and interests will change along with the amount of money budgeted for additions. It also takes a few years for a reference librarian to learn to be an effective selector of material. Not only is it necessary to be expert in distinguishing good reference books from inferior ones, but it also is essential to know one's library community. This requires study and the imagination to anticipate change. By all means, keep up with the new material and the tools for selecting them. But that is just the beginning. The next step is to bring the user and the source together and to see if the right match has been made.

REFERENCES AND SUGGESTED READINGS

American Library Association. *ALA glossary of library terms.* Chicago: American Library Association, 1943.

Bonk, W. J., & Magrill, R. M. National and trade bibliography. In their *Building library collections* (5th ed.). Metuchen, N.J.: Scarecrow, 1979, pp. 209–275.

Evans, G. E. Selection of books. In his *Developing library collections.* Littleton, Colo.: Libraries Unlimited, 1979, pp. 137–177.

Katz, B., & Tarr, A. (Eds.). The reference forms. Part II. *Reference and information services: A reader.* Metuchen, N.J.: Scarecrow Press, 1978, pp. 255–443.

Kister, K. Encyclopedia publishing: An update. *Library Journal,* 1978, *103*(April 15), 820–823.

Osborn, A. D. Reference work. In his *Serial publications: Their place and treatment in libraries.* Chicago: American Library Association, 1973, pp. 349–367.

Plotnik, A. They have created the ultimate reference guide in this room for decades, and very few outsiders know just how hard it's been; from Winchell's 8th to Sheehy's 9th. *American Libraries,* 1977, *8*(March), 129–132.

Seaholm, F. Winchell, Walford or Malclès? *College & Research Libraries,* 1964, *25*(January), 21–26,31.

Smith, A. Reference sources for children and young adults. *RSR,* 1977, *5*(October–December), 13–19.

Swenk, C., & Robinson, W. A comparison of the guides to abstracting and indexing services provided by Katz, Chicorel, and Ulrich. *RQ,* 1978, *17*(Summer), 317–319.

Walford, A. J. Compiling the *Guide to reference material. Journal of Librarianship,* 1978, *10* (October), 247–255.

Whittaker, K. Basic British. *RQ,* 1972, *12*(Fall), 1. 49–51.

Zink, S. D. Putting 'Reference' in the *Publications reference file. RQ,* 1980, *19*(Summer), 381–383.

CHAPTER 5

Desk Technique and the Library User

INTRODUCTION

PUBLIC SERVICE—THE GOAL OF ALL LIBRARY EFFORT

Discussions of new information delivery systems emphasize configurations of electronic devices and appliances that are umpteenth-generation descendants of Aladdin's lamp. Perhaps these will eventually bring information directly into an individual's living room the way television presently provides recreational and cultural material (Cherry, 1980). For the immediate future, however, much of the information from electronic systems will be delivered across a desk or counter to users who consider their information needs to merit the librarian's serious attention.

While library users obviously recognize that it is the library's function to provide information and cultural or recreational materials, most remain unaware of the extent to which librarians are able to help and advise them. While everyone is familiar with the circulation desk where books are checked out or discharged upon return, few are aware of other service points in the library. Commonly, libraries have a reference desk and as questions of specific types increase in number, separate information, serials, and reader's advisory or catalog information desks may be added. Whether operation of these desks will remain part of the reference function will be determined by the size, philosophy, and administrative structure of the particular library. In any case, the aim is to help readers to make maximum use of the material in the collection and, when appropriate, to alert them to additional resources. This person-to-person interaction will be considered as "desk technique" in this chapter.

Our discussion of desk technique is rooted in the following assumptions:

(1) Many people are not aware that information of interest or of use to them is generally available in libraries.

(2) As a reference librarian, one has accepted the responsibility of answering questions pleasantly, speedily, accurately, and, as nearly as possible, to the satisfaction of the inquirer.

(3) To discharge this responsibility requires mastery of a wide range and a large number of sources.

(4) The techniques or approaches discussed will allow librarians to elicit the information needed in order to proceed to answer the question while minimizing the danger that they will jump to personal conclusions rather than respond to what persons asking questions would like to know.
Interpersonal skills are discussed insofar as they directly relate to assumption (4).

There is much that could be and has been said about personal interaction. While this is not the place to review all the niceties of social graces, a general reminder or two may be in order. Everyone hopes to be treated with a basic minimum of respect and patience and should be prepared to treat others with the same. A reference librarian must maintain a pleasant expression (rather than a scowl that is easily read as disapproval of present company), speak clearly in a voice that can be readily heard but is not loud or abrasive, and dress to avoid appearing to demand comment, reaction, or restraint from others (unless one wishes to serve as a human billboard). There is no need to become self-effacing, but unrestrained self-expression is more appropriate to the stage or screen. In all public contacts, one strives to maintain a basic level of social grace by deploying the force and warmth of one's personality to ensure that the other person is at ease.

Professional responsibility requires giving priority to serving the public while at the reference desk. Working on a report, statistics, or other assigned tasks while on duty must never cause the librarian to give short shrift to a question. Furthermore, a personal interview should *not* be interrupted in order to answer the telephone. All of the processing, acquisitions, shelving, and record-keeping that is done in a library is for the purpose of making information available to those who need it. If at a critical moment any staff member is unresponsive to a user, all previous effort and expenditure has been wasted.

Uneasiness evidenced by some inquirers at the reference desk seems to stem from unfamiliarity with the personnel and service, and a fear of appearing ignorant. The discussion that follows attempts to present examples to permit recognition of this basic uneasiness. The examples show a variety of strengths and weaknesses from which one can cultivate a pattern of response to minimize tension and misunderstanding. The goal is to assist patrons to focus their attention on finding the answers to their questions. Without an effective technique, one's own mind can be so absorbed in trying to solve the problem that one's manner may become abstracted or abrupt.

Before proceeding with a discussion of how to *attract* persons with potential reference questions, it must be acknowledged that there are libraries whose major concern is how to cope with the excessive volume of inquiries they already receive. In general, these are the prominent libraries in their area: the Library of

Congress, the main libraries of large metropolitan areas such as New York and Los Angeles, major university libraries, and the more famous special libraries. In reference departments, as elsewhere, it seems that nothing succeeds like success. The reference department of a large library often becomes the avenue of first resort for questions that can be readily answered in smaller libraries.[1]

THE ARENA

Ironically, at a time when librarians are prepared to do more than ever before, it does not occur to most people to consult them. The experience at a reference desk is not so different from other day-to-day experiences. There are some interesting parallels between people with information needs and those with do-it-yourself or home repair needs. Levels of interest and competence in making home repairs vary, but everyone recognizes that such repairs are possible. There are various approaches, ranging from hiring a handiworker to asking advice from friends or, perhaps, a clerk in an old-fashioned hardware store. The virtue of such a store lies not only in its stock, but also in the understanding staff who know what gizmo is needed and can offer installation hints. Unfortunately, most of the population has not recognized the fact that libraries or librarians can provide similar services.

Once people come to the library, the design of the building should encourage them to consult with the staff. It should be clear where to ask for help and information. The catalog and the reference desk ideally should be readily discernible from the entrance to the building. No barriers should be placed between the entering user and a view of the reference desk. Library architecture is a subject unto itself, but the problems of drafts, staff comfort, and noise at a reference desk located near the entrance must be weighed against the value of high visibility and potential for supervision of the building with a minimum of staff.

Even when physical obstacles have been eliminated, psychological deterrents can remain. It is hard for an insider to perceive these. Some may be mistakes of placement and lighting, but others emanate from the staff and the way they conduct themselves at the desk. A balance should be maintained between businesslike reserve and approachability (Morgan, 1980). One eminent librarian remarked upon how odd it was that the unpopular reference desk at a university library was set upon a dais. It was not, in fact, but it was obvious why he had gained that impression. One wondered, did daring first-year students lose their nerve at the last minute and kneel as evidence that their audacity in approaching this ''holy of holies'' was tempered by the proper reverence?

The proliferation and variety of information resources and the fact that the public is increasingly diverse in background, education, skills, and expectations

---

[1]The referral of users is discussed on p. 125.

has greatly affected the role of the reference librarian or information specialist. There is increased scope for confusion and misunderstanding in the course of the transaction. It behooves the librarian to be as open and encouraging as possible and to be prepared to deliver the necessary information at any of a number of possible levels of sophistication. There are few library users, no matter how experienced, who cannot profit from consultation with a competent reference librarian.

THE REFERENCE TRANSACTION

The reference transaction can be considered as having two major and interdependent components: the intellectual and the interpersonal. The intellectual component is the central concern of the transaction: what is the question, what will constitute a satisfactory answer, and which sources and strategies should be used? Nonetheless, whether the transaction is concluded successfully or not may be determined by the effectiveness of the interview that is the interpersonal component. It is the purpose of the interview to elicit from the inquirer facts required in order to provide the information needed. The interview provides an opportunity to ascertain whether or not the *question* being posed expresses the inquirer's information *need* clearly and completely.

CATEGORIES OF QUESTIONS

Various definitions and categories have been suggested for transactions that occur at the reference desk. These have developed from an interest in reporting, measuring, comparing, and sometimes evaluating the amount of work performed at the desk. A simple, basic minimum reporting standard devised by the Committee on Statistics for Reference Services of the American Library Association's Library Administration Division, Library Organization and Management Section, consists of two categories: direction transactions and reference transactions (Emerson, 1977). A direction transaction can be completed without knowledge of or consultation of a source, while a reference transaction involves a source.[2] Lynch (1978, p. 126) reports that the New Jersey Measurement Study published in 1976 designates a similar but more elaborate set of four transaction categories: directional; library holdings; substantive; or moving from one kind of question to another.

Reference transactions can range from the ready-reference, or short-answer question, to the full-blown research inquiry establishing methodology and sur-

---

[2]The difficulty of categorizing questions and the need to measure other areas of reference service are discussed by Emerson (see References and Suggested Readings).

veying potentially useful sources. Of course, most questions fall somewhere between these extremes with the preponderance at the shorter end of the spectrum (López Muñoz, 1977; Wilkinson & Miller, 1978). Other categories frequently consider the length of time it takes to answer a question, type of user (adult, juvenile, and so on), type of resource used, form of request, and time of day (Ciucki, 1977).

The problem of differentiating among the transactions designated as reference questions has received attention from those interested in analyzing the reference process in order to develop a theory of reference service, to improve reference performance, or to teach others "what goes on at the reference desk"—sometimes in order to reduce costs by scheduling persons not professionally schooled. Broadly based observations and systematic analyses made from several perspectives seem to be converging and producing results that overlap in several useful ways.

From the analysis of some 5760 questions, Wilkinson and Miller (1978) developed a "step approach" to differentiate reference questions according to how many judgmental steps were required to answer them. They found that one-step questions comprised 31% of the total and included almost all of the directional questions asked. Two-step questions accounted for an additional 47%, and only 22% of the questions were considered multiple step. Their results provide some interesting parallels with those reported by Lynch (1978) from her analysis of more than 1159 transactions. Lynch's concern was with the reference interview and the "primary questions" librarians asked during the interview. She coded 35% of the transactions as not involving an interview because, as directional queries, they required no question to be asked *by* the librarian. While Lynch's primary questions cannot be assumed to indicate a Wilkinson and Miller step, the results suggest comparison. In those 269 transactions requiring interviews, Lynch found 52% (139 of the 1159 total) required only one question, while 24% (65 of the total) required two questions. Both these studies suggest that the response to most questions can be simple and straightforward. The question of how these observations relate to studies that indicate an appalling failure rate in reference service will be considered in a following section.

It may be that a "real" reference question is determined by the response of the staff member. Questions that take one into unfamiliar territory because the question or the subject matter is not understood require more thought and effort. Hence, an unskilled librarian can make a simple question unnecessarily difficult. It may be possible to elaborate and distort almost any simple request into a challenge, but persons who ask a simple question may only need an answer to exactly that question. However, they may have a question that they have yet to formulate or for which they cannot conceive the appropriate tool or method. One aim of this chapter is to indicate how reference librarians can respond to the need as expressed while prompting sufficient confidence and interaction to allow them to ascertain which of the full range of services available are most appropriate. Key words for this chapter might be responsiveness and responsibility.

THE INTELLECTUAL COMPONENT

Context of the Transaction

There is a general and a specific context for each reference transaction. The general context is provided by the kind of library and hence, the relationship of the librarian to inquirer and the level of service provided. It is the specific context of "what, who, why, and when" that is of concern here. "What" applies to the question asked or information sought. "Who, why, and when" determine what constitutes an acceptable answer. These facts are most often revealed during the interview, which will be discussed later. Here, the discussion will center on the intellectual implications of these questions.

Subject of the Question

The "what" centers on a clear understanding of the question asked. For instance, take the question,
     "Where can I find information about Waterloo?"
Unless one is in London or otherwise preoccupied with Waterloo railway station, the automatic connection is with Napoleon. Nonetheless, it is a good idea to check. This can be done directly by asking,
     "Do you mean Napoleon's Waterloo?",
to which the answer might be
     "Well, actually, the Battle of Waterloo."
Or, it could be done indirectly by asking,
     "Is there a particular aspect that interests you?"
There is some risk in proceeding immediately to the latter question, because the response may still obscure which Waterloo is involved. However, the answer,
     "I want to know the caliber of weaponry used,"
seems to make it clear enough.

At this juncture the question could be pursued in the context of Napoleon and French history, or alternatively with weaponry and military history. The nature and strengths of the library's collection may determine which research path is chosen. If the library's military history works do not provide the answer, one would try the French history approach. If the question were
     "When was (a particular weapon) first used in battle?",
the transaction assumes an entirely different complexion.

Requirements of the Answer

Many questions can be answered by a single piece of information. The recurring need for certain kinds of facts has resulted in various types of reference books such as dictionaries, directories, and almanacs. If a brief discussion of the subject is required, encyclopedias or yearbooks might meet the need. For more comprehensive consideration, a literature search may be required. Hence, one's approach to sources is influenced by the requirements of the answer.[3] It should be noted that not all factual questions can be answered from reference books. Recourse to the stack collection or consultation with a specialized agency may be required.

Who wants the information for whom is a factor to be considered. Perhaps the level of reading difficulty is important? Should the material be a film suitable for group viewing, something a partially sighted person can use, or something that can be reproduced? Why the information is wanted often influences the amount required and the time and energy that can be devoted to locating it. The approach may differ according to whether the person is preparing for a trip, settling a bet, beginning work on a 15-minute talk to a service club, or is undertaking to write a book on the subject. A deadline (the "when") may preclude following avenues otherwise desirable. The absence of time pressure may allow browsing through periodicals or large numbers of books.

Strategies and Sources: The Comprehensive Literature Search

There are useful elements in several of the various attempts to formalize and generalize search strategy or patterns of strategy. The approaches range from the simplicity of Josel (1971) through the more analytical and comprehensive of Taylor (1968) and Bates (1979). Various ways of analyzing the reference process are illustrated by the diagrams and flowcharts included in the Jahoda and Olson (1972) survey and by Carlson's model presented by Lancaster (1977, pp. 113–129). While each is instructive, none is exhaustive.

It is more useful to think in terms of "strategies" than of "a single search strategy." An effective response to a question requires (1) identifying potential sources; (2) choosing among these sources; and (3) searching within the source chosen. The strategies employed operate on several planes and are determined by a complex of variables for each question.[4] The strategy employed in response to one variable overlaps into and modifies that used in response to another. The culmination of these strategies might be considered the search strategy used for that question. For any given question several strategies may be possible, and the individual librarian may compensate for weakness in one area (identification of potential sources) by being especially effective in another (exploitation of the

---

[3]Jahoda and Braunagel (1980) discuss this at length in their Chapter 4.
[4]A detailed examination of these variables with examples and exercises can be found in Jahoda and Braunagel (1980).

source chosen). With training and experience, establishing strategies becomes nearly automatic.

The general routine to be followed for comprehensive literature searches encompasses the strategies used to identify potential sources for less ambitious questions. For subjects that one knows, it may be possible to think of the suitable source immediately and without consultation of listings of possible sources. In fields unfamiliar to one, it is advisable to proceed according to the routine outlined in the following. This routine also should be recommended to all who are preparing extensive reports, papers, or dissertations.

(1) Determine the intellectual context of the question. If the inquirer cannot provide the background information, use an encyclopedia or textbook. Determine the accepted relationships with other subjects as revealed in authoritative writings. In both print and nonprint files, synonyms and related terms must be consulted in order to identify all material of interest. In some instances searching must be done under broader headings. For very recent topics, periodical indexes or thesauri can reveal appropriate vocabulary.

(2) Identify the bibliographies and indexes for the field by consulting guides to reference works, *Bibliographic Index,* and the library's catalog.

(3) As the search proceeds, indicate exactly what has been checked. Make a careful record of the sources to be consulted. These notes should be clear and systematic enough to allow someone else to continue the work easily if that becomes necessary. A small check mark beside a heading can indicate that the heading was found in the source. A small zero can indicate that a particular heading was not found. For continuing bibliographies and works with supplements, indicate issues or volumes that have been checked and when headings were changed. On a long-term project or one that is interrupted, such a record—which can be made quickly—ensures that headings that prove fruitful in one source have been checked in the others. As information accumulates, one sees the question in a new light and becomes aware of new avenues to pursue. Care must be taken not to proceed too far without considering whether one has become sidetracked from the question.

(4) When a useful citation or fact has been found, copy the essential part and include an abbreviated reference to show its source. Such references, keyed to the record made in the previous step, allow easy rechecking for mystery citations and facilitate the verification required for interlibrary loan requests. Be sure to decipher all abbreviations of journal titles by referring to the key provided by the source.

(5) Check the local collection and note call numbers, and so on. Records for works that prove not to be useful should be so marked, and the records saved to prevent unnecessary rechecking. Works not on the shelf should be searched through circulation records to determine their status, and appropriate action should be initiated. Those "not on shelf" works which are declared missing,

lost, stolen, or otherwise not likely to become available should be requested on interlibrary loan (ILL). Works not owned by the library also should be requested on ILL. Such requests should be made as early as possible because of the many snags that can develop.

(6) Search continuing sources such as periodical indexes and abstracts. A recent *cumulation* will allow determination of current headings. Ordinarily one should then refer to the most recent issue and work back systematically, being alert to subject heading and vocabulary changes. Working back from the most recent issues may reveal reviews, rebuttals, and revisions before time is squandered pursuing outdated or refuted materials. Double-check for the arrival of recent indexes or abstracts. Finally, a check of current periodical issues that have not been indexed may be necessary.

Few reference departments actually perform manual literature searches for their clientele. The librarian usually advises the searcher about the sources and headings to use, and may suggest a retrospective search of an automated database and a SDI profile if subsequent updating is required.

Identifying Potential Sources

When a specific reference source is not apparent, a general subject approach must be used. If the subject's place in the library's classification scheme is not obvious, the index to the classification tables, a subject heading list, or the library's subject catalog should reveal it. Browsing in an appropriate section of the reference or stack collection may yield results. Guides to reference works, such as those by Sheehy and Walford, may suggest possible sources. If they do not, special subject guides or bibliographies may supply citations to potential sources.[5] Going back to our Waterloo question, a special or general encyclopedia may include useful titles at the end of an article on Waterloo, gunnery, or military science. These references often are listed because they are generally available. By this time, the librarian will know that the Battle of Waterloo was fought in 1815, and that "guns" (properly speaking) are cannon and machine guns, while small easily carried weapons are called "firearms."

Unless the question requires the most thorough search possible, the value of consulting bibliographies rather than simply relying on the library's subject catalog must be weighed against the time and effort it would involve. A reliable subject bibliography should cover the topic comprehensively. Not only will it present all material meeting its predetermined and stated criteria, but also, perhaps through its organization, reveal the implications of previous research on the subject. In the nature of things, the bibliography should cite more sources than most collections will have, and through annotations disclose the relative merits and strengths of the titles. Thus, the bibliography compensates for the

---

[5]These are discussed as "Lead-in Tools" in Chapter 5 of Jahoda and Braunagel (1980).

practical or accidental limitations of most collections, but in doing so creates demands for materials not immediately available.

Bibliographies perforce are limited in currency. If up-to-date coverage is needed, even the best bibliography must be supplemented by referring to the library's catalog and to on-going or current listings. Perhaps general trade or national bibliographies such as *Cumulated Book Index, American Book Publishing Record,* or the *British National Bibliography* may be the most up-to-date lists. Thus, a single bibliography covering materials published through 1969 may have to be supplemented by three or four other titles. In spite of cumulations, checking may require consultation of four or five volumes for each source. An attractive feature of computerized databases is their capacity for almost immediate updating and cumulation, which eliminates such cumbersome manual procedures. In the absence of a suitable computerized file, if the library has been actively acquiring materials on the subject, the catalog may be the most up-to-date and convenient subject listing of books. A direct appeal to the library's catalog will identify those most readily available.

Scope and Type of Information

To qualify as a potential source, a work must encompass the subject and have the type of information required. To answer a question about the weaponry at the Battle of Waterloo, a work would have to include European or French battles of the nineteenth century. While many delimitations of scope might allow for this, it is obvious that a work that concentrated on American or Renaissance or naval battles would not be useful. Usually the narrower the scope of the work, the more detailed the information presented will be. The title and subtitle may provide a strong indication of the potential value of the work. Thus, *The Encyclopedia of Military History; from 3500 B.C. to the Present* by R. Ernest Dupuy and Trevor N. Dupuy sounds promising as does *The Dictionary of Weapons and Military Terms* by John Quick. The subjects sound appropriate, and the words "encyclopedia" and "dictionary" promise presentations including significant facts. One might be disappointed to discover that although weaponry at Waterloo is discussed, only the number of guns and amount of ammunition used, rather than specific weapons, are mentioned.

Arrangement and Access

The arrangement of a work and its points of access to the information may determine its usefulness. Descriptive notes or annotations in guides and bibliographies may indicate arrangement and the kinds of indexes as well as the level of detail included in the entry. The principles upon which the entries in a work are arranged and the extent to which complementary access is provided by indexes determine the knowledge and effort required to locate the information sought. An index by name of battle would be necessary in order to locate speedily the

Waterloo entries in a work arranged by caliber of artillery. Such a name index could also be useful in works arranged by year the battle was fought or by place (region or country). One would compensate for lack of a name index by referring to more general sources to learn the year and to verify the location of Waterloo. Unfortunately decisions with respect to arrangement and corollary indexing too often are made for economic or other production reasons not directly related to the ease of using the work.

The table of contents should not be overlooked as a finding aid. In the Dupuy work, discussion of the particular battles is preceded by a useful commentary on military trends entitled ''Artillery of the Napoleonic Era,'' which is accompanied by line illustrations. Having discovered these illustrations, which are not mentioned in the text or index, one may also discover that the inquirer is more interested in firearms than in artillery. Perusal of the text in Dupuy has revealed that the Napoleonic handgun was the musket, with the English ''Brown Bess'' being noteworthy. Rifles were being developed and used in special situations.

With this information about firearms one might turn to Quick's *Dictionary* where the entries are arranged alphabetically by the name or type of firearm. There is no approach by name of battle or historical period. In this respect, the article ''Weaponry'' in the Macropaedia of the *Encyclopaedia Britannica* is more useful. It gives an historical account of the changes in weaponry. However, while Napoleon's influence is highlighted, specific weapons are not named or connected to a particular battle. At this point the inquirer may be satisfied with the information gained, although it would not be possible to state ''*x* caliber weapons were used at the Battle of Waterloo.''

Choosing Among Sources

Given several reliable and well-edited works of appropriate scope and access, ease of use is the primary basis for reaching for one reference book before another. In some instances, a second choice is used because it is close at hand. The potential availability of the materials cited also may weigh in the choice. One's first choice even may depend upon whether one is using the work oneself or is recommending it to another. It is well to bear in mind how easy or difficult it is to interpret the entries in the source in light of the user's expertise. A clear example is provided by a comparison of the entries in *Nineteenth Century Readers' Guide* with those in Poole's *Index to Periodical Literature*. Poole's dating and volume numbering requires consultation of special tables, and his ''correction'' of deplorable publishing practices makes his entries treacherous for the unwary and untutored. The *Readers' Guide* format is straightforward as well as widely known.

The influence of format on ease of use is readily exemplified by the difference between the first five editions of William Leonard Langer's *An Encyclopedia of World History* and the 1975 illustrated version. Over the years this title has established itself as a respected standard reference work of inestimable value. The format of the earlier editions successfully presented a great deal of information in a single volume. There were few tables and maps, and these were sometimes hard to locate, and the presentation by continent and country within large chronological periods meant some inconvenience at the beginning or end of the period. Nonetheless, it was a reliable workhorse.

The two-volume, large-page format of the illustrated edition presents an open vista of information enlivened with pictures and within generous margins. Each volume manifests the excitement of human history. Some aspects of the work are revised on the basis of new scholarship, but by and large the reliable and well-edited typesetting from previous editions has been preserved in a photo enlargement deployed in a new layout to accommodate the pictures. It appears as a modern book produced for a modern audience beyond the reference room.

The arrangement of the text always and quite reasonably has required use of the index. However, in the two-volume work this becomes cumbersome. By consulting the index under Waterloo, one finds the first reference is to page 629. One soon learns that is in Volume one, and one less easily discovers that the number on that page has been displaced (though not removed altogether, as on some pages) by a contemporary illustration "Blucher at Waterloo." One could easily prefer the convenience of the stodgy single-volume work—unless the illustration, which shows a field gun, reveals what the patron wishes to know! The two-volume edition is less attractive because it is less easy to use.

The revision and correction of reference works is an abiding concern to the librarian and the user, and is a very significant consideration at selection time. It is important *always* to consult addenda and supplementary portions of works. Overlooking a correction may completely nullify one's work and make one a malpractitioner. Perhaps the more revered and reliable the source is considered to be, the more reason to check the additions and corrections. A few minutes spent with the corrections and additions to the *Dictionary of National Biography* will reveal that although some changes seem very small and inconsiderable, others have major repercussions.

The preceding discussion has concerned the use of reference books—both factual and bibliographical, but consultation of the main stack collection should not be overlooked. When the reference collection fails or the question is broad in nature, the stacks may harbor exactly what is wanted. If, for some reason, no works on the Battle of Waterloo or on Napoleon were available, one's strategy would be to consider broader subjects that might include discussion of the subject. Thus, one would look to histories of the region surrounding the battle field, or biographies or histories of other principal figures, or the jurisdictions engaged in the battle.

With the interest in and the amount of material published about Napoleon and the Napoleonic Wars, more likely the problem will be to decide which of the many sources is most likely to include the information required. Certain biographers and historians have particular interests that make various dimensions of their work particularly strong. One writer may emphasize family and home life, another social connections, personal, and political maneuvering. Others may be counted upon to give details of buildings and interiors, and so on. If these aspects of a book have been highlighted by the title, subtitle, table of contents, or jacket blurb, they may be reflected in the subject headings or classification numbers assigned when the work is cataloged. Usually, however, failing one's own or the inquirer's knowledge of the people who have written on the subject, the table of contents and index of each book must be consulted. In such instances the attitude and disposition of the inquirer is important. Some persons who are passionately interested in the subject will be quite content to read or carefully browse through several works to locate the desired information. Others will not consider the question ''that important.''

Searching Within Sources: Manual and Automated

When the source has been selected, it is necessary to consider how to use it most effectively. The first thing to be determined is its structure, assumptions, and vocabulary. While these may be deduced by random examination, it is best to study the explanatory material describing the work. In a printed list this should appear as an introduction, preface, or statement on how to use the book. Library catalogs on cards and computerized files must provide that information by other means.

If the prefatory statement is not full or explicit enough, the structure of the work can be discerned through an examination of the table of contents, the order of arrangement of entries, the indexes, and by noticing whether filing terms are general, specific, or of mixed levels. Are cross references provided in the main arrangement, or is it necessary to use indexes? These approaches apply to all reference tools although bibliographic sources will be emphasized here.

There are several broad conventions that the trained librarian recognizes as standard for catalogs of library collections. These relate to the number and kind of entries, filing order, and the nature and number of references provided. Variations may be applied to the catalogs of individual collections, and reference librarians must be able to maneuver effectively within the conventions used.

The Structure and Vocabulary of the File. However experienced one is with a particular source, there are times when it is wise to review the explanation of its organization and the subject vocabulary used. This can be done while providing instruction to the inquirer. A useful example is provided by the *Library of Congress Subject Headings* in connection with the Waterloo search. Awareness of general conventions prompts one to try the specific topic rather than a broader one and also to try ''Waterloo, Battle of'' rather than ''Battle of Waterloo.''

Napoleonic Wars
   See Europe—History—1789-1815
     France—History—Revolution, 1789-1799
     France—History—1789-1815
     France—History—Consulate and Empire, 1799-1815
     Peninsular War, 1807-1814
   Second Coalition, War of the, 1798-1801
   names of battles, e.g. Waterloo, Battle of, 1815; *and specific*
     campaigns listed as subdivisions under Napoléon I, Emperor
     of the French, 1769-1821

Fig. 5.1. *Napoleonic Wars (from* U.S. Library of Congress Subject Headings. *1980.)*

Because one has sufficient background knowledge, albeit recently derived from an encyclopedia, the rationale of the *see-also* reference to "Quatre Bras, Battle of, 1815" and the note of a *see-also* reference from "Belle-Alliance, Battle of, 1815" is clear (U.S. Lib. of Congr., 1980, Vol. 2, p. 2521). The additional note that Waterloo is used as an example reference under "Napoleonic Wars" should arouse one's curiosity.

The information provided under "Napoleonic Wars" (see Fig. 5.1) is precisely the kind one needs in order to design an efficient and comprehensive search. Such elaborate information notes are few, but they provide patterns from which one can construct those appropriate to other topics.

The librarian's prior knowledge of a source or of the subject may compensate for the fact that few sources present even the scope notes provided by *LCSH*. In other instances, the entries found under synonyms and related terms should be sampled and the *"See"* and *"See also"* references should be followed up. Such sampling should precede the design of searches, whether of printed or computerized files.

The difficulties encountered in selecting appropriate headings for a search can be illustrated in the following example. A patron is interested in reading articles reflecting recent research into the characteristics useful for predicting marital satisfaction or success. Such a patron, interested in a serious but not highly technical discussion of this topic, can reasonably be referred to the *Social Sciences Index*. This tool is reputable and widely used, is based on standard conventions, and is presented in an easy to read and use format.

The untrained user might first consult the heading, "Satisfaction, Marital." Many searchers, although aware that library files often do not use natural word order, do not appreciate that inverted word order is intended to group citations on related topics conveniently and logically. The *"See"* reference that appears:

Satisfaction, Marital. See Marriage

tells searchers that the term consulted is not used by giving the alternative—in this case, "Marriage." The entries under "Marriage" begin with one citation to a general article followed by 14 *"See also"* references (Fig. 5.2.). After these references, the citations are grouped under such subdivisions as "Mathematical

Marriage

Macro- and micro-examination of family power and love: an exchange model. C. Safilios-Rothschild. bibl J Marr & Fam 38:355-62 My '76

See also

Australian aborigines—Marriage
Courtship
Divorce
Endogamy and exogamy
Engagement
Family
Family life education
Husband and wife
Intermarriage of races
Married students
Married women
Remarriage
Residence (kinship)
Sexual ethics

Mathematical models

Constructing increment-decrement life tables. R. Schoen. Demography 12:313-24 My '75; Reply with rejoinder. A. Rogers and J. Ledent. 13:287-91 My '76

Research

Familism scale: revalidation and revision. P. L. Heller. J Marr & Fam 38:423-9 Ag '76

Marital interaction and marital conflict: a critical evaluation of current research strategies. B. R. Glick and S. J. Gross. bibl J Marr & Fam 37:505-12 Ag '75; Reply. D. M. Klein and S. R. Jorgensen. 38:216-19 My '76

Measuring dyadic adjustment: new scales for assessing the quality of marriage and similar dyads. G. B. Spanier. bibl J Marr & Fam 38:15-28 F '76

Multivariate developmental model of marital satisfaction. B. C. Miller. J Marr & Fam 38:643-57 My '76

Research needs of a family life educator and marriage counselor. R. O. Blood. bibl J Marr & Fam 38:7-12 F '76

Burma

Marriage payments: a paradigm from the Burmese perspective. M. E. Spiro. bibl J Anthrop Res 31:89-115 Summ '75

Canada

Relationship of wives' employment status to husband, wife and pair satisfaction and performance. R. J. Burke and T. Weir. bibl J Marr & Fam 38:279-87 My '76

Sexual behavior in and out of marriage: an assessment of correlates. J. N. Edwards and A. Booth. bibl J Marr & Fam 38:73-81 F '76

Some personality differences between members of one-career and two-career families. R. J. Burke and T. Weir. bibl J Marr & Fam 38:453-9 Ag '76

Uganda

Formality of marriage: a Kampala case study. E. Mandeville. bibl J. Anthrop Res 31:183-95 Aut '75

United States

Dimensions of family alienation in the marital dyad. A. G. Neal and others. bibl Sociometry 39:396-405 D '76

Dimensions of marriage happiness: a research note. M. M. Marini. J Marr & Fam 38:443-8 Ag '76

Divorce and separation [symposium] ed. by O. C. Moles and G. Levinger. bibl J Soc Issues 32 no 1:1-207 '76

Evolving sources of happiness for men over the life cycle: a structural analysis. J. Harry. bibl J Marr & Fam 38:289-96 My '76

Historical trends and variations in educational homogamy. R. C. Rockwell. bibl J Marr & Fam 38:83-95 F '76

Invidious intimacy. J. Stiehm. il Soc Pol 6:12-16 Mr '76

Marital and family role satisfaction. B. A. Chadwick and others. bibl J Marr & Fam 38:431-40 Ag '76

Marriage and remarriage rates among older Americans. J. Treas and A. VanHilst. bibl Gerontologist 16:132-6 Ap '76

Marriage declines among U.S. youth. Futurist 10:165 Je '76

Overview of statistics on interracial marriage in the United States, with data on its extent from 1963-1970. T. P. Monahan. bibl Demography 13:223-31 My '76

Patterns of leisure and marital interaction. D. K. Orthner. bibl J Leis Res 8 no2:98-111 '76

Refined estimator of measures of location of the age at first marriage. T. J. Trussell. bibl Demography 13:225-33 My '76

Sex, marital status, and mental health: a reappraisal. G. J. Warheit and others. bibl Soc Forces 55:459-70 D '76

Fig. 5.2. *Marriage (from* Social Sciences Index, *Copyright* © *1976, 1977 by The H. W. Wilson Company. Material reproduced by permission of the publisher). (Figure is continued on p. 110.)*

models'' and ''Research.'' Under the latter heading, three of five titles imply a concern with marital happiness, but one suggests that the reader should be expert in sociological jargon. The bulk of the entries under the ''Marriage'' heading are subdivided by country. The 13 entries under the ''United States'' subdivision include three that seem to discuss marital happiness. One of these is for an article ''Dimensions of marital happiness: a research note.'' It does not appear under the ''Research'' subdivision. Perhaps it is a report on research rather than a discussion of methodology. The subdivision concludes with two ''*See also*'' references to ''Marriage'' used as a subdivision under other headings, and with one citation under the further subheading ''*History.*''

The ''*See also*'' references indicate how related topics are entered. Because

See also
Mexicans in the United States—Marriage
Negroes—Marriage

History

Crisis framework applied to macrosociological family changes: marriage, divorce, and occupational trends associated with World War II. J. Lipman-Blumen. bibl J Marr & Fam 37:889-902 N '75

West Indies, British

Mating patterns and adaptive change in Rum Bay, 1823-1970 [British Virgin Islands]. R. Dirks and V. Kerns. bibl Soc & Econ Stud 25:34-54 Mr '76

Marriage (Burmese law)

See also
Dower (Burmese law)

Marriage (Greek law)

Changes in property transfer among Greek Cypriot villagers. P. Loizos. Man 10:503-23 D '75

Marriage (primitive law)

Asymmetrical matrilateral cross-cousin marriage—the Love-du case. E. J. Krige. bibl Afric Stud 34 no4:231-57 '75

Dispersed alliance and the prohibition of marriage: reconsideration of McKinley's explanation of Crow-Omaha terminologies. R. H. Barnes. bibl Man 11:384-99 S '76

Measuring marriage preference. E. V. Fredlund and B. Dyke. Ethnology 15:35-45 Ja '76

See also
Bride price
Residence (kinship)

Marriage, Mixed

Intermarriage and unwanted fertility in the United States. F. D. Bean and L. H. Aiken. bibl J Marr & Fam 38:61-72 F '76

Jewish-gentile divorce in California. A. S. Maller. Jewish Soc Stud 37:279-90 Summ/Fall '75

Jewish intermarriage in Montreal, 1962-1972. J. C. Lasry and E. Bloomfield-Schachter. Jewish Soc Stud 37:267-78 Summ/Fall '75

Some social concomitants of interethnic marriage in Singapore. E. C. Y. Kuo and R. Hassan. bibl J Marr & Fam 38:549-59 Ag '76

Marriage contracts. See Antenuptial contracts

Marriage counseling

Abused wife problem. B. B. Nichols. Soc Casework 57:27-32 Ja '76

Assessment of marital discord in social work practice. W. W. Hudson and D. H. Glisson. Soc Serv R 50:293-311 Je '76

Behavioral exchange model of marital treatment. W. W. Saxon, jr. Soc Casework 57:33-40 Ja '76

Communication training program for couples [premarital counseling]. S. Miller and others. Soc Casework 57:9-18 Ja '76

Dyadic free association. S. Silbergeld and R. W. Manderscheid. Psychol Rept 39:423-6 O '76

Love-making—an act of murder: the Golem syndrome (G.S.) J. Bierer. Int J Soc Psych 22:197-9 Aut '76

Marital therapy when one spouse has a primary affective disorder. B. L. Greene and others. Am J Psych 133:827-30 Jl '76

Profiles of couples seeking sex therapy and marital therapy. E. Frank and others. Am J Psych 133:559-62 My '76

Review of behavioral marital counseling: has practice tuned out theory? D. H. Glisson. bibl Psychol Rec 26:95-104 Wint '76

Role of sex therapy in marital therapy. C. J. Sager. Am J Psych 133:555-8 My '76

Total separation treatment (T.S.T.) a method for the treatment of marital difficulties and disharmonies in patients suffering from the E.I.M.P. syndrome. J. Bierer. Int J Soc Psych 22:-206-13 Aut '76

Use of marriage enrichment programs in a family agency. H. Hunnicutt and B. Shapiro. Soc Casework 57:555-61 N '76

See also
Sexual therapy

Marriage customs and rites

Agnates and affines: studies in African marriage, manners and land allocation [symposium]. bibl maps Afric Stud 34 no4:231-316 '75

Continuity and change: patterns of mate selection and marriage ritual in a Malay village. H. Strange. J Marr & Fam 38:561-71 Ag '76

See also
Weddings

Fig. 5.2 (*continued*). *Marriage* (*from* Social Sciences Index, *Copyright* © *1976, 1977 by The H. W. Wilson Company. Material reproduced by permission of the publisher*).

"*See*" and "*See also*" references are not always included in each printed issue of a continuing source, cumulations should be consulted. Scanning "*See also*" references may suggest headings directly related to the search. The scope intended for headings may be suggested by the titles of the articles. The interpersonal dynamics of marriage are considered under the heading "Husband and wife" where nine of 34 titles refer to marital satisfaction or difficulties. One such title (Fig. 5.3) appears directly related to the question: "Perceptions of color preferences—a clue to marital prediction."

At some point in the search it may seem that the question is related to considerations of who should marry or what to do to increase the chances for a successful marriage. This line of thought leads to the headings "Engagement" and

Husband and wife

Behavior exchange theory and marital decision making. J. Gottman and others. bibl J Pers Soc Psychol 34:14-23 Jl '76

Cessation of marital intercourse. J. N. Edwards and A. Booth. Am J Psych 133:1333-6 N '76

Community and propinquity in a city. J. C. Everitt. maps Assn Am Geog Ann 66:104-16 Mr '76

Comparison of weighted and unweighted decision-making scores. S. Price-Bonham. bibl J Marr & Fam 38:629-40 N '76

Compatibility [simulation game]. A. A. Zox. Simulat & Games 7:227-30 Je '76

Concurrent sex therapy and psychoanalytic psychotherapy by separate therapists: effectiveness and implications. A. Levay and others. Psychiatry 39:355-63 N '76

Course of love: a cross-sectional design. R. S. Cimbalo and others. Psychol Rept 38:1292-4 Je pt2 '76

Husband and wife—*cont.*

Differential contribution of stature phenotypes to assortative mating in parents of Philadelphia black and white school children. W. H. Mueller and R. M. Malina. bibl Am J Phys Anthrop 45:269-75 S '76

Dimensions of family alienation in the marital dyad. A. G. Neal and others. bibl Sociometry 39:396-405 D '76

Disclosure of problems and tensions experienced by marital partners. R. J. Burke and others. bibl Psychol Rept 38:531-42 Ap '76

Divorce and separation [symposium] ed. by O. C. Moles and G. Levinger. bibl J Soc Issues 32 no 1:1-207 '76

Dyadic free association. S. Silbergeld and R. W. Manderscheid. Psychol Rept 39:423-6 O '76

Education, wage rates, and the division of labor between husband and wife. G. Farkas. bibl J Marr & Fam 38:473-83 Ag '76

Elderly couples and the institution. R. Locker. Soc Work 21:149-50 Mr '76

Family structure and society. P. Heintz and others. bibl J Marr & Fam 37:861-70 N '75

Gender roles and the process of fertility control. J. Scanzoni. bibl J Marr & Fam 38:677-91 N '76

Husband/wife comparisons of price-quality relationships in the post-purchase situation. G. W. H. Scherf and G. F. Kawash. J Soc Psychol 100:99-106 O '76

Identity and stability within the marriage relationship. J. Askham. J Marr & Fam 38:535-47 Ag '76

Marital communication and sexism. L. Alsbrook. Soc Casework 57:517-22 O '76

Marital interaction and marital conflict: a critical evaluation of

current research strategies. B. R. Glick and S. J. Gross. bibl J Marr & Fam 37:505-12 Ag '75; Reply. D. M. Klein and S. R. Jorgensen. 38:216-19 My '76

Multivariate developmental model of marital satisfaction. B. C. Miller. J Marr & Fam 38:643-57 N '76

Occupational positions and class identifications of married working women: a test of the asymmetry hypothesis. K. V. Ritter and L. L. Hargens. bibl Am J Sociol 80:934-48 Ja '75; Reply with rejoinder. J. W. Schneider. 82:411-17 S '76

Perceptions of color preferences—a clue to marital prediction? D. G. Dean and others. J Psychol 93:243-4 Jl '76

Physical attractiveness and marriage adjustment in middle-aged couples. B. I. Murstein and P. Christy. bibl J Pers Soc Psychol 34:537-42 O '76

Presterilization interviewing: an evaluation. R. G. Carey. J Counsel Psychol 23:492-4 S '76

Professional pair; husband and wife psychologists. R. B. Bryson and others. Am Psychol 31:10-16 Ja '76

Psychological reaction to infertility. V. R. Wiehe. Psychol Rept 38:863-6 Je '76

Relationship of wives' employment status to husband, wife and pair satisfaction and performance. R. J. Burke and T. Weir. bibl J Marr & Fam 38:279-87 My '76

Role relationships between husband and wife in rural Ghana. S. van der Geest. bibl J Marr & Fam 38:572-8 Ag '76

Social standing of a married woman. L. B. Nilson. bibl Soc Prob 23:581-92 Je '76

Theory of power relationships in marriage. B. C. Rollins and S. J. Bahr. bibl J Marr & Fam 38:619-27 N '76

Transition to parenthood: a decade replication. D. F. Hobbs, jr and S. P. Cole. J Marr & Fam 38:723-31 N '76

When love is blind: maintaining idealized images of one's spouse. J. A. Hall and S. E. Taylor. Hum Relat 29:751-61 Ag '76

Work integration, marital satisfaction, and conjugal power. T. D. Kemper and M. L. Reichler. bibl Hum Relat 29:929-44 O '76

See also

Divorce

Marriage

also

Alcoholics—Family relationships

Brain damaged—Family relationships

Cancer patients—Family relationships

Emotionally disturbed—Family relationships

Mentally ill—Family relationships

Victims of crimes—Family relationships

Fig. 5.3. *Husband and wife (from* Social Sciences Index, *Copyright © 1976, 1977 by The H. W. Wilson Company. Material reproduced by permission of the publisher.)*

"Premarital counseling;" the latter advises "*See Marriage counseling.*" Reference to Fig. 5.2 shows that entries under the phrase "Marriage counseling" are filed after all the subdivisions of "Marriage," after "Marriage (primitive law)" and "Marriage, Mixed."

The structure of the list found under "Marriage" reveals widely used and often effective conventions taught in cataloging courses. Citations for general articles precede subheadings on aspects of the topic. A special sequence of subheadings, in this case geographical, but often chronological, follows. As shown in Fig. 5.2, these headings may be further subdivided by topic as in "Marriage—United States—*History.*" A quick scan of the headings and subheadings will indicate whether or not one is on the right track for the question and which subheading(s) are important in reducing scatter in the files when they are merged by cumulation and interfiled.

Such conventions are so ingrained in American library practice that it is easy to forget they are not self-evident. Even users who have spent a lot of time with indexes may not understand the relationship of *"See"* and *"See also"* references, and the way the subdivisions are used. Indeed, these conventions are not always consistent in their logic or application. It is unsettling to discover under "Happiness" (Fig. 5.4) two titles that are dispersed under the many marriage-related headings. Moreover, the most directly related title appeared among many dissimilar "Husband and wife" entries (Fig. 5.3). Effective searchers learn to consider alternatives and to know the value of assessing the entires found under various headings.

A good search is designed to gain greatest results for the effort expended. A little time spent looking through the terms used in the source will help to refine the terminology and to focus the question to best reflect the interests of the inquirer. One wants to avoid searching unlikely headings, but not to ignore productive ones. Given the constraints of a search and the structure of a file, some minimally productive headings might even be excluded.

The conventions used in the assignment of headings or access points are equally important in computerized files. Printed files have emphasized pre-coordinate indexing. The subject headings are used to group similar citations, and cost usually dictates that the headings chosen be few in number and reflect the overall content of the item. Even in computer files that allow post-coordinate searching (a search for all entries associated with "marriage" *and* "happiness" without concern for the order in which the terms are assigned), the search terms must agree with those used in the file. A richer choice of terms means that for full recall, either the searcher or the program must make connections between all the

Happiness

Evolving sources of happiness for men over the life cycle: a structural analysis. J. Harry. bibl J Marr & Fam 38:289-96 My '76

Matched samples analysis for item responses. G. D. Faulkenberry and R. G. Mason. Pub Opinion Q 40:256-60 Summ '76

Measuring dyadic adjustment: new scales for assessing the quality of marriage and similar dyads. G. B. Spanier. bibl J Marr & Fam 38:15-28 F '76

Social agents in children's happiness. U. R. Sidana and others. J Soc Psychol 99:289-90 Ag '76

Subjective measures of well-being. A. Campbell. bibl Am Psychol 31:117-24 F '76

Fig. 5.4. *Happiness (from* Social Sciences Index, *Copyright © 1976, 1977 by The H. W. Wilson Company. Material reproduced by permission of the publisher.)*

terms. The search can be broadened by adding a synonym (marriage *and* happiness *or* satisfaction). Broadening must be carefully considered to avoid picking up too many peripheral or unrelated items. Unwanted items are called ''noise'' and reduce the search's precision. However, adding the term ''research'' (research *and* marriage *and* happiness *or* satisfaction) would suppress citations in which research was not highlighted. If the search instructions were ''marriage *and* happiness *or* satisfaction *or* research,'' articles dealing with marriage and research, but not necessarily also with happiness or satisfaction, would be included. This capacity to search on coordinated terms using the ''and, or, not'' statements of Boolean logic is a very attractive and useful aspect of computerized searching.

Computerized files may have useful capabilities in addition to ease of searching on coordinated terms and full cumulation previously mentioned. They may provide points of access beyond the assigned descriptors (subject headings) and key words of the title embodied in the printed version. It may be possible to search on fields in addition to those for author and title, and/or on the text provided in the abstract. Search statements must reflect, however, the requirements of the database and the vendor. Unless the service is used regularly and frequently, it is difficult for a searcher to maintain efficiency.

The decision of whether to do a manual or a computer-assisted search should be reached after the complexity of the search and the time and effort involved in the manual search has been weighed against the time and effort necessary to record the search statement, the expense and, if printing is done offline and results mailed, the delay of doing a computerized search. A straightforward manual search might be completed in less time than it would take to formulate a request for a computer search.

Participation of Requester. The main change that computer assistance has made to reference service is in the duration of the presearch interview and the patron's attitude. These library users will make an advance appointment and will participate in a fairly rigorous examination of the nature of their question or need and the results that they expect or will find acceptable. Such interviews differ from the customary ''catch-as-catch-can'' reference desk interviews mainly in the open acknowledgment that the patrons have questions they wish to have seriously and professionally considered—at length, if necessary. The librarian is attempting to elicit the same necessary information in each case (Somerville, 1977).

Experience suggests that clients are more satisfied when they have been present and have participated in the online search. Some searchers, however, confident of their knowledge of the database and their interview skills, or nervous in the presence of clients, consider them to be intrusive. The uninitiated may be easily distracted and prone to browse in peripheral or tangential material. Such sightseeing while online increases the cost of the search. Other searchers are equally convinced that only the presence of the client can ensure maximum recall. Inevitably in the course of the search, new avenues are suggested that should be explored. These searchers consider that the time spent in determining whether or not the new areas are productive is well-worth the additional cost.

Presentation of Results

Most manual searches will be completed by the interested party; however, most computer-based and all delegated searches require presentation of results. When possible, presentation and delivery should include an opportunity for the requester to discuss the search and the citations.

The person receiving the material should know what has been done and the relative weight that has been given to specific factors. Inclusion of some peripheral items may help to indicate the extent of the recall achieved. Such reassurance becomes particularly important if the inquirer has not sampled the file, either in a printed format or in browsing online.

Whether the individual pays for the search directly or the cost is absorbed by the institution, scrupulous accounting procedures should provide cost information for the individual and the library. Included with the results should be the library unit with office phone number and hours of service and the name of the person to contact.

The results of a delegated manual search also should be appropriately formatted and include a statement as to sources and headings consulted. The basis for decisions and alterations made during the search should be recorded. A summary comment on the research trends observed may be useful and welcome.

If delegated manual searches are frequent, time and trouble may be saved by a photocopy of the pages of the bibliographic sources, or by the design and duplication of worksheets or slips for recording references. If these forms are neatly filled out during the search, they can serve as the reporting sheets. Obviating the need to recopy citations not only saves time, but also reduces the opportunities for introducing errors. The merits of keeping a copy of the search on file for reference or for use in training must be weighed against the cost of storing and maintaining such a file if it is rarely consulted.

Presentation and delivery of results afford an opportunity to show what the library can do. It is worth some time and trouble to strike the right note of pride and frugality.

THE INTERPERSONAL COMPONENT: THE INTERVIEW

The interview is the first stage in the reference transaction. It may extend to nothing more than the user's asking a question and the librarian's providing the suitable source. It may become a fairly complex social and intellectual exchange. The interview provides an opportunity to discover and satisfy the inquirer's information need even when this may differ from answering the question as asked. If there is no contact between the library user and the reference librarian, users may remain unaware of available resources. Improving the public's recognition of its information needs and its awareness of the library's scope and potential is a constant challenge to librarians. The interview meets that challenge on a one-to-one basis and may determine the success or failure of the reference transaction (Jennerich, 1980; Rothstein, 1977).

A complete interview encompasses greeting the user, receiving and refining the question, matching it to the appropriate source, insuring that the user retrieves the information from the source, and following through to ascertain that the information meets the user's needs—not merely answers the question. Patrons must feel confident and open so that they are willing to share the information they have and to acknowledge when there is uncertainty about its validity. The librarian sometimes must probe to discover the context of the question and to be able to discuss various possible approaches and explore their merits. If patrons feel unsure and threatened by the tone of the interview, they cannot participate so usefully. Without demeaning the inquirer it should be clear that the librarian has a definite contribution to make in meeting the information need.

Greeting the Inquirer

The librarian at the reference desk should appear productively occupied but interruptible. While the exact nature of assigned desk duties will vary, responsibility for the general area is usually assumed. Work that requires consistent and undivided attention should not be brought to the desk. Desk duty sometimes is seen as an opportunity to read professional literature. One seasoned supervisor, an experienced budget defender, insisted that in order to appear businesslike, staff reading while on desk duty should hold a pencil. She knew that the public would not always associate reading with work duties. It is important to look around frequently with a pleasant and encouraging expression showing one's willingness to respond to people. Those who approach the desk should be given full attention.

Approach, Body Language

It should be clear to inquirers that they have the librarian's interest. This can be done by making eye contact and putting aside one's work. The significance of such body language and its importance are now widely recognized. The basic elements of body language as they relate to the reference interview have been discussed by Jennerich and Jennerich (1976) and López Muñoz (1977). Genuine interest in helping to answer questions can be perceived by the user, but it may have to be augmented by acquired skills. Videotaping is an excellent way to see oneself as others do, but observation of others also can be helpful in minimizing one's own distracting or offensive mannerisms. Self-discipline will ensure an acceptable performance even on days when one is ill or especially tired.

There are many interview styles and the one with which the librarian is most comfortable will be modified by the institutional setting and the pace of business at the desk. The interview should be a responsive interaction. The librarian who can enjoy an informal, if brief, discussion while eliciting the standard complement of facts required to pursue the information need, exemplifies the art of the reference interview.

Accompanying the person to the recommended source can be a valuable technique. It diffuses the stiffness, formality, and nervousness of inexperienced librarians and the users by providing a more informal situation for eliciting information. A casual, indirect exploration of a question and the individual's ability to pursue it may save time in the long run.

This walking technique can be used readily only when one is not ''tied'' to the desk. When only one person is on desk duty, it may be worthwhile to devise a way to indicate that the librarian soon will return. When several people are waiting and the question posed seems to be long and involved to answer, it may be possible to tell the inquirer to investigate one or two works and return to the desk—either with more information or with the reference work itself. It often is advisable to say, ''If that doesn't work, come back and we'll try something else.'' In the interval one can cope with some of those waiting.

Accompanying persons to sources is an opportunity to explore their information need in more depth. ''Need'' here is used to mean both why and how much information they want and also their understanding of the subject and of how to use the reference materials. Do not just march off full-tilt in front of them. Looking at an encyclopedia or textbook with inquirers can reveal a great deal about them relative to the subject. If they are novices, the search should proceed meticulously, step by step; if they are sophisticated, shortcuts may work. Special attitudes they have to the subject may be important. If they are persuaded that the traditional approach to the subject is misleading and in error, then the whole search process could become very difficult. Consulting general sources with the inquirer provides an opportunity to learn about the subject without weakening the confidence of the person. Making general observations on the material or subject may draw out the patron so that one can learn more about their question or interest in the subject.

Unless the desk is consistently busy, one does not have to wait for the user to initiate the interview. While scanning the area under supervision, the librarian may detect persons who appear restless or puzzled. If there is an opportunity, one should approach such persons and tactfully initiate the interview. This should be done without presumption. ''Can I help you?'' or ''Do you need anything?'' can sound as if the persons look lost, incompetent, or otherwise conspicuous. Such approaches are easily deflected by a hasty, perhaps automatic and ill-considered, ''Oh, no thanks.'' This response may be regretted almost immediately, but it is difficult to retract. The interest may be appreciated, but the persons who have not found what they wanted still may not know what to ask for. "Have you found everything you need?" might be a preferable approach. It recognizes a measure of self-sufficiency and possible success on their part, but is open for continuation in several ways. While librarians expect to help with a wide range of information needs and problems more demanding than helping to locate a particular book, the extent of the service they are willing to provide generally remains unknown.

Ideally, the level of service provided to library users will be determined by their needs or the requirements of the answer. When trying to determine the extent and level of information required and what level of sophistication might be acceptable, there are hazards. Persons with a casual or personal interest may feel that it is not legitimate for them to take up the librarian's time and attention with a subject they are "just" interested in. Highly educated and research-oriented users may feel that they should know what they do not, and their attempts to save face may complicate the question-answering process. Specialists also may create problems by assuming that librarians have more subject expertise than is the case. The librarian must ask them for a clarification and simplification of the terms of the question.

Students often are reluctant to admit that their questions are related to courses. They may feel suspected of cheating or of trying to get their work done for them. Their reluctance may result from past experience of tension created when the librarian envisioned three dozen classmates descending like locusts upon the library. Anticipating the frustration caused by multiple demands for essentially the same material, librarians may automatically give students with library assignments a prefunctory response such as "check the encyclopedia."

In a private or special library, policies may specifically dictate the levels and extent of service to be rendered to categories of legitimate users. These considerations may be predicated upon the level of governmental or industrial security clearance or the person's rank within the organization. Within the firm the situation will be broadly understood by the clientele of the library. It will be necessary to be gracious when accepting what seem to be peripheral assignments from a company vice president. When refusing lower-echelon staff members, rather than reminding them that they are not of exalted enough rank, adopt a "you-could-check-in-such-and-such" approach.

Receiving and Refining the Question

> *Everything has two handles:*
> *that by which it may be borne,*
> *and that by which it may not.*
>
> —*Epictetus*

Determining the "Need"

In the reference interview as elsewhere, success follows from asking the right questions in the right way. This is true for the patron pursuing the question and for the librarian endeavoring to help. The librarian's first challenge is to determine the full question or information need. One must accept and be responsive to the question as stated, but conduct the interview so that, if necessary, it moves into other areas.

First, the librarian has to determine what the question "really is." Someone may ask "What do you have on the Middle Ages?" when she is looking for information about Abelard and Heloise. "Where are your medical books? is a straightforward directional question that could be answered by library graphics, whether printed floor plans or signs. By responding with another question, "Are you looking for something specific?", the librarian may elicit the admission, "I really want to know the symptoms of muscular dystrophy." However, the patron's response might have been "Oh, no. I just want to know where the medical books are." In that case, after providing the directional information, the librarian might say, "If you don't find what you want, come back." The returning patron may ask a more sharply focused question.

It may be difficult to respond effectively to a question such as "Where's the *Readers' Guide?*" Certainly one indicates where it is, but one also tries to determine whether or not there are more helpful sources. One's expression and the tone of voice in beginning the interview are very important. The tack taken will depend on one's estimate of the inquirer. What will be useful with one person may not work with another. The objective is to elicit enough of a response that a clearer picture of the question emerges. In an educational setting, after indicating where the *Readers' Guide* is, one might add "Are you writing a paper?" Even if the answer is negative, the person still might reveal the topic of the search. In other settings, the question "Have you used it before?" (in a tone that shows willingness to assist) provides an opportunity to continue discussion.

Directional questions should be answered pleasantly and with one's full attention. Library users asking directional questions may be testing the environment. If they find it courteous and helpful, they may begin to trust and rely upon the librarian. Staff members should avoid telegraphing boredom or impatience with uninteresting or routine questions. More difficult to convey is a willingness to help without suggesting that users lack the ability or knowledge to cope by themselves.

The interview should provide an opportunity for inquirers to bring their needs into focus and formulate a question that can be searched and answered. Taylor (1968) has discussed the difficulties that individuals experience in knowing what questions to ask. Taylor (p. 182) postulates four levels of information need or question formulation existing as points along a continuum:

(1) The visceral need—the actual but unexpressed need for information;

(2) The conscious need—the conscious, within-brain description of the need;

(3) The formalized need—the formal statement of the need; and

(4) The compromised need—the question as presented to the information system.

These four states are useful ways of considering information needs, but librarians soon recognize that the questions presented to them may not correspond to visceral or actual needs. During the interview the expressed need should be brought into the greatest possible congruence with the actual need.

Consider the question,

"Where can I find out about Clones?"

That seems easy enough, and the answer

"*The New Columbia Encyclopedia*"

may seem like a snappy, precise, and efficient response. But such a response is deficient, not only because it is abrupt, but also because it makes no attempt to get behind the question. A better initial response might be:

"What is it you want to know about Clones?"

This response clearly repeats the key words and rephrases the inquiry providing an immediate opportunity to discover a misunderstanding. Perhaps the word was *cloves* or *drones*. There is a delightful story of the person who appealed to the librarian for "Darwin's oranges and peaches." Listening to oneself repeat the question gives a sense of what the question probably is, and it may be possible to exercise the required courteous self-control while saying, "Darwin's *Origin of the Species?*"

To return to the Clones question:

"I want to know where it is and what it is famous for."

This statement may truly startle one whose head is full of the exciting potential of biological cloning.

Since the person is not interested in biological clones, the librarian should continue to explore the subject.

"How did you hear about it?"

Such open-ended questions can be very useful (Emerson, 1977). They do not assume very much and do not cut off possibilities.

"In an exhibit catalog."

If an expectant silence is maintained, the person may continue,

"It's a place where some (Celtic) art objects were found."

If the person does not say "Celtic," they nonetheless may be able to provide an idea of the probable general area in which Clones is to be looked for.

Similarly open-ended would be the question,

"How did you come to be interested in Clones? Is it a personal interest of yours?"

The tone of voice should suggest that the inquirer's interest demonstrates something positive about the person—if not charm, wit, or intelligence, then perhaps earnestness. Professional responsibility requires suppression of negative responses and attitudes toward the person or the question. Persons pursuing a casual interest may have the leisure to explore peripheral but pleasant byways in the course of the search. They should not be made to feel that their questions are unimportant.

At this point the librarian knows that Clones is a place, and that art objects found there have been discussed in an exhibit catalog. It may be located in Ireland. What is needed now is an indication of the level and extent of information the inquirer would like.

Even indirect questions may elicit an indication as to whether the person is preparing for a trip, settling a bet, or beginning work on a five-minute report or a full-scale research project. Based upon knowledge and awareness of the total library and client environment, the librarian may decide on a personal approach that assumes that the person is studying the subject—either formally or informally.

"Are you studying art (or Irish history)?"

Eventually, experience with people allows cultivation of a shrewdness that prompts specific suggestions more often than not appropriate to the individual. But, while people are complimented by having their interests recognized, very often they deeply resent being summarily categorized or stereotyped.

Time might be saved by a more direct approach that establishes a commonly recognized framework.

"Is this for a course?", or

"Is this for Professor Shaw's course?"

One wants to keep one's position open and encouraging by an intonation that conveys interest and support; avoid closing off any possibilities. A flat "no" to a question about Professor Shaw's course leaves uncertainty as to whether one was mistaken in the professor or in the suggestion that it was for a course. In such situations an attentive silence following a "no" may be more productive than adding to the confusion by throwing out more false leads.

A difficulty arising from asking the wrong kind of question is the need to clear away the erroneous material and all the vestiges of the misunderstanding that it gathers in its wake. Moreover, care should be taken that the question asked solicits the information desired and that one does not proceed to make assumptions beyond established facts. For example (to use a question more likely in a social than in a professional setting), asking where someone was born is not a sure-fire way of finding out what their accent is and may lead to erroneous assumptions. If one does grasp the question by the wrong handle, it is not always easy to relinquish it quickly and smoothly. Open questions reduce this danger.

Once the question as stated is understood, there may be little more to the interview. General sources provide very little information on Clones. The biological clone has driven Ireland's Clones out of current encyclopedias. The basic information found might satisfy the inquirer or be the basis for a wide-ranging search through sources on Irish and art history.

Matching the Question to the Sources

Seasoned researchers have learned to ask questions in ways that permit informative answers. Usually when such researchers come to the reference desk, it is for guidance in fields peripheral to their major area of work. Because of their experience, they are aware of the kinds of sources that might be available and may have shaped their question on that basis. Should they have misjudged the availability of such a source, they can anticipate alternate approaches. If they seek advice from the librarian, it will be for specific kinds of resources that will satisfy identified requirements.

Those who are not trained researchers rely more heavily on the librarian to define or shape the question. Most individuals have a variety of questions and little opportunity to build up expertise in any particular field. Helping them recognize their question is a major service or responsibility of the librarian. In one's eagerness to answer the question, it is important to remember what the inquirer's needs are. As each bit of information about the question accumulates, several approaches may seem possible. Do not proceed too far without confirmation from the inquirer. It is important to ensure that one is pursuing the patron's question and has not gone off on another track.

As the question is being refined, the librarian should be considering the structure of potential information sources (books, statistical tables, maps, or computerized data sets) and the access provided by their arrangement and indexes. The needs of the inquirer should be matched against the characteristics of known sources. The sensitive questions required to discover who needs the information, why they want it, and how quickly they need it can be asked unobtrusively as one proceeds with the interview or even the search.

The young man who was interested in characteristics that predict success in marriage might have asked:

"Do you have anything on marriage or happy marriages?"
The response,

"What do you want to know about happy marriages?"
should begin a productive exchange, but the range of potentially interesting material is enormous.

"I want to know what personal characteristics are most likely to lead to a successful marriage."

There are several problems with such a question. How are successful marriages identified? Which of a myriad of personal characteristics of individuals happily married are significant? But, at least for the time being, statistical and demographical sources can be ignored. By making suggestions that represent specific kinds of material, the librarian can provide a comfortable way for unsophisticated patrons to indicate the kind of information they are looking for. By mentioning the title of a popular marriage manual or a book about a famous couple, one might learn that the question was sparked by a newspaper account of recent research. Further conversation might make clear that a list of the characteristics that are considered an indication of a happy marriage is not what is wanted. By locating the original news story, one might gain helpful information and discover where the study or report was published. In most libraries, however, the likelihood of obtaining a recent account of research is slight. One must look for work of a similar nature.

It has been established that the individual does not have a specific goal such as a talk or term paper, and is willing to spend some time and effort looking for the information. He does not want a sensationalized piece of popular journalism, but is not an expert or subject specialist, so highly technical material would not be a first choice. It can be assumed that he has a somewhat better than average education and apparently adequate reading skills.

Suitable information might be found in an encyclopedia or textbook on marriage and the family. However, given the characteristics of the inquirer and the apparent recency of the research reported, periodical articles might discuss the question at the proper level and length. This, of course, means consultation of a periodical index. If a reasonable number of references gleaned from *Social Sciences Index* will be found in the library, then that index would be a better source to consult than the *Readers' Guide to Periodical Literature,* which features magazines of a more popular nature. Depending on the material available in the collection, other indexes might be considered appropriate first choices.

If the available information is unsuitable and if the patron is not interested enough to pursue the question to other collections or to wait for material to be borrowed on his behalf, then continued effort is pointless. Such situations provide a direct test of the effectiveness of the library's selection policy and collection building *vis-à-vis* that type of inquiry.

Insuring Effective Use of Sources

But before sending users off to any sources, the librarian should have a fairly clear idea of what they will find there and should suggest some headings. For some subjects, as the previous discussion of the marriage question has shown, choice of headings and their relationships is not clear, and it is very helpful if the librarian can spend a few minutes with the user at the source. Even when the subject seems fairly straightforward, it is important to ascertain if the user is familiar with the source and knows how to use it. It is preferable to ask, "Have you ever used that index before?" rather than "Do you know how to use it?" The response to the first question may be a "No, but . . .", which is nonetheless reassuring. The response to the second usually will be a confident, "Oh, yes." However, even readers who have used *Readers' Guide* or similar indexes in school seldom recognize the importance and utility of the *"See"* and *"See also"* references; moreover, it is not always clear why articles appear under one heading rather than another. Therefore, unless readers have considerable experience or seem ready to return with questions, there is much to be gained by spending a few minutes at the index with them. Encouraging readers to check back with the librarian after they have consulted the recommended source provides an opportunity for them to ask questions that may arise from that consultation and for the librarian to evaluate its success.

EVALUATING EFFECTIVENESS OF RESPONSE

Effective reference service has been provided when the most appropriate tool has been consulted in the manner that yields a reliable answer with the least expenditure of time and effort. The question is received, a source is consulted, and the answer is discovered as expected. If the sources for the collection have been well-selected and if there have been no social blunders committed during the transaction, the service may be judged to be as good as the answer is accurate. There may be no apparent need or way to judge the efficiency of a response. Indeed, in his fine discussion of formal evaluation of reference services, Lancaster (1977) notes that real evaluation "has rarely been applied to reference service." But his following discussion shows that evaluation demands serious attention. While librarians may report a 90% success rate, a variety of studies indicate that when accuracy is considered, the *highest* success rates range between 50% and 55% (Lancaster, 1977, pp. 79–109; Childers, 1980; Peat, Marwick, Mitchell, 1975). This success rate must be raised in every library.

Reviewing Answered Questions

Reviewing questions and discussing alternate sources and approaches are important ways for every reference librarian to improve performance. Four major qualities (in addition to cost, response time, and accuracy of citation) are considered in the evaluation of literature searches. These qualities are

(1)   Completeness of coverage;
(2)   Recall (total recall would indicate that every useful item was retrieved);
(3)   Precision (complete precision would mean that only useful items were retrieved); and
(4)   Novelty.

The aim is to achieve the balance of qualities appropriate to the demands of that particular search. If the reader only wants one or two items to give a basic overview, completeness and high recall would not be important. Usually, however, one will want to consult first the source with the best coverage. The decision to stop a search is made when successive files yield fewer and fewer new items (that is, provide little novelty). Colleagial discussion of completed searches allows consideration of different approaches and combinations of sources. It promotes staff flexibility in response to successive searches.

When a fact and not literature about a subject is required, the discovery of particular tables, appendices, or a concentration of illustrations may refine strategies for handling subsequent questions. If the search has been time-consuming and the question can be expected to recur, a note should be made for the use of other librarians. As mentioned before, reference departments often maintain files of such nuggets of information. It is well to become acquainted with that file and to review it regularly. Direct consultation with colleagues—in both public and technical services—can alert one to appropriate sources one might have overlooked. But even when the question has been satisfactorily answered, there is much to be learned. Without colleagial exchanges and con-tinuous review of the collection, it is hard to improve efficiency in choice and exploitation of sources.

Unanswered Questions

The three main reasons a question cannot be answered relate to deficiencies of the librarian, the collection, and the question itself. To be specific: (a) the librarian overlooks the answer in an available source, (b) the answer is not available in the collection, or (c) the question has no definitive answer.

Answer Overlooked

The first situation is the most frustrating. All too often inquirers have been told there is no answer or were given erroneous answers even when the resources for an accurate response were available (Lancaster, 1977, pp. 91–108). There is no substitute for knowing one's resources, including the entire collection and special files and indexes. When one cannot answer a question, the perspective and knowledge of colleagues can be invaluable. Often they "just happen to know" something essential. If unanswerable questions of a similar type seem to be recurring, one should try to discover their basis and consider acquisition of suitable materials.

Even if the question must go unanswered, the approach that is taken during the interview and search can build goodwill and confidence. Supervisors must devise training, monitoring, and review methods that minimize the number of desk failures. Evaluation should be viewed as an opportunity for professional im-provement. The librarian who joins a library with such a program is fortunate.

A conscientious searcher may be haunted by the possibility that the answer "must be there," and must learn when it is reasonable to stop. This becomes easier with experience. The reference policy manual should provide guidelines indicating the kinds of questions staff members can accept and how much library time can be devoted to them. Once the priorities and level of service have been determined, it is up to the staff member at the desk to implement them evenhandedly and without regard for the personal charms of the inquirer or the intrinsic interest of the question. The temptation to continue with a question and to look in a series of "one last" places is great, but must be resisted.

If one is sure of the question and its facets, has confirmed spellings, and has double-checked four or five sources—including those suggested by Sheehy and the library's catalog—without turning up the answer, it is time to consult. The perspective of a colleague may be all that is required to break the stalemate. Until one has conferred with colleagues, one does not say that there appears to be no answer in available sources. Beginning librarians can be astonished by the depth and variety of information available in the few hundred basic reference works introduced in library school courses.

When one is the only librarian on duty, inquiries can be passed on to the next shift. The inquiry is written down and annotated with the avenues tried. Inquirers should be advised to leave their names and phone numbers or to check back after staff members have had time to consider the question. There should be an established routine for completing referrals. While the presence of the librarian who received the question should not be necessary, one should follow up to see what the results were and that they were conveyed to the inquirer.

Following through may be strictly an internal matter to discover what has happened to the book that could not be located, or insuring that the latest supplement has been ordered, or otherwise clarifying an obscure locational note. It may or may not require contacting the patron in order to modify information provided previously.

Answer Not in the Collection

If the desired information cannot be located, perhaps it is readily available elsewhere. The proper way of proceeding may be predetermined by the library's participation in cooperative or networking agreements. The protocol established under such agreements should be strictly followed. If adhering to such protocol proves cumbersome, mutually agreeable modifications should be effected. In lieu of formal agreements, appeal might be made to local libraries with special strengths. A quick check of Lee Ash and Denis Lorenz's *Subject Collections* or local directories will provide suggestions. Avoid sending people to the obvious, large general collections that inevitably are overworked, unless there is no *appropriate* alternative collection.

Agencies other than libraries may specialize in certain types of information and a particular library may serve as the local Information and Referral center. A phone call may be all that is required. If one can identify governmental, commercial, or association offices interested in the matter of concern, they may be able to provide useful fugitive or unpublished material. It should be remembered that commercial firms often have an interest in collecting special subject materials and may respond to an inquiry as an investment in goodwill.

Whenever a referral is made, certain amenities are expected. The basic work of defining the question and verifying the terminology should be done as far as local resources will allow. Moreover, in order to save unwitting duplication of work, sources that have already been checked should be indicated. When possible, availability of the service at the library to which the user is being referred should be confirmed in advance by a telephone call. This not only saves the user's time, but also expands the librarian's knowledge of other collections.

Question Has No Definitive Answer—Some Haystacks Don't Have Needles

There usually is no point in personally trying to correct misconceptions that may be the basis of some questions. Such questions may be based on a false premise, for example, "In what Italian city did Hannibal meet the pope?" An efficient and effective answer would be provided by reference to a source that indicates that Hannibal crossed the Alps into Italy in 218 B.C. Less obvious traps are presented by those with a fastidious concern for the one right answer. For example, it may not be possible to determine how some medieval names "were really spelled." Practices varied and an appropriate standard authority should be chosen and followed consistently.

An effective response may be to express one's doubts about there being a neat answer and to refer to a source that addresses the particular, or perhaps the general, question. One might also suggest that the inquirer return with the source to confer about the results. Sometimes the problem is that the questions require interpretations of facts as well as considerable research: "Did the United States drop the atomic bomb on Hiroshima in order to prevent Russia's entry into Asia?" or "Are nuclear power plants safe?" Attempts to correct basic ignorance orally often only embroil the librarian in discussion or arguments that literally are interminable (see discussion of the problem patron that follows). To handle these questions successfully requires tact and inspiration.

SPECIAL CONCERNS

PROBLEM QUESTIONS

Two broad categories of questions create special problems for libraries: questions received by telephone and questions that impinge upon areas of expertise such as law, medicine, and appraisal of property. A sound policy with respect to these categories requires a clear sense of the library's function and priorities. To implement this policy without creating resentment requires firmness and sensitivity.

Telephone Inquiries

Ideally, full telephone service should be given with restrictions only on questions that either require too much staff time or are too likely to provide opportunity for misunderstanding and errors in relaying the question or information. To prevent callers from continuously receiving a busy signal or having to hold for extended periods may require several incoming lines and the personnel to answer them.

Every library has a potential problem with questions received by telephone. The main objection to such service is the extent to which it disrupts service to those who have come to the library. The mere ringing of the telephone and the necessary conversation on it create a considerable level of noise. Moreover, it is rude to break off work with a library user who is present in order to answer the telephone. Some libraries refuse to accept any telephone questions and may not even have a telephone at the public reference desk. Others will accept questions only during slack hours and have arranged to have the telephone ring muted and an answering device explain that telephone service is not available at that particular time.

The telephone provokes a range of interesting problems, and one hopes not to offend callers but rather to minimize the distraction of telephone transactions. One does not want to obstruct traffic while relaying information. The phone should be in a sequestered place with a writing surface, a place to rest the book or books being consulted, and a chair.

If the library offers telephone service, pleasant, efficient responses can enhance its image. One should answer the telephone clearly and pleasantly—not in a bored voice or in slurred haste. Briefly identify the library office and service point. Most telephone questions require simple, factual answers but callers may have two or three related questions. Time and return trips to sources can be saved by not rushing off immediately after the first question. Instead ask, ''Is there anything else you'd like to know about it?'' It is often wise to bring the reference source or the catalog drawer to the telephone just in case.

Use the hold button rather than leaving the line open. There is no need to share desk conversation with the waiting caller. Estimate how long it will take to find the answer, and if the desk is busy the inquirer can be asked to call back after a stipulated time. If the library can afford it, take a number at which to call back with the answer. It may be useful to have preprinted forms that help to ensure one has taken all the necessary information: deadline for answer, name and phone number of caller, the question and its particular requirements, intended use of information, and caller's affiliation with the institution. The last two items can be useful in answering the question appropriately and in supporting funding requests, respectively. Both questions, however, are potentially offensive to the caller.

Because callers are unaware of the work situation in the library, it may be necessary to state clearly that there are other people waiting. One must be polite but firm. This is a particular challenge with the dear old soul whose primary aim is to chat and regale one with colorful stories from the past or special insight into the future. If a statement about waiting patrons or a summoning supervisor does not serve to break off the visit, it may be necessary to interrupt with a firm "I'm sorry but we cannot accept long questions on the telephone." However frantic one might feel, one should maintain a pleasantly calm and authoritative manner.

Questions Not to Answer

In these days of heightened awareness of individual rights, the traditional librarian's hands-off attitude to the provision of legal and medical advice is more frequently challenged within the professional literature. At the very time when legal and medical aid is more informally available than before, librarians may be tempted to take a more active role. Many hazards exist, however. The legal system depends upon interpretation of statutory authority and case law. Moreover, the medical profession encompasses a spectrum of opinions as to the efficacy, value, and danger attendant upon various regimens and courses of treatment. It is folly for the librarian to venture an opinion on such matters.

The library should have basic medical and legal reference books of attested quality, and the librarian should expect to help people to use these tools as any other sophisticated reference source. Giving advice, opinion, or interpretations should be avoided as should speculation about symptoms. The interested party should be encouraged to seek competent professional help. A local professional association will give sound advice about referrals regardless of the individual's ability to pay. For questions involving social services or legal technicalities, one can determine the appropriate agency or appeal to a local Information and Referral service (see Chapter 1).

The policy with respect to appraising books and other property should be similar—indicate the standard sources and explain their use. Library policy may forbid staff members from giving appraisals. In any case, one should not provide an opinion unless one is well-acquainted with all aspects of valuation and market prices and is prepared to support the valuation against that of an opposing expert in an Internal Revenue Service hearing. People are particularly sensitive in matters involving money. Extreme caution should be taken to avoid appearing to advise in investment or financial matters. One wishes to be helpful without misleading the inquirer.

PROBLEM PATRONS

Increasingly, librarians are willing to admit that some patrons can be problems and can create trouble in the library. Attitudes about personal and institutional responsibility to individuals behaving objectionably and to other library users run a multifaceted spectrum colored by social training, education, past experience, and physical and psychological condition. Intricate philosophical and legal questions may be involved in any action to remove an unwelcome individual from a public facility. Anyone assuming responsibility for desk duty should be clear about the library's policy and the accepted steps of response (escalation), and should be informed of presumed liability. (See discussion of legal sanctions in Chapter 6.) A fundamental rule must be that the individuals are unwelcome not because of who or what they are, but because of disruptive or intolerable behavior that can be specified and documented. The librarian's concern is to protect the safety and rights of both the general public and the individual ("The Troublesome Patron," 1978).

Essentially, problem patrons can be considered in three groups: (1) the dangerous or apparently dangerous; (2) the patron who disrupts readers; and (3) the nuisance whose focus is the librarian.

Coping with the nuisance usually requires only well-developed but routine social skills; coping with the disruptive person requires additional fortitude and even special knowledge and skill. A situation involving the dangerous or apparently dangerous person (perhaps someone reportedly carrying a gun or knife) requires the librarian to summon expert help.

The Dangerous

Assessing the potential for danger is one of the most difficult aspects of dealing with problem patrons. Prompt responses are required to bomb threats and reports of such dangerous or criminal conduct as sprinkling acid on chairs or clothing, mutilating books, tampering with the card catalog, or obscene behavior. But in some situations threatening persons or property, the danger may be increased by the direct intervention of someone untrained. Do not become a self-taught social engineer, but do consult with mental health experts, local law enforcement and public safety personnel, and your institution's attorney. One requires guidance on how to meet the situation on site, information about support agencies skilled in behavioral areas, and an understanding of the legal aspects from personal, public, and institutional standpoints (Calif. Lib. Assoc., 1976; "Sex and Psychos," 1980).

In specific terms:

(1) Learn to recognize signs of dangerous disorders. Some loud loonies are not dangerous while others may be; one wants the best advice on how to guess which is which.

(2) Develop appropriate and nonexacerbating responses to violent or common disruptive behaviors.

(3) Establish a working understanding with the local agencies trained to respond promptly to a bad situation. The reference department policy manual should indicate criteria for selecting the appropriate agency. Consideration may

be given to how the cost of such service is met and what contact with the agency means for the individual receiving the attention.

(4)   Establish a close relationship with law enforcement officers to insure maximum cooperation. Learn how to describe or report a situation in terms that allow law enforcement personnel to understand what action is appropriate. What kind of report and evidence is required if persons wish to enter formal complaints or press charges?

(5)   Learn the nature and extent of the legal responsibilities and liabilities of both the individual staff member and the institution. Determine what the library's policy is and what support will be given to the individual performing in accordance with that policy. What are the specific policies and how is one expected to implement them?

The information acquired and the policies developed should be included in the policy manual as guidance for the staff.

The Disruptive

When a patron is accused of improper conduct and does not appear to present a danger, do not immediately confront the person with the accusation. Solicit the facts as calmly and as firmly as possible. Some complaints arise from misunderstandings, unreasonable expectations, or ignorance of what constitutes an acceptable standard of behavior. Nonetheless, be prepared to insist that the undesirable behavior cease and, if indicated, that the offender leave the premises. Always proceed warily anticipating violent behavior.

The Nuisance

Nuisance patrons demand more service or more of the librarian's time than is equitable. Often they are garrulous, even quarrelsome. Here, as elsewhere, one applies a second rule of thumb: retain self-control. Do not encourage the nuisance by giving attention craved and avoid creating an incident where none has developed. If one is confident and firm without being provocative, one's problems are minimized. Do not provide ammunition for prolonged discussion. Alas, some of our colleagues seem to be magnets for such unpleasant attention by being appeasing or tentative in their response.

One common nuisance is the reader who demands a quiet environment but is unwilling to move away from the companionship provided by the activity in the reference area. After ascertaining that the noise level in the area is reasonable, one can only suggest alternate locations for the person with the complaint.

Also unfortunately common is the lonely soul who visits interminably with whomever is on the desk—and occasionally with other readers. However compassionate, courteous, and unpressed for time one is, it becomes necessary to move on to other duties. There are few ways of doing this without being rude, although one wonders if someone as inconsiderate as is the interminable visitor has any right to be as sensitive to a chilly reception as they sometimes indicate they are.

An even more difficult problem is posed by persons making extraordinary demands for service. They may feel justified because they are transacting business. However, they monopolize one's time, and it is not easy to break away. For whatever reason—affection, respect, or spite—these demanders of super service often latch on to a specific staff member.

When possible, the preferred victim should disappear upon the approach of the nemesis. If one spots the *bête noir,* one signals for immediate replacement or alerts the preferred victim to stay out of sight. If one cannot disappear, then one can appear to be engaged in a telephone transaction that will allow moving away from the desk with the comment: "Excuse me a minute, I'll check on that." Or, one can seek help from other staff members. After a suitable interval, which gives the *persona non grata* fair and equitable time, another staff member can telephone the desk or otherwise provide an interruption that gives the victim the opportunity to terminate the session cleanly. Most persons trained to be polite, and not having been driven to desperation by these situations, must practice such a routine in order to make it effective. If there is no one to perform a rescue, then it may be necessary to state clearly that one cannot devote any more time to the individual.

Do not nurse a troublesome patron. However much of a helping profession librarianship is, most librarians do not have the training for counseling and should avoid gratuitous tampering with the lives of library patrons. Have the unit supervisor explain to the individual that monopolizing of attention cannot be permitted. Similarly, if one has observed questionable behavior or has had an unpleasant exchange with a user, or if one has committed a blunder of some magnitude, then it is good policy to inform one's supervisor. An informed supervisor is better prepared to cope with the situation should it become necessary.

In general, while on desk duty one must be aware of what is happening in the vicinity and notice who is coming and going. Persons who appear nervous or out of place should be approached. They may appreciate your help, or upon the indications that they have been noticed, they may retreat (to the street, one hopes, and not merely out of view).

THE ENVIRONMENT

There are several reasons why the persons on duty at the reference desk are assigned special responsibilities. As the desk is likely to be centrally located and highly visible, it should be an obvious place to turn for assistance. Moreover, during extended hours, when the library's administrative officers are unavailable, the reference librarian may be responsible for the entire building as well as for reference service. Manuals delineating policy, providing equipment service phone numbers, and appropriate emergency procedures should be at hand. The reference desk should have an operating telephone that allows contact with the world beyond the institution. Any library offering service or allowing staff members to work hours during which the switchboard is not in operation should arrange to have the switchboard operators plug the reference phone into an outgoing jack when they close. This is a necessary personal safety and security precaution.

The reference desk will attract persons trying to do business with the library as well as those with complaints about facilities, service, and personnel. These persons should be referred to the appropriate staff member. If that librarian is not present, it may take some skill to avoid becoming a practice opportunity for a salesman with a new line. Complaints should be received according to established policy. If immediate action is not appropriate, the name of the person, the name of the business or group, and the telephone number should be taken with a note about the subject of the visit. While it may be helpful to indicate when the staff member is generally available, care should be taken not to obligate others.

Good judgment is particularly important in response to complaints about materials or displays perceived to be offensive. The library should have a thoroughly considered and thoughtful policy safeguarding freedom to read, and this policy should be understood and faithfully followed. Refer to the Resolution on Challenged Materials reproduced in the Appendix following.

Equipment Failures

Many complaints received at the reference desk concern malfunctioning equipment. The responses given in great measure influence attitudes toward the library. The response should always be cordial and positive in style, whether or not an immediate remedial action is possible. The most effective response will be determined by the particulars of the situation, whether it be the terms of an equipment lease or service contract, attitude of service personnel, knowledge and dexterity of the staff member, or potential danger to equipment or people. While staff should be able to perform some routine tasks, such as the replacement of bulbs in microfilm readers, the maintenance and adjustment of equipment should not be allowed to absorb staff time. A log in which equipment "downtime" is noted will provide documentation useful for the justification of replacements or the arrangement of suitable maintenance schedules.

Crises

Equipment failures may precipitate an emergency or crisis. Learn what to do when there is a power outage and how to respond to the alarms that signal stuck elevators or that activate security or sprinkler systems. It is important to know what police or fire responses are triggered by alarms and how that reaction can be aborted and the alarm silenced. Reduce the potential for error by anticipation and prior systematic consideration of alternative actions and their consequences. In an emergency, good information about the building is second in importance only to good judgment. The appropriate prompt action—perhaps with the proper fire retardant from a readily available fire extinguisher—may prevent a mishap from becoming a catastrophe.

People are the first concern in any emergency. Often a crucial decision is whether or not to clear and close the building. Undue haste and panic can be minimized by calm, purposeful behavior that is reassuring to the public. There can be many dangers associated with evacuation, and the procedures must be determined by local conditions. Consideration should be given to structural hazards and the best way to channel traffic. Particular attention should be given to the needs of the infirm, the handicapped, and/or the injured. A thorough knowledge of emergency procedures should prepare one to provide guidance and directions that do not contradict the information being given by others on the staff.

Administrators are sensitive to the value of having disaster and emergency plans. These procedures should be coordinated with municipal and regional plans for responses to natural disasters and major fires. Within the library, it should be decided and generally made known which files (shelf lists, authority and circulation files, financial and employee records) and which collections and stack areas are to receive priority. The steps to be followed in the reclamation and restoration of library materials should be set out, and the authority for making on-the-spot decisions clearly designated and understood (Bohem, 1978; Waters, 1975).

All librarians must be concerned with these essentially administrative responsibilities, but because of extended hours and assigned responsibilities of the reference desk, it most often falls to the reference librarian to put these policies into practice.

RESPONSIBILITIES TO OTHER LIBRARIANS

While discharging responsibilities to the inquirer at the reference desk, bear in mind obligations to colleagues. Various aspects of professional courtesy already have been touched upon, and most of them involve simple common sense, consideration, and doing one's fair share of the work. Coworkers at the desk expect one to arrive promptly and not create unnecessary complications in the scheduling or demand special favors or treatment. Errors in colleagues' work should be brought to their attention tactfully and not in the presence of others. Do not interrupt an interview to give ideas on how the search should be conducted. Assist inquirers in order of their arrival and try not to linger unduly with questions while others cope with the bulk of the work.

Exercise discretion when making referrals, whether to other units in the library or to other libraries. Be sure that the necessary background has been provided. When referral to other libraries becomes an established practice, resist the temptation to refer questions automatically to a special collection. Referrals should be a step in the library's service, not a refusal of service.

THE VALUE AND USE OF THE POLICY MANUAL

The policy manual should provide a clear statement of departmental (and perhaps library) policy and even procedures. Appropriate responses to minor disruptions and emergencies should be simply and clearly stated. By presenting procedural guidelines that delineate authority and responsibilities, the policy manual establishes the expected level of service and conduct.[6]

Such manuals are life- and face-savers for new staff members and those who perform some departmental services only occasionally. At first, new staff members may not realize how many "odd" or "interesting" questions and situations recur often enough to have been made the subject of a policy statement. It is advisable to become thoroughly acquainted with the manual and to refer to it as the occasion arises. Because of the institutional support it gives to individual responses, the manual should be clearly written, well-organized, and continuously updated. It is a touchstone for the librarian facing the demanding and exhilarating responsibilities of providing desk service.

REFERENCES AND SUGGESTED READINGS

Alexander, C. Technique of library searching. *Special Libraries,* 1936, *27*(September), 230–238.

Bates, M. Information search tactics. *Journal of the American Society for Information Science,* 1979, *30*(July), 205–214.

Bohem, H. *Disaster prevention and disaster preparedness.* Report of the University Task Group on the Preservation of Library Materials. Berkeley, Calif.: University of California, Systemwide Administration. Office of the Assistant Vice President—Library Plans and Policies, 1978.

California Library Association. Annual Conference (78th), December 2–6, 1976, Los Angeles. Reference and Information Services Chapter. *The library and the problem patron: Legal and psycho-social aspects.* Session M3, Monday, December 6, 1976. Northridge, Calif.: On·The·Spot Duplicators, Inc., 1976. (Cassette)

Cherry, S. S. Telereference: The new TV information systems. *American Libraries,* 1980, *11* (February), 94–109.

Childers, T. The test of reference. *Library Journal,* 1980, *105*(April 15), 924–928.

Ciucki, M. Recording of reference/information service activities: A study of forms currently used. *RQ,* 1977, *16*(Summer), 273–283.

Criner, K. and Johnson-Hall, M. Videotex: Threat or opportunity. *Special Libraries,* 1980, *71* (September), 379–385.

[6]See Appendix for "Draft Outline of Information Service Policy Manual." American Library Association, Reference and Adult Services Division, Standards Committee. *A Commitment to Information Services: Developmental Guidelines, 1979.* Appendix A.

Emerson, K. National reporting on reference transactions, 1976-78. *RQ,* 1977, *16*(Spring), 199-207.

Firschein, O., Summit, R. K., & Mick, C. K. Planning for on-line search in the public library. *Special Libraries,* 1978, *69*(July), 255-260.

Heinlen, W. F., & Midbon, M. A. Data base management on a budget. *RQ,* 1978, *18*(Fall), 50-52.

Jahoda, G., & Braunagel, J. S. *The librarian and reference queries: A systematic approach.* New York: Academic Press, 1980.

Jahoda, G., & Olson, P. E. Analyzing the reference process: Models of reference. *RQ,* 1972, *12*(Winter), 148-156.

Jennerich, E. J., & Jennerich, E. Z. Teaching the reference interview. *Journal of Education for Librarianship,* 1976, *17*(Fall), 106-111.

Jennerich, E. Z. Before the answer: Evaluating the reference process. *RQ,* 1980, *19*(Summer), 360-366.

Jensen, R. J., Asbury, H. O., & King, R. G. Costs and benefits to industry of online literature searches. *Special Libraries,* 1980, *71*(July), 291-299.

Josel, N. Ten reference commandments. *RQ,* 1971, *11*(Winter), 146-147.

King, G. B. The reference interview: Open and closed questions. *RQ,* 1972, *12*(Winter), 157-160.

Knapp, S. D. The reference interview in the computer-based setting. *RQ,* 1978, *17*(Summer), 320-324.

Lancaster, F. W. *The measurement and evaluation of library services.* Washington, D.C.: Information Resources Press, 1977.

López Muñoz, J. The significance of nonverbal communication in the reference interview. *RQ,* 1977, *16*(Spring), 220-224.

Lynch, M. J. Reference interview in public libraries. *Library Quarterly,* 1978, *48,*(April), 119-142.

Morgan, L. Patron preference in reference service points. *RQ,* 1980, *19*(Summer), 373-375.

Peat, Marwick, Mitchell, & Co. *California public library systems: A comprehensive review with guidelines for the next decade.* Los Angeles: Peat, Marwick, Mitchell and Co., 1975.

Rothstein, S. Across the desk: 100 years of reference encounters. *Canadian Library Journal,* 1977, *34*(October), 391-399.

Schell, C. Preventive medicine: The library prescription. *Library Journal,* 1980, *105*(April 15), 929-931.

"Sex and psychos" in An odd euphoria: The 99th annual conference of the American Library Association. *Library Journal,* 1980, *105*(August), 1596-1597.

Somerville, A. N. The place of the reference interview in computer searching: The academic. *Online,* 1977, *1*(October), 14-23.

Strong, G. E. Evaluation the reference product. *RQ,* 1980, *19*(Summer), 367-372.

Stych, F. S. Decision factors in search strategy: Teaching reference work. *RQ,* 1972, *12*(Winter), 143-147.

Taylor, R. S. Question-negotiation and information seeking in libraries. *College & Research Libraries,* 1968, *29*(May), 178-194.

The troublesome patron: Approaches eyed in N.Y. *Library Journal,* 1978, *103*(December 1), 2371-2374.

United States Library of Congress, Subject Cataloging Division, Processing Services. *Library of Congress subject headings* (9th ed., 2 vols.). Washington, D.C.: Library of Congress, 1980.

Warden, C. L. Online searching of bibliographic data bases: The role of the search intermediary. *Bookmark* (New York State Library), 1977, *36*(Winter), 35-41.

Waters, P. *Procedures for salvage of water-damaged library materials.* Library of Congress Publications on Conservation of Library Materials. Washington, D.C.: U.S. Government Printing Office, 1975.

Wilkinson, J. P., & Miller, W. The step approach to reference service. *RQ,* 1978, *17*(Summer), 293-300.

CHAPTER 6

Administration

Those who become enamored of reference librarianship and its challenges usually succumb to its lure before discovering all of its parts. The image of the reference librarian, as portrayed by Katherine Hepburn in the film, *Desk Set,* suggests the superb flair and intellectual acumen with which reference librarians would like to dazzle their patrons. However, close attention to the role of the computer specialist, as played by Spencer Tracy, and to the interaction of these two principals (excepting the love scenes!) provides a glimpse of the world behind the reference desk and reveals more of the character of reference activities.

IMPORTANCE OF ADMINISTRATION

Administrative decisions, which are made behind the scenes sometimes outside the purview of a reference department or section, usually determine which reference services are offered, as well as determine the mode. Standards of reference and informational services, such as those developed by the Standards Committee of the Reference and Adult Services Division of ALA and The Library Association's *Standards for Reference Services in Public Libraries,* provide illuminating guidelines against which a reference department's services can be measured. But if a library cannot afford to offer all of the services that are deemed necessary, the administrative decisions as to which services will be offered loom even larger in importance.

In this chapter, the administration and management of reference services will be considered, with the terms used interchangeably. The student should be aware, however, that administration is a term usually applied to the functions of goal-setting and long-range planning for an organization. Management is a term that is usually applied to the execution of the objectives determined by administration. Prospective reference librarians must be prepared to involve themselves in all aspects of support for reference services, of which the administration and management are among the most important. No matter how small the library, careful attention to sound administrative practice is imperative.

Happily, there is no dearth of sophisticated management and business administration literature for those who wish to explore the subject from the overall perspective. Most library school students have read Rothstein (1955), Hutchins (1944), and Green (1876) on the theory, development, and practice of reference work. But there is very little literature of enduring significance on the administration of reference services *per se*. Here, the authors of this text are presenting their own highly personal viewpoint in order to delineate administrative concerns toward which beginning reference librarians sometimes may be nonchalant.

Although it would seem to be only "common sense" to attempt to understand administrative policy and practices in a library in which one aspires to work, many students graduating from library school and seeking jobs profess disdain for administrative responsibilities not only within the reference section, but also within the library as a whole. Those interviewing prospective reference librarians hear so often that it is the "intellectual challenge" and the "gratification of providing personal assistance" that constitute the attraction of reference librarianship—not administration, which is viewed as "paperwork." Few seem to realize that their ability to work and to achieve personal satisfaction in an institutional setting will be closely tied to their own understanding of administrative goals and functions.

Basic decisions as to which services should be offered through a reference unit in a particular library will affect the unit's organizational scheme. For example, the library's periodicals and indexes may be the responsibility of the reference department, as may be the interlibrary loan function, government documents services, and computer-based literature searching; or, each of these services may be organizationally separate.

Frequently these decisions are predicated on the funding available, but, most importantly, the *level* of service decided upon for the different reference functions is always dependent upon the allocation of funds in accordance with the library's priorities. Perhaps the library cannot afford to expend staff time in providing additional bibliographic searching for interlibrary loan requests received; in such a case, the interlibrary loan function may be handled by a non-librarian in the loan section who will be instructed to return requests for materials that are not immediately identifiable saying, "Nil as cited." Ideally, decisions as to which services will be offered and how much money will be allocated for their support will be based on known data, clearly indicating needs and priorities. Contributing to the development of this data is one of the functions for which reference librarians should prepare themselves. A new reference librarian may well be asked to draft a questionnaire that can be used to assess library users' success with library catalogs; or, (following a budget cut) to determine at which hours reference service could be curtailed with the least devastating effect on the greater number of library users. Reference librarianship is similar to going on stage; a tremendous amount of behind-the-scenes activity must be skillfully done in order for the play to succeed. One may begin with very little responsibility for the whole production, but one must have an understanding of what the director wishes to accomplish and be able to contribute whatever is necessary to the collective effort.

IMPORTANCE OF PERSONAL ATTRIBUTES

The nature of the administration of a reference unit within a larger institution such as a corporation, a school, a public library, or a university will necessarily be dependent on the administrative structure of the parent organization. But as would be expected, given the differences in personalities and management styles that inevitably distinguish administrators in all professions, the personal attributes of the library's administrators have a direct effect upon the management of the library and should be of great interest to the new librarian. It sometimes happens that the overall administration of a library may be tolerant, encouraging, and actually dependent upon staff participation in management decisions, while the head of the reference or cataloging unit may run that section like a marine drill sergeant. Conversely, the overall management may be strictly authoritarian and desire no staff "input," although a section head may run a particular library unit as if it were a committee, providing for full staff participation. In either of these instances, so long as the unit carries out its responsibilities well and violates no regulations governing institutional policies and procedures, there is little likelihood that the library director will attempt to impose his or her individual style of management on the independent section head. It behooves a new librarian, however, to ascertain the administrative styles of the library director and the librarian's immediate supervisor, because an understanding of these "dynamics" will help the reference librarian to contribute more effectively to the library's operation. If the reference head does not like to be surprised by formal memoranda suggesting changes in policy or procedure, it would be wise, for example, to ask informally whether it would be helpful to outline a few possible policy or procedure changes for discussion purposes. If the new reference librarian can avoid appearing to be aggressive in a manner that threatens the reference head or the director of the library, innovative ideas are usually more readily accepted.

If an organization is sufficiently small so that the library director knows every staff member, then one can expect that the prevailing management style will be that of the director. It is to be hoped that the director, in addition to professional competence, possesses "common sense, energy, a reasonable share of tact, imagination, and ingenuity, and the ability to make decisions, yet appreciate many points of view, delegate authority, communicate, persuade, and most importantly, enjoy achieving through others" (Darling, 1970, p. 35). The importance of ethical conduct, displaying no favoritism or bias, and the ability to separate approval or disapproval of another's ideas from one's regard for the individual are personal attributes that must be cultivated by everyone who works with others. With a responsibility for contributing to the successful operation of reference services, all reference librarians should develop the capability of being able supervisors as well as effective support staff. It is not unusual for a new librarian to be assigned supervisory responsibilities immediately.

More often than not, the interaction of librarians with each other, with paraprofessionals, and with the library administration will determine the success of a particular management scheme. If some people do not interact in a civil, constructive manner, it is more likely that a rigid administrative structure will be employed to minimize their disruptiveness. Even though others' ideas may seem unacceptable, one should always assume that their motives are pure. Healthy differences of opinion serve the library well when they are aired with tolerance for opposing views. However, some individuals, operating under the impression that they are virtuously "outspoken" when they have the courage to dissent, are simply rude and insensitive. These people usually do not realize that it often takes greater strength of character and heroic self-discipline to refrain from changing feet every time one opens one's mouth. Denigrating the ideas of others is just one step away from a personal attack and reflects the speaker's ineptness. Those who perform in this manner can be characterized as those who would "rather fight than win," and it is to be hoped that no one aspiring to be a reference librarian would indulge in this practice.

To be an effective reference librarian requires a constructive and positive view of problems and alternative solutions. Lean to disagree *agreeably*. Problems are never solved by doomsday proclamations and categorical statements of "That won't work." Also, to become emotionally wedded to a particular view is to eviscerate one's effectiveness in achieving a workable solution. Idealism is laudable and essential, but those who are rigidly idealistic and cannot compromise seldom accomplish even the first steps toward the ideal. Further, one cannot successfully force an idea whose time has not come. Perhaps the idea of noting the library's call numbers in the list of books indexed by the *Essay and General Literature Index* is dependent on receiving more money for casual assistance. Until additional funds are forthcoming, it is not helpful to "push" such a plan, unless one can tactfully convince one's supervisor that another task presently being performed is unnecessary. It is neither helpful nor politic to advocate a course of action (or to disparage a prospective course of action) if one cannot present a viable alternative in a constructive manner.

Skilled administrators know that they cannot tackle all problems and achieve optimum solutions all at once. New reference librarians must also learn to select the problems for study and action that are not only immediate but that are also susceptible to the means at hand. In the library world, as in all others, some of the objectives that we recognize as being of critical importance may only be accomplished after our retirement. But if the groundwork for these accomplishments can be laid with patient, constructive efforts, that contribution is more important than presiding over the final act. There will always be administrative battles lost, but reference librarians should never let temporary reverses occasion loss of morale. The new librarian will learn to appreciate the administrator who cultivates in the staff a respect for the entire library system and encourages a long-range view of any setbacks. If loyalty toward the institution and its goals is nurtured, the administrator is doing a better job than if he or she tries to inspire personal devotion. Administrative personnel change many times, and the morale of the individual reference librarian should never be dependent on any one supervisor or library director.

MANAGEMENT SYSTEMS

Entire books are devoted to management systems and styles, and it is not the intent of this chapter to provide a detailed analysis or description of any particular management scheme. Rather, the continuum of administrative structures, from the hierarchical to participative management systems, will be discussed in terms of general characteristics and effects. As will be evident, most hierarchical management schemes utilize information-gathering mechanisms that may be virtually the same as those used in "participatory" arrangements. Most participatory schemes still retain hierarchical lines of authority.

HIERARCHICAL MANAGEMENT

In the most obvious version of a hierarchical management scheme, the chief reference librarian may function virtually as a dictator. There are advantages to such a concentration of power, because the staff is never in doubt as to who makes decisions, and the decisions are usually made without large expenditures of staff time in consultation. With luck, unilateral decisions made by a skillful reference administrator may benefit the library user and the reference staff.

Most hierarchically structured administrations, however, provide formalized information channels as an overlay to the administrative lines of authority. These communication channels permit the dissemination of information both up and down the vertical organization scheme from the lowest ranking clerical assistant to the head reference librarian. This administrative structure gives the head the opportunity to make informed decisions without setting up separate advisory groups, and recommendations made by concerned and knowledgeable staff are appreciated by good administrators. Admittedly, a few reference heads (and other library adminstrators) have been known to invite recommendations from their staff, even though they have already determined the course of action they will take and will not be deterred from it. Obviously, to seek advice with no intention of using it engenders disappointment, contempt, and is self-defeating. Beginning reference librarians should listen willingly to the proffered advice of even the lowest level of assistant on the staff, and if the advice cannot be followed, then professional courtesy dictates that the reasons for the contrary decision be fully explained.

In a hierarchical management structure, the head must depend on established channels for management information, and if some deputies or section chiefs lack administrative skill and the confidence to seek and to relay advice from their staffs, the head will not get the best information. Conversely, reference librarians may receive insufficient information from their supervisors or the head, thereby making it difficult to do their jobs well and to provide necessary data and useful recommendations. Perhaps, for example, the city council initiated a program to provide special education in personnel management, requiring extensive use of library resources, for some of the city's managers. If the head of reference services is advised of this but does not pass along the information to the staff, the opportunity to mount a special effort to meet the managers' information needs is lost, and the reference librarians, by being uninformed, will undoubtedly not make as good an impression on the important city managers. Such circumstances are rare, but they are personally and professionally exasperating when they do occur. Although a reference librarian may exercise superb diplomatic skills, such a situation may be corrected only when the bottleneck boss leaves. When there is strict adherence to hierarchical lines of authority and communication, the personal attributes of supervisory reference librarians are even more important.

PARTICIPATIVE MANAGEMENT

There is more opportunity for direct staff participation in the process of enumeration, evaluation, and decision-making about alternatives with the introduction of various degrees of participative management. The two main forms of this administrative system range from staff advisory, or study groups, to staff decision-making bodies. Appointments to committees or study groups are often made of reference librarians who may be outside the administrative channels. Unless the primary purpose of the participative management scheme is to provide an opportunity for staff development and education, these persons usually are appointed to special study or working groups for their relevant expertise. One hopes, however, that a reference head will not overlook the benefits to be gained by selecting for service on a task group a librarian with "potential" but little experience. The "old boy" technique of running things can work well for a time, but the "old boys" must provide for an infusion of younger blood and ideas if they want the library to prosper. Bringing new blood to the forefront, even that of "young Turks," is certain to make life more interesting for everyone. Young librarians must be prepared to participate in committees and study groups in a constructive manner without resorting to confrontation tactics. The latter approach is more likely to defeat a good idea that the "confrontationist" is advocating than any opposing argument.

In addition to advisory groups, there may be decision-making committees. Sometimes a head reference librarian or library director will delegate authority to certain committees and permit these groups to make decisions and policies in specified areas ranging from collection development to staff travel funds. While deputy administrators are frequently involved *ex officio* or as chairpersons of these groups, the chief librarian usually will reserve the final decision-making authority on major issues to him or herself. This is because the chief librarian is personally accountable to the next higher level of authority such as the mayor, the city council, the hospital director, or the university president. This is not to say that a library or a unit within the library cannot be governed by a committee, but it is not a usual procedure. Decisions reached by committee are often achieved in an astonishingly cumbersome manner, if the committee can reach a consensus at all. Furthermore, if the library's governance system is guilty of poor performance, it is more difficult to induce corrective action from a committee than from one person, who can be more easily removed for just cause.

Personal accountability and responsibility are important factors in insuring that a governance system will respond to needs. Although participative management systems sometimes utilize rotating section heads, just as is seen in academic departments of universities, such rotation has not been notably successful. Individuals who know that they have a limited time to exercise authority sometimes avoid facing unpleasant responsibilities. If there is a "changing of the guard" too frequently, the reference section loses the benefit of experienced direction with a long-range view. The development of good administrative skills takes most people several years, and a library facing ever increasing financial problems needs sophisticated and experienced librarian/administrators to run its reference services.

Another aspect of a participative management scheme of which a new reference librarian should be aware is that, in order to provide opportunities for all staff to participate, the library director must provide more information to more people than would be required in a hierarchical system. The "need to know" maxim for determining who must see copies of the minutes of meetings and budget proposals becomes expensive if the staff are to be "informed" and to offer recommendations. Young librarians should also recognize that the more management information that is passed on to staff to solicit their contributions toward decisions, the higher the level of expectation the staff develops that their recommendations will be adopted. Disappointment and disillusionment easily can accompany a participative management system where, despite the sincere and thoughtful recommendations of reference staff, contrary decisions sometimes are made. If there is no free choice in a matter, the reference head should make this clear to the staff. If there are alternative courses of action and the head elects a course that is different from that recommended, one would hope that the compelling reasons for a contrary decision are made known.

Advocates of participative management point out that the advantages of providing opportunities for the staff to contribute to the governance process may well outweigh the burden of inefficiency. Ideas from the lower eschelons can be refreshingly valuable, and reference staff cannot avoid being better educated about the overall mission of the library. Ideally, a new reference librarian should begin his or her career in a library that strikes a productive balance between hierarchical and participative management systems. Knowing precisely who is responsible for specific library services and who will make decisions relieves the uncertainty that can be particularly vexing to a neophyte (and paralyzing to library services). At the same time, the opportunity to participate in committees that are working on reference service problems is instructive and beneficial to a librarian's professional development.

RESPONSIBILITY AND AUTHORITY

A sense of responsibility and the courage to act decisively at an appropriate time are qualities that must be cultivated by anyone in public service work. An important rule-of-thumb that one hopes is practiced by one's reference supervisor is to be sure that each member of the staff has the authority to carry out assigned responsibilities. Unfortunately, not all supervisors and library directors will delegate the *authority* as well as the responsibility. A reference librarian may be held responsible for a particular unfortunate occurrence, without having been authorized to institute the procedural changes or to make exceptions to library policy. Perhaps a new reference librarian enraged the mayor by refusing to allow the mayor's secretary to borrow a noncirculating population report. If the reference head is the sole person authorized to make an exception to the lending policy (and the head is out to lunch), the unpleasant encounter must be handled by the new librarian with as much courteous dignity as possible. If doubt about the extent of one's authority hinders performance, clarification should be sought from one's supervisors. Reasons for requiring authority to discharge certain responsibilities should be clearly delineated.

In ordinary circumstances, it is probable that the authority for many critical decisions must remain at a higher administrative level than that of a reference librarian. But if referrals to higher authority are frequent, they may signal a need to modify the regulations. Perhaps the authority should be delegated to the new librarian, who should explore and discuss all the options with his or her supervisor. Paralysis of library services can occur when an administrator wants to retain the authority for making a preponderance of operational decisions. Usually administrators who are so loathe to delegate will be unable to advance very far in library administration because they are so busy making small decisions that they do not have time to work in a larger arena. This is slight comfort, alas, for the beginning reference librarian, but it is a good example not to follow.

DECISION-MAKING

No matter what combination of management systems is utilized in a library, librarians at all levels are expected to make certain decisions. Ideally, as was mentioned, responsibility should to assigned and decision-making should occur at the lowest possible level of responsibility for a particular function so that action can be taken without delay. Regrettably, some people have considerable difficulty in facing up to responsibility and they procrastinate; others become notorious for making snap judgments. Ideally, each librarian should have appropriate data so that an *informed,* timely decision can be made. Staff analyses, special surveys, statistical studies, and outside consultants all contribute to sound decision-making on high administrative levels, but if a crisis precludes normal data-gathering, administrators usually must initiate appropriate action immediately and accept the responsibility.

New reference librarians ordinarily will not have responsibility for making decisions that have a direct bearing on policy and services; they are expected instead to make continuous impromptu decisions within their sphere of responsibility for assisting library users. Nevertheless, it is important for the new reference librarian to be cognizant of the mechanics of decision-making. For example, if the library has decided to offer computer-based reference service, decisions will have to be made on whether the library must recover some or all of the costs, which databases will be searched, which classes of patrons will be served (i.e., the "primary clientele" only, other affiliated groups, or all comers), and which methods of payment, if necessary, can be accepted. A decision as to the location of the terminal must be made, giving consideration to the advantage of placing it in a prominent, open location so that all library users will be aware of its existence versus the disadvantage caused by the need to be able to conduct searches in a quiet atmosphere conducive to concentration. Adequate security for the expensive equipment must also be provided for in this decision, and a secluded back room, a remote phone cut-off switch, or a removable keyboard may be mandated. Lastly, decisions must be made as to how many and which librarians will be trained to offer these services and whether each will specialize in certain databases. If the number of requests for computer searches is not anticipated to be very high, it obviously will not be cost-effective to train more than a minimum number of librarians. Continual practice is necessary for a reference librarian to develop and maintain proficiency with these expensive tools.

One maxim that is not always evident to a new reference librarian is that many problems resolve themselves more satisfactorily if a precipitate decision is not made. One distinguished librarian of our acquaintance was noted for glancing at the contents of his ''in'' basket with great rapidity and culling out the three or four ''action'' items. The rest of the stack was put in the bottom drawer of his desk, there to repose for a year. His theory (which worked very well for him) was that if no one asked him about any of the material in the drawer during the year, it was not worth reading and could be safely discarded.

While this practice cannot be recommended, supervisors do find it prudent to postpone some actions and decisions until the ''time is right.'' Sometimes, for example, by not immediately liening funds for an expensive reference work that is just announced, one may benefit from reviews or an opportunity to examine the work before commiting the money. Then, the reference librarian has better justification to buy and perhaps to induce others to contribute to the purchase.

In some situations it is possible to test the result of a decision before it is irrevocable. Spectacular consequences may be avoided when contemplating the withdrawal of a title from the library's reference collection by temporarily removing it to the office. If after a few months, no one has needed the book, a decision can be made more comfortably about withdrawing or transferring it.

Some librarians feel compelled to decide arbitrarily certain matters so as to avoid ''loose ends.'' Publications in series, for example, may appear irregularly and out-of-sequence. If one cannot get a response from a publisher, particularly one in a foreign country, it is very tempting to close the entry in the catalog and to note ''no more published.'' But until one ascertains that a publication is in fact discontinued, a penciled note on the catalog card that a publication is temporarily suspended is better than unconfirmed surmise that a publication has ceased.

Acting decisively when the situation requires it is equally important. If someone reports that a member of the staff is drunk while on the job, the supervisor must immediately set in motion the prescribed personnel procedures for verifying the charge, issuing a warning, observing and documenting future performance, and, if necessary, initiating a dismissal action. If the budget is cut and expenses must be reduced before the end of the fiscal year, the librarian must be capable of making a prompt decision as to which services must be reduced and to what level. This kind of decision should be based on the best available data and advice from concerned staff, but it ultimately may be predicated on the administrator's judgment as to which of the library's operational spheres is more likely to see funds restored the next fiscal year.

After the necessary decisions have been made, the reference librarian, like the chief librarian, must learn not to agonize over them. It is important to concentrate on the present and the future. When mistakes are recognized, one then makes decisions about remedial actions. Errors in judgment are inevitable and will not diminish one's professional standing unless they are frequent. New reference librarians must be willing to accept responsibility for their own mistakes, and be tolerant of the inevitable mistakes of colleagues, supervisors, and subordinates.

ORGANIZATION

The varied operations of a library that are frequently assigned to a reference librarian have been discussed in Chapter 1. These functions are important from an administrative point of view, not only because of implications for space, facilities, and the library budget, but also because of their impact on the administrative organization of a reference unit.

In one-room, one-person libraries, reference librarians must budget their own time and cover all functions. If there is a large reference staff, individual librarians may be assigned as heads of different units, overseeing reference desk activity and training, providing bibliographic and library use instruction, handling interlibrary loans, selecting acquisitions, or other responsibilities such as computerized reference services. One may also have these responsibilities divided between the head and only one or two other persons. In a complex operation, a middle management level team of section heads can be very productive and prevents the administrative burden from being entirely borne by the head. In order to be a success, this more complex scheme requires that the section heads keep the head fully informed as to their problems and objectives, just as the head must keep them informed about all the developments at the highest administrative level. This need for necessary information is genuine in any organization scheme, but it becomes more difficult to meet where there are numbers of people and complex activities involved. Regular staff meetings, in which full discussion of matters ranging from broad policy considerations to techniques for handling a difficult patron, are an important aid for the entire reference staff.

For the new reference librarian, there are distinct advantages and disadvantages to be found in the various organizational schemes depicted in the following three charts. Generally, if a librarian has a chance to participate in all of the reference functions, as in Organization Chart I (Fig. 6.1), it is a good developmental experience. However, if the head of the reference division does not involve the other staff in acquisitions work, as is the case described, the reference librarians will have less instructive assignments. No librarian on that hypothetical staff has any designated responsibility for working with technical services librarians; and consequently, unless their work on the public services desks involves occasional work with the cataloging and processing units, a new reference librarian would miss this valuable experience.

In Organization Chart II (Fig. 6.2), it might be assumed that the bibliographer

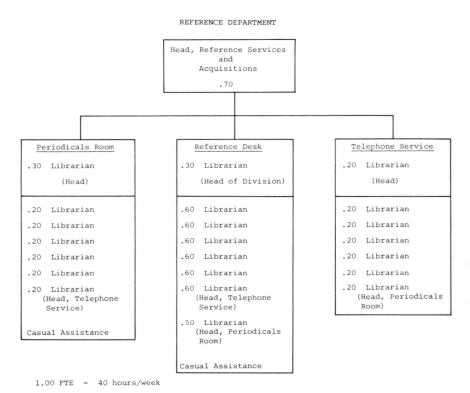

Fig. 6.1. *Organization chart I: Medium-size public library (7.00 FTE).*

responsibilities carry with them the necessity to work closely with technical services staff in acquisitions, cataloging, and serials areas. Except for the fact that there is little clerical assistance for the librarians and no real "back-up" in case of a lengthy absence, this arrangement would give the subject specialist/ beginning librarian an excellent first professional experience.

Organization Chart III (Fig. 6.3) shows an organization that is sufficiently large that most of the reference librarians who work in the reference department's Collection Development division have the responsibility of working regularly with technical services units. This division also sends .25 of a librarian to assist in the Interlibrary Loan division on a rotating basis. The Interlibrary Loan division however, apparently cannot spare a librarian to work in another division, except for the .10 full-time employee (FTE) used in Computer Reference Services. The facts that there are several paraprofessionals on the staff and that Interlibrary Loans participates in two special "ILL" networks provide additional opportunities for a new reference librarian to learn supervisory skills and to learn

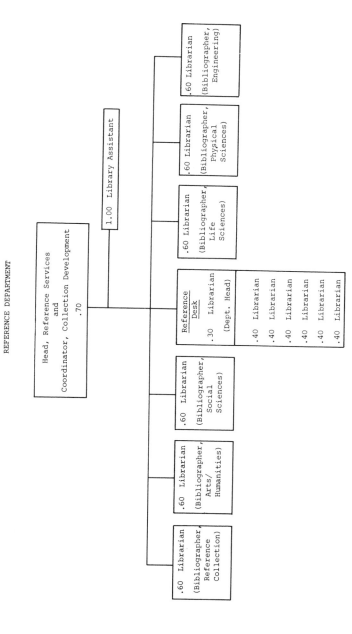

1.00 FTE = 40 hours/week

Fig. 6.2. *Organization chart II: Medium-size academic library (8.00 FTE).*

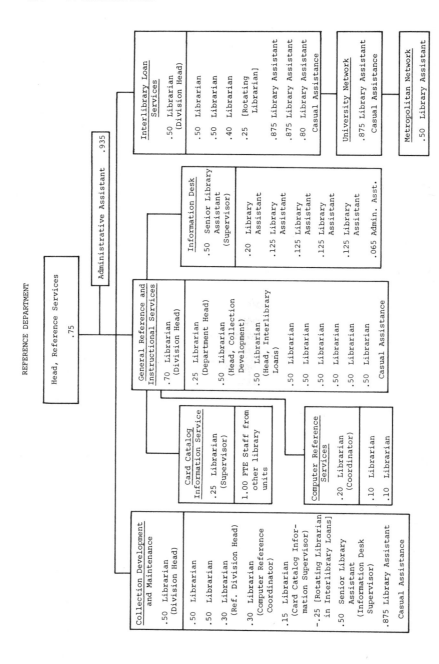

REFERENCE DEPARTMENT

| Head, Reference Services |
| .75 |

Administrative Assistant   .935

Interlibrary Loan Services

.50 Librarian (Division Head)

.50 Librarian
.50 Librarian
.40 Librarian
.25 [Rotating Librarian]
.875 Library Assistant
.875 Library Assistant
.80 Library Assistant
Casual Assistance

University Network

.875 Library Assistant
Casual Assistance

Metropolitan Network

.50 Library Assistant

General Reference and Instructional Services

.70 Librarian (Division Head)

.25 Librarian (Department Head)
.50 Librarian (Head, Collection Development)
.50 Librarian (Head, Interlibrary Loans)
.50 Librarian
.50 Librarian
.50 Librarian
.50 Librarian
.50 Librarian
Casual Assistance

Information Desk

.50 Senior Library Assistant (Supervisor)

.20 Library Assistant
.125 Library Assistant
.125 Library Assistant
.125 Library Assistant
.125 Library Assistant
.065 Admin. Asst.

Card Catalog Information Service

.25 Librarian (Supervisor)

1.00 FTE Staff from other library units

Computer Reference Services

.20 Librarian (Coordinator)

.10 Librarian
.10 Librarian

Collection Development and Maintenance

.50 Librarian (Division Head)

.50 Librarian
.50 Librarian
.30 Librarian (Ref. Division Head)
.30 Librarian (Computer Reference Coordinator)
.15 Librarian (Card Catalog Information Supervisor)
-.25 [Rotating Librarian in Interlibrary Loans]
.50 Senior Library Assistant (Information Desk Supervisor)
.875 Library Assistant
Casual Assistance

1.00 FTE = 40 hours/week

Fig. 6.3. *Organization chart III: Large research library (17.50 FTE).*

a little about budgeting (assuming the division head delegates some of the responsibilities or at least involves the staff in planning).

What is not clear from these charts, but which is of great importance to an aspiring reference librarian, is what style of administration is employed by the reference heads and assistants. There may be a very flexible communication system that overlays the administrative structure, or there may be a fairly rigid pattern of communication that adheres to the administrative lines of authority. Decision-making may be an open process with invigorating staff discussions, or it may be carried on in private between the reference head, the section heads, and/or the head of the library. All of these questions should be explored by a prospective reference librarian who wishes to work for a particular library.

Within each unit, detailed functional organization schemes, which we have not attempted to depict, should make clear who has responsibility for specific duties, and where the final authority for decision-making lies. No one on the reference staff should be in any doubt about whom to consult concerning a particular problem and to whom to go next if the first person is not there. In Organization Chart II (Fig. 6.2), it is not clear what would happen if one of the reference librarian/bibliographers broke a leg. Libraries ordinarily have only a small staff ''cushion'' to provide for sickness, vacation, and compensatory days off. When the reference librarians also have major responsibilities for service and acquisitions in a particular subject field, other reference librarians may well have to substitute for each other in alien fields. An important corollary to this is the need to keep departmental files in good order, with careful retention of necessary records so that one's successor can see the basis for particular policy decisions. Compromise organization schemes, making allowances for weaknesses of individuals, will naturally be put in place as necessary, but reference heads, like other administrators, will generally work toward establishing the ''ideal'' scheme based on functional responsibilities—and not based on the current personnel roster.

GOALS AND OBJECTIVES

Long-range goals and specific objectives are the primary components of the planning and budgeting process. If the library or reference unit is part of a larger institution, it is necessary to understand the goals within the framework of the institution's *raison d'être*. It may be that a reference librarian is employed by a law firm or a motion picture company solely to support that organization's profit-making efforts. Perhaps the reference librarian is responsible for a branch of a city or county library with a wide-ranging clientele from a large geographic area that includes special user groups such as those who speak only languages other than English or those who are blind, deaf, or otherwise handicapped. Or, perhaps the reference librarian works in a school, college, or university library where the library's efforts are aimed at supporting courses of instruction at that institution and/or the research of faculty and advanced students. Clearly, the purpose behind the library's existence will affect the particulars of a reference unit's goals and objectives, and these, in turn, will affect the prospective reference librarian's opportunities to use special skills as well as to develop new areas of expertise.

These goals and objectives usually are presented in some kind of time frame, with the ultimate goals being in the future, and specific objectives for achieving the goals laid out in stages. An example would be a library determining to establish a more formalized and better publicized Information and Referral (I & R) program as a goal to be realized within one year. The first objective may be to secure additional funding from state or municipal governments in order to hire an I & R specialist, who would be asked to develop a file or directory of outside resources. The second objective may be for the I & R specialist to train present staff to perform more "in-depth" interviews to determine the users' needs and to take the appropriate next step, such as calling an outside agency for an appointment. The final objective may be to embark on a promotional program featuring radio and tv spots, attractive advertisements placed on city buses, and brochures.

PROCEDURES AND PROGRAMS FOR MEETING OBJECTIVES

Policy Statements

Policy statements are an aid to the accomplishment of a library's goals because they govern and explain its operations. Sometimes, the policy statements are in-house documents used by staff as part of a reference manual, and are seldom shown to the public. Sometimes, they are part of a carefully executed publicity effort. The statements can take many forms such as a statement or brochure on interlibrary loan borrowing; a comprehensive statement of the reference unit's goals and all policies governing specific services provided; or, a card file, used to govern reference acquisitions. Ingredients of such policy statements may include the library's program for meeting the requirements of the Rehabilitation Act of 1973 concerning access to public buildings by handicapped persons; maxims about the length of time one can give to telephone inquiries (or to one individual when others are waiting); under what circumstances the removal of books from the reference room can be permitted; eligibility of interlibrary loan borrowers; or related requirements such as postage fees or published sources of reference. The *Reference/Information Service Policy Manual for the Staff of the Chicago Public Library* is an excellent example of a policy statement.

All types of written policies contribute to a better awareness on the part of reference staff of what they should and should not be doing. How useful it is to have policy statements that are deliberately designed for posting or for distribution to the library's clientele will depend on circumstances. If there are frequent questions from library users about particular reference services and their limits (for example, reading services for the blind), it is desirable to have policy statements about these services available for consultation or distribution. Such a practice will not only save staff time but also can provide "authority" for hard-pressed reference staff who must explain why they cannot read lengthy excerpts from the United States Constitution over the phone or why they cannot perform mathematical calculations for a student. If a library wishes to attract more users, publicity brochures can describe in glowing terms the library's public service policies.

Rather than giving an interested library user a large document that covers every aspect of reference service policy, it can be more effective to have separate leaflets on particular services of interest. A large document can amount to using a shotgun approach to the user's problems, and in fact, may be better used as an in-house tool. Smaller public relations-oriented handouts on specific services offered can provoke a more positive response from a user, and necessary limitations of service can be delineated separately as necessary. For example, a brochure on computerized reference services can be used to explain the nature of the subsidy that funds the program, or conversely, why the library must charge fees to recover the costs incurred in providing the service.

Many reference units never develop a comprehensive policy statement because they lack sufficient time to devote to any but the most essential tasks. This is not to say that such a comprehensive policy statement is not of use to the library administration and to the reference staff. Another reason that some reference units may not develop a comprehensive written policy of reference service is that the policy statements must necessarily declare limits of service, and this is a negative aspect of the reference librarian's public relations responsibility. All reference units probably wish to provide as much (or more) service as their level of funding permits, with the usual exceptions for not undertaking unsanctioned activities, such as doing a student's homework. But usable policy statements should declare the limitations of reference service in sufficient detail so as to avoid misunderstandings. A prospective new reference librarian can learn much by inquiring as to the policies that may or may not exist in a reference department.

Use of Legal Sanctions

A library's objectives can be accomplished without legalistic study of the statutes, codes, or municipal ordinances that may establish the library or have some bearing on its functions. Nevertheless, a conscientious reference librarian should be aware of the applicable provisions of the law that may be usefully invoked to protect the rights of library users, staff, and library materials. Every state has its own statutes and codes that may make the theft or mutilation of library materials a misdemeanor or even a felony. Certain obligations of public and university libraries and publicly supported library networks often are also spelled out in statutory form (e.g., the Rehabilitation Act of 1973, which requires access for the physically handicapped). Awareness of the services that one is legally obliged to offer—and to whom—is as essential for reference librarians as it is for library administrators.

A conscientious reference librarian will also seek to be informed about the statutory limits of acceptable behavior. Reference supervisors have a responsibility to protect their staff as well as other library users from the unpleasant, abusive behavior of some persons. If a reference head is prepared to deal with unpleasant situations and has properly trained the staff in appropriate procedure, this type of problem can be handled relatively smoothly. While it is never pleasant to have a cite a particular section of the appropriate municipal code to an offender, the fact that a reference librarian knows the law and quietly insists that it be observed can ease some distressing situations.

Naturally, it is essential that the library administration and the reference librarian develop a coordinated policy of how the relevant statutes and ordinances shall be applied. In a large library system employing many staff, it is more difficult to ensure consistent interpretation and application of the laws governing library services, materials, and the behavior of individuals, but such consistency should be considered an essential element of public service policy. The staff must understand the limits of conduct in which they are allowed to operate, just as they must know the limits of acceptable conduct for library patrons. Because reference librarians so often serve as the "buffer" for the library when a patron is dissatisfied, they must be prepared to handle all kinds of complants, soothe the frustrated library user, and, if necessary, defend library staff who have had the misfortune to have to explain the noncirculating policy for reference books to a patron who considers the policy to be a personal affront.

Publicity

Objectives for a reference unit frequently include a program for making services more widely known to the appropriate clientele. Sometimes such public relations efforts become part of an outreach program wherein the reference librarian may visit classes, travel in a bookmobile, and give lectures, workshops, or story hours. Brochures and leaflets advertising services are handed out or even mailed to the target clientele.

While the publicizing of a library's services is generally worthwhile, it sometimes happens that a library's ability to meet the demands engendered by the publicity effort may be diminished by an unanticipated high volume of use, and service to all may suffer. Therefore, it is important for the new reference librarian to understand that not all reference units can absorb the greater workload occasioned by successful publicity efforts. If a reference section is already at the saturation point, the reference head would probably be considered irresponsible if a program were to be mounted to attract new users when inadequate funding existed to meet the needs of the present clientele. In such a situation, it becomes essential to determine whether other users might not be more appropriately served in other libraries, and the heavily used library may wish to join in publicity efforts of other libraries in the metropolitan area to equalize the load. College and university libraries, in particular, may have to develop programs to encourage the general public to use their public libraries before seeking access to the college and university collections.

Measurements of Activity

Measurements of activity in a reference unit can be used to determine whether the unit is meeting its goals or whether additional support must be sought. Statistical measurements are most commonly used because numbers and percentages can be more readily incorporated into budget preparation. Sometimes, however, the recorded activity clearly indicates that modification of current policies and staffing is in order rather than the seeking of additional funds. Perhaps, for example, more people are taking advantage of a metropolitan interlibrary loan network, and a library experiences a drop in the number of persons visiting the library but a sharp rise in the number of volumes lent on interlibrary loan. In such a case, some staff from the stack maintenance section may be shifted to the ILL section.

While there are many efforts to measure and evaluate reference service, there are few studies which reflect the careful analysis that is required. One of the best was reported by Balay and Andrew (1975), as it was carried out at Yale. In this analysis, variables such as the day of the week, time of day, duration of inquiry, mode of inquiry (i.e., telephone, person, or library department), patron affiliation, search location (i.e., stacks, card catalog, bibliography room, and so on), and 18 different types of inquiry were recorded on the worksheet. The resulting data were tabulated by computer and provided valuable information for management decisions.

While this study has demonstrated a practical methodology for determining patterns of library use, so far there is no notable methodology developed to permit us to analyze the quality of reference service (i.e., how successful are we in providing the relevant, accurate information required—and in what time frame?). One can easily conduct sample studies of user satisfaction, but user satisfaction is not necessarily related to the accuracy and relevance of the information provided. With fiscal constraints looming large on the horizon for most libraries, the reference librarian who develops an economical method for assessing the quality of reference service will become a legend in the annals of reference librarianship.

Because recording statistics of use devours staff time, and because it is difficult to record accurately the number and type of users, questions, type of questions, length of search time, and mode (in person or by telephone) at a busy reference desk, reference administrators generally try to keep the data-gathering to a minimum. Most importantly, reference heads must anticipate which measurements will be useful to themselves and to the library administration in preparing a new budget and justifying additional resources. Adherence to nationally agreed-upon measurements of a reference activity is also important for comparative purposes (Emerson, 1977).

When one know which statistics are needed, then the determination can be made as to whether those numbers can be derived from a sampling taken at appropriate times during the year, or whether, alas, it is necessary to record certain statistics throughout the entire fiscal year. Sometimes, instead of performing a major study, as was done at Yale, the reference librarian must be prepared to conduct special surveys or studies of particular aspects of reference service. If one is concerned about the staffing patterns at the reference desk, statistics may be kept on an hourly basis for a time; if one wonders what percentage of phone calls are, "Does the library own . . ." questions, a special tally of that type of phone question may help determine whether the library needs a separate station for catalog information. Remember also, in this instance, that the identity of the callers may be important, and one may have to categorize the users as well. Perhaps the library administration is in no position to subsidize service to a high proportion of "outside" users. If a study must be conducted of the use made of the reference room, apart from activities at the reference desk, hourly head counts, shelving statistics, and inquiries as to the users' school or industrial affiliation may be employed.

In measuring reference activity, one should not be dismayed when results of studies indicate unexpected conclusions. An information desk, established to "screen" questions so that reference desk personnel will not have to answer many directional inquiries, may have no effect on the numbers of directional questions still received at the reference desk. This is not necessarily bad news. The number of appropriate reference questions asked may rise dramatically as a result of referrals from the information desk. Perhaps one learns that the information desk seems to have no useful effect at all; one can then happily conclude that it is unnecessary. It is equally important to use measurements of activity to eliminate unnecessary services, because if the library administration can rely on a reference librarian's judgment as to what is really necessary to meet the user's needs, the reference librarian will be more successful in securing administrative support for necessary services. It may well be that in a particular year, if budget allocations give the library only one new FTE, the library's users will be benefited more by the use of that FTE in a cataloging unit rather than a reference unit. After all, if a library's technical service responsibilities are well-met, it makes the work of a reference librarian much easier and less time consuming!

Space and Facilities

In order to meet the objectives of a reference unit, thoughtful consideration must also be given to the use of space and facilities. Whatever functions are assigned to it, a reference unit should be clearly visible and its services identifiable to a newcomer entering the library. Consideration should also be given to the entrance to and the exit from the reference room so that control of the collection can be easily maintained and a security system installed, if necessary. Even though it may be initially planned to have reference service available the entire time that the building is open, use statistics may indicate that almost no one asks for reference assistance after a certain hour, although many persons use the library as their "sitting room" or community center. In such an instance, budget constraints may well dictate an earlier closing of the reference room, even though the main building is open.

Long-range planning is essential, even though short-term arrangements may be appropriate. and necessary as emergency measures, or as first steps in a staged plan of remodeling. In all libraries, skillful arrangement of facilities and furniture is mandatory. Great ingenuity must be exercised to ensure that there is a logical scheme behind the placement of the library's catalog, various reference tools, the materials they index, and related public service stations. The needs of special clientele such as children and the physically handicapped must also be considered. Arrangements that facilitate a good pattern of research methodology will also save time for the reference staff.

Within a reference room, there is a universally followed rule-of-thumb that dictates that reference materials used most often are kept in a "core" or "desk" collection. However, reference librarians should beware of keeping in a core collection the type of reference work that is more often consulted by library users than by the librarians (unless there is a need to protect a title that constantly "walks"). Library administrators have good reason to question statistics that reflect a high circulation of popular reference titles from the core collection. Unless the reference librarian needs to consult the popular works frequently, library patrons may be better served by having such works as the Oxford Companion series and automobile repair manuals available on the shelves in the reference room. If funds permit, it may be desirable to have second copies of the items that are used frequently by both the library's clientele as well as by the reference staff.

Facilities employed in giving reference/information service must be given as much thought as the use of space. Signs are of tremendous importance, and it is no secret that attractively executed, judiciously placed signs reduce user frustration and the diversion of staff time to giving repetitious responses to simple directional questions. Whether or not to install a telephone on a reference or information desk may well be determined by the nature and volume of reference activity. Perhaps one can afford to have telephoned inquiries handled at a separate station, or alternatively, to have telephone answering equipment that can tell the caller that the reference librarian is busy. As previously mentioned, whether one has a computer terminal installed in a visible public service area may depend not just on wiring costs and available space, but also on whether one can provide adequate security for the equipment. Now that various annals of crime include instances of fraud and felonious thefts perpetrated via computer (not to mention the theft of equipment), librarians must anticipate needs for safeguarding automated files as well as the equipment.

Whatever decisions are required concerning space and facilities, reference librarians should avail themselves of every opportunity to observe arrangements in other libraries. Inevitably, solutions devised in other institutions may be beneficially adapted to one's own library. It is also helpful to inquire of other librarians what justification was used for successful budget requests for such items as carpeting, draperies, and telephone answering devices. Carpeting and draperies, for example, may be considered desirable features in one library simply because they are attractive, but another library may well justify them on the basis of acoustics and insulation.

BUDGET PREPARATION AND FUNDING MECHANISMS

With adequate data about the library's goals, objectives, and activities, preparation of a budget proposal for a reference unit is not difficult. The types of budget preparation usually employed may be generally categorized as falling into four genres with considerable variation and overlap among them. These are line item budgeting, program budgeting, zero base budgeting, and formula budgeting (Prentice, 1977).

Although one's library administration may be interested only in a line item or "object of expenditure" budget wherein the reference unit's anticipated costs for the next year's operation are simply itemized (based on the present year's expenditures with an inflation factor added), it is useful for planning purposes to conceive of reference needs in terms of specific service programs. This is particularly true in years with a tight money situation, because it is easier to justify line items on a budget request if they are tied in to a particular program that has been determined to be of high priority for the library. Thus, one may have a list of equipment, supplies, and training sessions, all of what are needed in order to inaugurate computerized reference services; but if one lists all these items individually along with other items intended for the overall operation of reference services, they may not get the attention they deserve. By assembling a budget proposal for each program, such as computer reference services, the reference librarian can show the real costs of operating such a service. Anticipated income from grants or direct search fees can be shown in relation to ongoing costs for equipment rental/purchase and service, electrical and telecommunication costs, paper costs, training costs, and so on.

If program budgeting is utilized, one should be prepared to analyze the various alternatives that might be employed to meet program objectives and to indicate the anticipated cost benefit for each alternative. The goal here, of course, is to devise a budget scheme that will provide the greatest benefit for the least cost. Perhaps one can arrange for experienced computer searchers in another library to do a training workshop that would cost less than one arranged by a commercial vendor. If a mechanism for evaluation of the program in relation to the library's goals and objectives is also incorporated into the budget plan, then the budget format is known as PPBS (planning, programming, budgeting system).

Although a very expensive, time-consuming method of budgeting, zero base budgeting can be useful if the reference librarian wishes to start from scratch and analyze and justify the cost of each element of a reference service. Because the assumption in this method is that none of the preceding years' operations are worth continuing unless they can be shown to be necessary, zero-base budgeting can be useful for paring out the deadwood of obsolete or uselessly extravagant programs. Using such a method, a reference librarian would have to evaluate and cost out every activity, such as telephone reference and the indexing of local publications, and then decide what should be proposed in the new budget and at what cost. One would hope, however, that such a costly process would not be undertaken except at intervals of several years.

Formula budgeting is another mechanism that is frequently used and must be reckoned with. Libraries in educational institutions usually are faced more often with this technique which relates enrollment figures to library support. The formulas can be very complex and tie in such factors as enrollment of students in various academic disciplines with the number of degrees offered at different levels and the distance between collections in the same system. Public libraries, however, also are affected by formula budgeting if they receive any money from the state or federal government to finance specific programs such as a metropolitan interlibrary loan network or special late-hour telephone service.

Outside Funding

Because of the soaring costs of library materials, construction, and personnel, libraries increasingly must look for sources of outside funding to accomplish their goals. The growing financial burdens have been recognized by federal and state legislation, e.g., the Library Services Construction Act (LSCA, 1956) and the California Library Services Act (CLSA, 1977). Such legislation frequently helps to fund the establishment of networks and consortia to develop structured interdependent library relationships. Grants from private sources, e.g., the Council of Library Resources and private foundations, also are used to develop better library service programs. The Office of Education and the National Endowment for the Humanities furnish additional support for various programs that include bibliographic projects and conservation efforts, and the Department of Labor administers the Comprehensive Employment and Training Act (CETA), which permits the hiring and training of unemployed workers at little cost to the employing institution.

A reference librarian must be alert to opportunities for the library to benefit from such funds. Quite apart from special grants for such projects as training the reference staff in computer searching or testing an expedited interlibrary loan system, certain statutes, such as CLSA, permit reimbursement to libraries within appropriate areas for every person served from a separate jurisdiction or every book lent on interlibrary loan. Many grants available from local sources will assist a reference librarian to provide bookmobile programs, library instruction in the schools, or subsidized computer searches.

Fees

A debatable source of outside funding is the collection of fees for services rendered. Most librarians agree that ideally all library services should be subsidized in recognition of the importance of free access to information, but the financial plight of libraries sometimes requires that fees be charged to recover partial or full costs for "extra" services. Computerized literature searching, paging and delivery, and photocopy services are the most obvious examples. These services (exclusive of photocopy) are frequently funded on a "start-up" basis by a grant, but the ongoing service must somehow be funded by the library. A library may decide to subsidize its computer search services so that anyone can have a search performed, but usually this means that the library must curtail its expenses in another area of operation. Perhaps the weekly, monthly, or quarterly production of the serials list will have to be foregone if search services are to be subsidized.

In analyzing the "trade-offs," the reference librarian must be careful to establish priorities. Some librarians believe that it is better not to offer services for which one has to charge a fee, thus preserving in practice the concept of free library service. Others believe that a library should not leave the provision of desired services to commercial establishments and research firms who must make a profit. These firms are unlikely to advise a user of the fact that computer searches usually retrieve information that is already available in printed versions of the databases that can be searched manually without cost in a library. It can be argued that paying for a computerized literature search or delivery service is analogous to hiring a research assistant. By shifting the efforts of the research assistant from gathering to evaluating the material, a computer search may be more cost-efficient.

In the evolution of libraries as an important social institution, it is to be hoped that services that are essential for the public good will be so recognized and made freely available to all. Reference librarians should not be discouraged if their libraries cannot at first afford to provide some of the costly new services. As the services prove their value and as librarians and their clientele continue to push for subsidization, society and the legislators will gradually accept the notion that at least some of these new expensive services are deserving of support. Already there is a strong support for this cause from leaders in the library profession as can be seen by this statement made by Russell Shank in an address to the California Library Association in December 1977:

> . . . Not only must we fight for and retain the right for the community to own and operate the freely accessible library, but we must convince society that this important new technology must be funded as part of the subsidized service. . . . Whatever we do, we must not let the powerful new technology in the information service field slip behind the greenback curtain, there to be an exotic tool for the exclusive use of the well-heeled. (Shank, 1978, p. 119)

UTILIZATION OF STAFF FROM OTHER SOURCES

Volunteers

When a reference unit needs additional staff to man an information desk, to conduct tours, or to provide catalog assistance, it is not uncommon to make use of volunteers. These may come from other units within the library (if their supervisors give permission) or from outside groups, such as library support organizations or students. Reference librarians should be aware, however, of some problems that can occur with the use of unpaid staff.

Because volunteers are giving their time, they may feel less compelled to meet the required public service schedule. "No shows" are frequent among volunteers who lack a career commitment and sometimes forget their scheduled work periods. Also, once a library accepts volunteers, it is difficult to turn away those whose qualifications are inadequate. Training is expensive, and one can spend large amounts of time providing orientation and in-service training, only to have some of the volunteers discover that the work does not meet their expectations of a pleasurable pastime. For this reason, volunteers are almost never used, except in nonprofessional work that requires little investment of training time. To nave to fire an unsatisfactory volunteer is awkward and can result in bad public relations. Further, special arrangements that often must be made to accomodate volunteers, such as parking, may be more costly than the volunteer service is worth. Naturally, there are always a few retired librarians who constitute the exception to the rule. Many libraries are beholden to their retired ''volunteers'' who return to perform special cataloging or bibliographic research projects.

Paid Assistance from Library Staff

If the reference section is part of a large library, it is sometimes possible to acquire the services of staff from other library units on a funded basis. That is, instead of using allocated funds to staff an information desk or card catalog station with a newly hired reference librarian or paraprofessional, the reference section may recruit staff from other units and reimburse those units for the staff time. Naturally, this type of program requires the endorsement of the library administration and the cooperation of other library unit heads.

The advantages of utilizing staff who are on the payroll are twofold. First, staff applicants can be selected and evaluated with established personnel procedures. The need for proper training and orientation for such staff is still very real, however. Second, the opportunity for staff development and the exchange of ideas and knowledge can be of great benefit to the individuals from the participating units and thereby to the library as a whole. Reference librarians can learn more readily of constantly changing cataloging and acquisition procedures or new branch library services and regulations. Similarly, staff from technical processing units and branch libraries can become aware of the problems and the needs of library users. Such a cooperative venture can result in a healthy, close liaison between reference staff and other library units and makes collaboration on important policy formulation much more productive (e.g., whether to discontinue classification of acquired materials and shelve by accession number).

PERSONNEL

REQUIREMENTS

The one requirement for reference work that does not vary with the number and complexity of responsibilities assigned is that the individual must have a pronounced ability to relate well to others. Just as one should not become a police officer for the personal satisfaction of being in a position of authority, one should not become a reference librarian in order to demonstrate intellectual superiority. A reference librarian not only must be a master of research methodology and reference sources, but also must have the instincts of a social welfare worker. A good reference librarian is tolerant of the ignorance of others and patient with their idiosyncracies and occasional unpleasantness, always remembering to draw the line between constructive assistance to those who really need help and indulgence of excessive demands.

In selecting reference personnel, however, it is important not to employ a reference librarian who has an emotional preference to be a social worker. Unfortunately, few libraries are staffed to provide as much reference assistance to each person as is needed, so reference librarians must have the capability of kindly and tactfully disentangling themselves from hangers-on who would monopolize their time, to the detriment of others. Reference librarians who have a strong nursing tendency should ask themselves if they are really helping the pitiable cases by spending so much time with them, or if perhaps they are just making themselves seem wonderful and indispensable to these people. If, however, the reference librarians are not just "doing the work" for the people, but are methodically coaching them in the rationale of the "search," then the time is well-spent.

Education and Expertise

When a job is posted, the levels of education, expertise, and experience should correspond to the actual duties and responsibilities of the position. In addition to the master of library science (MLS) degree, it is a great temptation for a reference supervisor to require high levels of experience and expertise, because experienced personnel can usually become effective in a new position faster than the uninitiated. Nevertheless, for budget reasons as well as for long-term staff development needs, it is often wiser to fill an open position with a librarian whose qualifications match, not exceed, the basic requirements of the job. The practice of bringing in new staff at junior or entry level is a healthy one and provides for the training and development of future reference supervisors and administrators in anticipation of the eventual loss of senior staff. If a prospective reference librarian has demonstrated the interest and ability to learn whatever is necessary for the job, then that person is likely to be a better "risk" for a reference department than a more experienced reference librarian who is content with his or her present mastery of librarianship.

Some reference functions, apart from support tasks, do not require personnel with an MLS degree. With the proper supervision, paraprofessionals and student assistants can play important roles in direct public service. They may be used to staff information desks, catalog information stations, and, under certain conditions, even reference desks. Again, the single most important qualification for anyone is the ability to deal agreeably with the library's clientele without pretending to imagined expertise. If students and/or paraprofessionals are used in any direct public service, they must be trained to recognize questions that should be referred to a librarian.

On the other hand, it is more than likely that a new librarian can and must learn a great deal from an experienced paraprofessional. A good reference librarian recognizes that every job is equally important (the variation is in complexity and level of responsibility) and that nonprofessional staff members make a comparable contribution to the services of the library.

Subject Backgrounds

Much has been made of the importance of subject backgrounds and expertise in various languages for reference librarians. There is no doubt that the more one already knows about a subject, the more quickly substantive reference assistance can be provided. Instead of just knowing the most likely sources, one may already know that the sources disagree and when the reader should be cautioned. Subject backgrounds in reference staff also prepare them to evaluate, select, and catalog materials in those specific subjects or language areas. In-depth research and fulfillment of advanced course requirements are excellent preparation for assisting students and faculty with similar projects. Naturally, within a reference unit, staff specializations should complement each other.

Nonetheless, there can be drawbacks to subject specialization. It is difficult to make sure that a library has enough subject specialists so that there are no "gaps" in areas where no one takes any interest or responsibility. Also, a subject specialist may well be bored with having to assist people with inquiries about subjects outside the special field and may suffer from "tunnel vision" with the result that interdisciplinary connections may not be recognized.

While some believe that general reference service is not at as high a level as that found in libraries that use specialists, the merits of general reference assistance should not be overlooked. General reference is in itself a speciality and requires a staff of great breadth and depth of interest and education. Good general reference services employ librarians who have complementary subject/language specialities, comparable to bibliographers, but the focus is on the interdisciplinary nature of all of the subjects. Each librarian enjoys giving skilled reference assistance to all library users and calls upon the special strengths of other colleagues only after all of the obvious reference sources have been consulted. In a sense, the general reference librarian can be viewed as a renaissance ideal who deserves everyone's admiration.

Full Time versus Part Time

The problems attendant upon the use of volunteers have already been discussed, but it behooves us now to give some attention to the question of full time versus part time staff. It is very difficult to build a career as a reference librarian when working only part time. Full-time work is ordinarily much more desirable for the new librarian as well as for the reference unit, because of the opportunity it affords to immerse the librarian in all aspects of the job. A librarian who works only part time can seldom supervise other staff satisfactorily, whereas a full-time librarian cannot only assume responsibilities for ongoing operations, but can also participate more easily in other extra-reference activities such as committee work. Part-time staff members are handicapped in terms of ''keeping up'' with all that is essential for their work and in participating in library-related activities.

Assistance from part-time librarians should not be totally discounted, however. In an emergency situation when someone is ill or must take a leave of absence, sometimes the best help available will come from librarians who are able to work only part time. Many outstanding reference librarians are unable to work full time because of other responsibilities, yet they can make a valuable contribution. However, even though one may be able to hire several experienced librarians who can work only part time, it is safer for a reference head to have no more than one position filled on a part-time basis. Split responsibilities and variant work schedules can compound operational difficulties for the reference department as well as make the progress of a career more difficult for the reference librarian.

Recruitment and Selection of Staff

The processes by which librarians are recruited, interviewed, and selected in any institution are usually outlined and defined explicitly in the personnel and affirmative action regulations. These procedures not only should be fully understood, but also every effort should be made to comply with them when one is a reference supervisor. Making sure that notices of open positions are widely circulated, posted, and advertised is the best method of assuring that the library has a good pool of applicants, as well as demonstrating conformity with laws and regulations.

When there is a vacancy in the reference section, it is an opportunity to reevaluate the organization scheme and the workload. It may be that a more effective utilization of manpower will require a change in the position's responsibilities and a corresponding upgrading or downgrading of the classification. A reference librarian should assist the department head in making an honest, well-documented assessment of needs and learning as much about the process as possible. If the budget will not permit staff augmentation, then the reference librarian must help the department head to make the most of available resources.

In the selection process, all personnel involved in the activities of the unit should have an opportunity to contribute their opinions of the qualifications needed for the job in question. Although it is desirable for a staff to meet candidates, the interview process is perhaps best limited to a small group or committee of knowledgeable staff who can represent appropriate concerns. It is not desirable to subject candidates to ''gang'' interviews or to have large numbers of a staff spend their time on matters that can be responsibly delegated to a few. On the other hand, a prolonged sequence of interviews can be equally stressful, and ''free time'' should be interspersed with the successive appointments.

Care should be taken also to ensure that the interviews and evaluations of the candidates are conducted in the most objective manner possible. A structured interview in which the same questions, perhaps each with a particular weight, are asked of every candidate, can produce a numerical rating of each applicant that can be helpful in reaching a decision. Questions that might be relevant to ask include the following:

(1)   What gives you the greatest pleasure in the work you have previously performed that is similar to this job?

(2)   What do you find least satisfying about the jobs you have held (or the library school curriculum)?

(3)   How do you prefer to organize your responsibilities?

(4)   How do you prefer to deal with interruptions of your work?

(5)   Are there any aspects of this job for which you feel less prepared than you would wish?

(6)   What do you hope to accomplish in this job?

Obviously, certain questions relating to personal data are not only improper but also illegal. Such questions include:

(1)   Are you married (divorced, single, separated)?

(2)   Are you planning to have a family?

(3)   Are you a member of a union?

With the ever-increasing number of complaints being filed by disgruntled applicants for jobs, documentation of recruitment, selection, and evaluation procedures is of tremendous importance. One must be able to prove that a new staff member was selected with due process and with clearly delineated criteria that were communicated to candidates at an early stage in the proceedings.

The selection process may be affected by several other factors. Persons from other library units, the city council, the board of directors, or from the academic senate may sit on the selection committees. Among academic librarians, peer review is becoming more commonplace and has contributed a great deal to the advancement of members of the profession who might have otherwise been held back by rigid administrative structures. At the same time, such reviews not only are very time consuming but also tend to result in increased requirements for promotion and merit increase that go above and beyond job performance. Because libraries are service organizations, few of them can afford to have heavy emphasis put on professional activities that may be more directly related to professional development and extra-library matters than to productivity and effectiveness on the job.

Orientation/Training/Continuing Education Programs

In-house programs for reference staff are of two types: (1) orientation for incoming staff to acquaint them with the entire institutional setting, reference policies and procedures, and the location of works in the reference room; and (2) staff development programs for new and continuing staff. The latter may need to learn new skills in order to improve their job performance or to develop capabilities that will enable them to handle more complex assignments. Unfortunately, it is unlikely that all new reference librarians (or even all old ones!) can receive as much additional training as would be desirable and of interest. Libraries can seldom afford to train all the reference librarians to perform computer searches, for example. It usually happens that those few who have demonstrated a "flair" for it in initial training/demonstration sessions—or those who happen to work in a small unit where each librarian *must* be trained—are the ones whom the reference supervisor must send for thorough training. Reference librarians who receive such special training should plan on developing sufficient competency to begin to train their colleagues, as necessary, in-house. Other special training sessions in the giving of workshops or coping with the new cataloging rules can be passed on to staff who could not attend by the presentation of oral or written reports and the routing of workshop materials.

Staff development can be best accomplished by the use of experienced staff as coaches, tutors, and supervisors. Procedural manuals covering all of the various reference activities are also useful and usually indispensable. Depending on funding capabilities and audiovisual resources, orientation and training can be greatly helped by the use of such devices as films, tape/slide shows, and perhaps even videotaping of reference transactions. There is no better way for reference librarians to see how their efforts are perceived by library users than to see themselves in action—blunders and all. But neophytes should not be discouraged if they feel a little inadequate from time to time. A healthy practice is to observe what is effective in others whom one admires and to try to emulate their methods. One should also feel free to discuss with one's supervisor problems of inadequacy or institutional frustrations and seek advice on achieving one's own goals and objectives.

Another training method for both new and experienced reference librarians is to rotate duties among staff at scheduled intervals. In a large library, it may be possible to bring new librarians into a type of internship program in which they spend an initial few months in cataloging, then move to acquisitions, interlibrary loans, the card catalog, the reference desk, and so on. If all newly appointed librarians could be given this rounded training, assuming their "permanent" positions later, it would be a boon to the profession and to libraries alike. Usually, only appointees to small libraries have a chance to perform so many primary duties.

Rotation of staff has many benefits but is time-consuming and costly. The cost is usually seen to be recoverable, however, in terms of long-range staff development and "back-up" capabilities. The question then becomes whether the library can afford to finance a program in which the benefits cannot be immediately seen and which cannot be shown to be of direct benefit to the library's users. If the library director has to choose between funding a staff development program involving rotation of staff and funding a new film-lending service, the staff program may have to wait. Obviously, if one rotates personnel, the library must continuously provide training for those moving into new responsibilities, while losing the expertise of those who have mastered one assignment and are ready to move on to the next. Further, some librarians are able to perform well in certain jobs but not in others. Providing an opportunity for librarians to work just a few hours each week learning other duties is a compromise arrangement allowing those hired for particular talents to continue to perform in the jobs for which they are most suited. Ordinarily, one should avoid simultaneous "exchanges" of personnel between units for training purposes, however, because it is a hardship for any library section to try to train a new person while one of their "regulars" is gone at the same time.

As is true with all professions, additional training may necessarily take the form of continuing education. If a class is sponsored or paid for by the library, it would be considered a staff development effort. If the librarian enrolls in and pays for courses without compensation in time or money from the library, such an effort would be viewed as continuing education. Attendance at professional workshops, seminars, and institutes can provide invaluable education at the post-MLS level. The taking of specific classes in languages or subjects relevant to one's work is also important. It is not necessary to be enrolled in a degree program to learn much that will be valuable on the job. Those who find themselves as heads of reference units should encourage all types of continuing education if they want to be proud of their staffs and confident that the reference service offered is maintained at a high level. Further, a reference administrator should be alert to funding possibilities in order to assist the librarians to attend job-related classes. At the same time, Page Ackerman, former University Librarian at UCLA, observed that, "The individual is responsible for his WHOLE LIFE career. The organization is responsible for furthering this career during the time the individual is in the organization" (Librarians Association of the University of California, Berkeley, p. 29). Beginning reference librarians should take the initiative in obtaining whatever additional education may be necessary to meet their long-term career goals.

Evaluation and Review

As with the selection process, evaluation and review procedures are often tied to specific rules and regulations. There may be requirements for peer review, mentioned earlier, for which a reference head must prepare careful documentation. Even in instances, however, in which there may be no specific time for review and in which the decision as to a merit increase or promotion may be made arbitrarily by a reference head or the head of the library, it is still important to have an evaluation process. A reference head cannot develop the greatest potential in librarians without mutual discussions of their strengths and weaknesses. Some libraries use forms and evaluation procedures to categorize the supervisors' observations, and provide the formal consistent basis for a yearly assessment of progress. But it is only on a day-to-day basis, with informal communication between supervisor and those supervised that one can effectively reinforce and encourage the standards of excellence toward which we all strive. No supervisor should be a tiresome nag, but the achievements and failings of a person's performance deserves mention in a constructive way at timely, regular intervals, and a supervisor should ask the reference librarian for a personal assessment of his or her stronger or weaker points at some time in the evaluation process. If the supervisor does not take the initiative, the new reference librarian should try to establish a continuing dialogue about the supervisor's perception of one's weaker or stronger points and obtain suggestions for enhancing one's performance.

Naturally, if one is a supervisor, one finds that a difficult staff member requires more time in counseling and supervising. It is especially important in such cases to document instances of both good and poor performance, and if necessary to record verbal instructions, warnings, and so on with a memorandum to the individual and a copy in the person's file. If events take an unfortunate turn and a dismissal action must be initiated, the supervisor must make certain that the applicable personnel rules and procedures have been followed. If a library has a personnel officer, close liaison is essential.

Fortunately, reference librarians as a genre are marvelous, scintillating, and dedicated professionals and are usually their own worst critics. To instill a certain sense of one's own fallibility, there is nothing like an exhilarating hour at the reference desk where one is asked an array of provocative questions. Any librarian responsible for reference service has an exciting job with boundless opportunities. The most rewarding part of being a reference administrator is in creating the opportunity for one's staff to perform work that they love in an invigorating, pleasant environment. If the reference administrator can so design the unit's operation so that staff members can demonstrate and develop their talents within a framework of high professional standards, the administrator will be more than repaid by high staff morale for all the trouble-shooting and unglamorous behind-the-scenes planning. Administration of reference services is an absorbing challenge, and no reference librarian should fail to take advantage of the opportunities offered by the inevitable assignment of some administrative duties. As Ambrose Bierce noted in *The Devil's Dictionary:* "What is worth doing is worth the trouble of asking somebody to do it" (Bierce, 1972, p. 199).

REFERENCES AND SUGGESTED READINGS

American Library Association. Library Administration Division, Personnel Administration Section. *Personnel manual: An outline for libraries.* Prepared by the Ad Hoc Committee to Revise the

ALA Personnel Organization and Procedure Manuals. Chicago: American Library Association, 1977.

American Library Association. Reference and Adult Services Division, Standards Committee. *A commitment to information services: Development guidelines, 1979.* Reprinted in *RQ,* 1979, *18*(Spring), 275–278.

Balay, R. & Andrew, C. Use of the reference service in a large academic library. *College & Research Libraries,* 1975, *36*(January), 9–26.

Bare, A. C. Staffing and training: Neglected supervisory functions related to group performance. *Personnel Psychology,* 1978, *31*(Spring), 107–117.

Berger, P. An investigation of the relationship between public relations activities and budget allocation in public libraries. *Information Processing & Management,* 1979, *15,* No. 4, 179–193.

Berkner, D. S. Library staff development through performance appraisal. *College & Research Libraries,* 1979, *40*(July), 335–344.

Bierce, A. *The devil's dictionary.* New York: Limited Editions Club, 1972.

Chicago Public Library. *Reference/information service policy manual for staff of the Chicago public library,* 1978, Mimeographed.

Cogswell, J. A. On-line search services: Implications for libraries and library users. *College & Research Libraries,* 1978, *39*(July), 275–280.

Cooper, M. D., & DeWath, N. A. The effect of user fees on the cost of on-line searching in libraries. *Journal of Library Automation,* 1977, *10*(December), 304–319.

Darling, L. 'Administration. In G. L. Annan & J. W. Felter (Eds.), *Handbook of medical library practice* (3rd ed.). Chicago: Medical Library Association, 1970, pp. 32–70.

De Gennaro, R. Library administration & new management systems. *Library Journal,* 1978, *103* (December 15) 2477–2482.

Emerson, K. National reporting on reference transactions, 1976–78. *RQ,* 1977, *16* (Spring) 199–207.

Evans, G. E. *Management techniques for librarians.* New York: Academic Press, 1976.

Gardner, T. A. Effect of on-line data bases on reference policy. *RQ,* 1979, *19*(Fall), 70–74.

Green, S. S. Personal relations between librarians and readers. *The American Library Journal,* 1876, *1*(November 30), 74–81.

Hilton, R. C. Performance evaluation of library personnel. *Special Libraries,* 1978, *69*(November), 429–434.

Hutchins, M. *Introduction to reference work.* Chicago: American Library Association, 1944.

Librarians Association of the University of California, Berkeley. *LAUC seminars on career development for academic librarians,* edited with an introduction by Richard S. Cooper. Berkeley, 1977, Mimeographed.

Lynch, M. J. Academic library reference policy statements: Towards a definition of service. *RQ,* 1972, *11*(Spring), 222–226.

Martin, J. K. Computer-based literature searching: Impact on interlibrary loan service. *Special Libraries,* 1978, *69*(January), 1–6.

Nitecki, D. A. Online services. (Column beginning) *RQ,* 1980, *19*(Summer).

Pollet, D., & Haskell, P. C. (Eds.). *Sign systems for libraries: Solving the wayfinding problem.* New York: R. R. Bowker Co., 1979.

Prentice, A. E. The lingo of library finance. *American Libraries,* 1977, *8*(November), 551–552.

Rothstein, S. *The development of reference services through academic traditions, public library practice, and special librarianship.* Chicago: Association of College and Reference Libraries, 1955. (ACRL Monographs, no. 14)

Sampson, G. S. "Staffing model for telephone reference operations. *Special Libraries,* 1978, *69*(May–June), 220–222.

Shank, R. As quoted in *Library Journal,* 1978, *103*(January 15), 119.

Shaughnessy, T. W. Participative management, collective bargaining, and professionalism. *College & Research Libraries,* 1977, *38*(March), 140-146.

Simon, B. E. To ask or not to ask: Personnel selection practices: Applications and interviews. *American Libraries,* 1978, *9*(March), 141-143.

Standards for reference services in public libraries. *The Library Association Record,* 1970, *72* (February), 53-57.

Stone, E. W. Continuing education for librarians in the United States. In *Advances in librarianship,* Vol. 8. New York: Academic Press, 1978, pp. 241-331.

Warner, A. S. & Eddison, E. B. Volunteers in libraries. *LJ Special Report* No. 2, 1977.

CHAPTER 7

Current and Continuing Issues

INTRODUCTION

This chapter is intended to stimulate classroom discussion of problems that are not exclusively those of reference librarians but extend to the whole profession. However, because public service personnel frequently represent the profession to the world at large, it is especially important for reference librarians to have given prior consideration to these pervasive and difficult questions. In their daily transactions with library users, public service personnel subtly define policy.

These issues are intertwined and discussion of one easily slips into consideration of others. Similarly, philosophies expressed and policies developed in the context of one problem may color the perspective in which another of the problems is viewed. To facilitate discussion, the issues have been presented in broad groups. The first three categories bring together issues that respectively concern (1) the nature and extent of the reference service that a library will support; (2) the more narrowly defined professional concern with what distinguishes librarians from nonlibrarians; and (3) the broader social responsibilities of the library that are subject to the direct influence of the individual librarian. To provoke discussion, strong statements, both pro and con, are given. The last two concerns, censorship and technical services issues, describe particular problems for which only positive statements seem appropriate.

The brief reading lists that follow some of the statements are meant to make it easier for a class to gain a common basis for discussion. Unfortunately, some of these issues have not been separately considered in the professional literature, and others have not been well-treated. Published material is scattered and often is repetitive, or is a mere recording of an incident considered newsworthy. The citations given are for items considered to provide useful background, to illustrate the problem, or to present representative, cogent arguments.

The problems aired in this chapter require the balancing of personal, institutional, and professional values and loyalties. The appendix ''Responsibilities and Ethics: The Profession's View'' provides important policy statements issued by library groups in the United States. Notoriously, it is easier to reach apparent agreement in principle than to agree on action or behavior in specific instances. These appended statements provide a background against which personal views of the issues can be measured.

PHILOSOPHIES OF REFERENCE SERVICE: THE INSTITUTIONAL VIEW

EDUCATION OR INFORMATION?

Issue: "The real future of library reference service lies in the direct provision of comprehensive and accurate information to satisfy user demands; instructing the user in the technique of information-searching is an important, but secondary, goal and is not necessarily a reference function." (Schiller, 1965, p. 60—Reprinted from *Library Quarterly* by Anita Schiller by permission of the University of Chicago Press.)

Pro: It is time to give up trying to make everyone into amateur librarians. More than a few hours of bibliographic instruction are required to make sound use of library resources. In addition to obscuring the professional competence involved in providing information, such courses often reinforce a "do-not-disturb-the-librarian" attitude. People want and need information, not personalized instruction. Providing such information should not be disdained as spoon-feeding. The complexity of obtaining and evaluating the information necessary to make informed decisions in all areas of modern life provides librarians with an important responsibility that extends beyond traditional library responses from printed sources. Electronic media now make it possible to provide information about community services and events, social and personal services, legal and regulatory matters that is up-to-date and reliable without requiring every branch library (or service point) to devote hours of staff time to maintenance. Combinations of electronic devices can overcome the physical barriers between the library and isolated or handicapped individuals. It is the librarian's responsibility to provide information to a wider range of people in a greater variety of ways.

Con: The finest tradition of American librarianship grows out of a respect for the individual and seeks to foster self-reliance. This tradition aims to minimize user dependence on an information-specialist intermediary. Librarians should acquire and provide access to information and reject the role of guardian and dispenser of information. Librarians should assist individuals in evaluating data, by explaining the basis for it and the nature of the source providing it, but they should shun making exclusive choices. Freedom rests on choice, and the individual must retain the prerogative for accepting the information most suitable for the given circumstances and values. Thus, the library remains an educational rather than a prescriptive institution.

Responsiveness to the individual allows individuals to move at their own pace and makes the library an invaluable, unique social resource. Any reluctance to provide a facile answer is not based on judging or disciplining the individual; the librarian will provide whatever help is required without obtruding into the process. For the individual, the opportunity to discover unsuspected information resources may be much more important than being presented with a neat, preprocessed answer. Moreover, experience suggests that systems which provide neat answers effortlessly are directly responsive to economic and group pressures. Often this means provision of only those services easily or cheaply offered or widely sought (market demand), and the individual loses the option of investing time and effort in discovery of information sought; it is just no longer available.

References and Suggested Readings

Childers, T. The future of reference and information service in the public Library. *Library Quarterly*, 1978, *48*(October), 463–475.

Lubans, J. R. Library literacy. *RQ*, 1980, *19* (Summer), 325–328.

Schiller, A. Reference service: Instruction or information. *Library Quarterly*, 1965, *35*(January), 52–60.

Smith, E. T., & Winnick, P. Your library: Neighborhood ombudsman. *American Education*, 1976, *12*(November), 6–11.

Thrasher, J. & Shields, J. The adult independent learner project of the Westchester library system. *Bookmark* (N.Y. State Library), 1978, *37*(Spring), 74–79.

BIBLIOGRAPHIC INSTRUCTION

Issue: Librarians should stick to the job they were trained for and hired to do, and stay out of the classroom. The library is not a teaching institution, and librarians are not teachers.

Pro: To take the phrase "the library is an educational institution" too literally is a mistake. It may prompt public libraries to divert resources into general education programs, which insofar as they are public service endeavors, concern the reference department. In schools and colleges, libraries are more likely to promote courses in bibliographic instruction. The rationale that such instruction is an efficient way to reduce the number of individual questions often is mistaken, because those who know something of the library's resources and procedures may make more demands of the staff. Whether in the public library or a school or college library, neophytes underestimate the work involved in preparing for and meeting a regularly scheduled class. It is difficult to maintain even routine reference desk service when energies are being channeled into course preparation and the evaluation of student assignments. How is desk duty to be scheduled when librarians are regularly drawn into the classroom? The public service efforts of the library can only be shortchanged by librarians playing the role of instructors.

Untrained as teachers, most librarians are not very effective before a class. Their clumsiness in a course obscures their professional competence and turns people away from the library.

Con: Formal bibliographic instruction is more efficient than piecemeal advice given to individuals on an ad hoc basis. These presentations can be much more carefully prepared with good examples tailored to the objectives of the group. By systematic, step-by-step consideration free from the pressure to hurry to the next waiting individual, the number of false assumptions can be minimized. Often instructors will be willing to have librarians speak to classes, but wider audiences can be reached if librarians themselves offer courses in library research methods and how to prepare term papers. The institution's procedures for insuring course quality and instructional competence may require that a teaching department sponsor such courses. The effort involved in creating an hospitable niche and in reaching an understanding with suitable departments (perhaps even devising an accounting mechanism to allow FTE compensation to the library) is repaid by the stimulus such courses provide to staff members. Opportunities for new kinds of contact with the library's clientele improves the staff's appreciation of, and ability to respond to, user needs and problems. Bibliographic instruction courses can convey the message that the basic methodology of finding information can be widely applied to various subjects or disciplines. Thus, individuals learn that there is a wealth of information available and can be encouraged to consult with librarians. The background and understanding gained during the course will help students to make the interview process more efficient.

References and Suggested Readings

Newman, R. T. Instructing the out-of-school adult in public library use. In J. Lubans, Jr (Ed.), *Educating the library user.* New York: R. R. Bowker Company, 1974, pp. 59–68.
Patterson, T. H. Library skills workshops for support personnel. *RQ,* 1980, *19*(Summer), 351–353.
Rosenblum, J. Reference service in Academia—*Quo Vadis? Journal of Academic Librarianship,* 1980, *6*(July) 151–153.

Special Services

Issue: Libraries should increase their direct value to the community by providing services that meet special needs such as those of (1) the business community and (2) handicapped individuals.

To the Business Community

Pro: Immeasurable recognition can be gained from increasing the library's responsiveness to the business community. Its members are influential in civic affairs, and they are organized and easy to contact. Their needs are readily identifiable and many libraries already have the sources to meet them. Considering the taxes paid by business and industry, they are entitled to receive basic services. A public library business section can provide convenient, comprehensive coverage of economic and demographic information and maintain background and historical files. Cooperation among libraries and governmental offices will strengthen the local economy and be mutually beneficial. The quality and extent of service a librarian can provide and the immediate value to the company will win substantial recognition and support for the library in general.

Con: Providing information to business is exciting, but it requires a change of attitude in addition to an investment in materials that are expensive to maintain and to keep up-to-date. It is an inappropriate use of public money. To win the confidence of the business community, the library has to perform at a very high level. Merely having the materials available will not provide the desired boost to the library's stature unless the collection is exceptional. If there is any doubt that the library will have the information, alternate sources will be consulted instead. Businesses work to deadlines that put a premium on convenience and ready availability. Reliable use of the complex, densely formatted business sources requires training and experience. A business collection needs specialized staff and means for high-capacity telephone service. This requires money. Firms can consider the expense of such service as part of the cost of doing business; the public library cannot, and the children's section should not have to compete with the business service for public funds.

References and Suggested Readings

Campbell, M. J. Information for business: Problems of availability and access—Public libraries. *ASLIB Proceedings*, 1978, *30*(September), 337–341.
Publicizing library service to business. *RQ*, 1974, *13*(Spring), 239–240.
Ripin, A. L. How to serve the information needs of businessmen. *Unabashed Librarian*, 1975, *16*(Summer), 19–20.
Slanker, B. O. Public libraries and the information industry. *Drexel Library Quarterly*, 1976, *12*(January–April), 139–148. Rebuttal: Blake, F. M., & Irby, J. The selling of the public library. *Drexel Library Quarterly*, 1976, *12*(January–April), 149–158.

To Handicapped Individuals

Pro: The library should increase its social contribution by responding to the special needs of individuals. With the growing awareness of physical barriers to access, one hopes for a committment to eliminate unnecessary steps and areas too cramped for walkers and wheelchairs. But service to the physically handicapped should not stop there. Staff members should be prepared to handle catalog drawers, manipulate microform readers, carry materials, and if necessary, read to the blind. A clear need also exists for service to shut-ins who, upon discharge from a hospital, no longer receive reading matter but cannot travel to the public library. The reading may or may not be part of a bibliotherapy program relating to the illness or disability causing the immobility. Often simply maintaining or establishing social contact with the outside world is a most important factor. Such contact is also important for a group that can be referred to as the socially disabled, who sometimes may be categorized as "problem patrons." Many of these people are odd, but harmless and only mildly or occasionally disruptive.

Recently, librarians have more readily recognized the relationship between Reader's Advisory or Reader's Guidance service, routinely provided for less needy library users, and bibliotherapy as it is practiced in a medical setting and through the patient libraries of hospitals. Librarians should accept the responsibility of recommending material designed to help individuals meet the crises and stresses of everyday life. Librarians only are making suggestions for reading rather than writing prescriptions. It requires very little more than compassion and, perhaps, advice and cooperation from mental health professionals for the library to play a positive role in making it possible for individuals to improve their abilities to function socially.

Con: Libraries cannot provide staff devoted to any individual, handicapped or otherwise, for extended periods of time. Individuals requiring readers or attendants to push wheelchairs and handle materials should apply to other social agencies for such help. Similarly, the library has neither the public mandate nor the trained personnel to provide the type of personalized service required by the shut-in or the socially disabled.

Bibliotherapy is not a mere extension of recommending a book for recreational reading. It is a clinically supervised activity that is part of a structured rehabilitation program. Few librarians have the training required to assess an individual's need for therapy, and seldom does a library situation allow the confiding and sensitive interview necessary for such an assessment. Given the librarian's training and situation, it is difficult to see how the individual would benefit, and it is easy to anticipate potential danger. Even if librarians feel secure because it is the individual's decision to accept or reject a reading suggestion, the material may add to the confusion and anxiety of a person already troubled. The needs of the variously handicapped are better addressed by the expertise of the social or mental health worker through institutions with more appropriate conditions and facilities than the public library.

References and Suggested Readings

Lucioli, C. Role of public and institution librarians in helping the patient transfer from institution to the community. In M. E. Monroe (Ed.), *Reading guidance and bibliotherapy in public, hospital and institution libraries: A selection of papers presented at a series of Adult Services Institutes, 1965-1968*. Madison, Wis.: Library School of the University of Wisconsin, 1971, pp. 63-70.

Monroe, M. E. Reading guidance as a basic library service. In M. E. Monroe (Ed.), *Reading guidance and bibliotherapy in public, hospital and institution libraries: A selection of papers presented at a series of Adult Services Institutes, 1965-1968*. Madison, Wis.: Library School of the University of Wisconsin, 1971, pp. 1-11.

Rubin, R. J. *Using bibliotherapy: A guide to theory and practice*. Phoenix, Ariz.: Oryx Press, 1978.

Weinberg, B. The Kurzweil machine: Half a miracle. *American Libraries*, 1980, *11*(November) 603-604, 627.

FREE OR FEE?

Issue: Public libraries have never been "free." They are supported by tax dollars. Augmenting that support by charging fees not only is fiscally sound, it is equitable.

Pro: Charging fees for personalized or customized services is an equitable way of continuing and expanding public library services. It is hard to justify large public expenditures for library facilities and services used by only a small percentage of the population. Some European countries charge fees for the use of their "public" libraries. As tax-supported services come under closer scrutiny, it becomes clear that even to continue to provide the most basic and traditional services will require revenue from new sources. A fee structure for services not only funds them, but it also provides evidence that the service adequately meets real needs. There is a built-in evaluation component. Moreover, the cost is paid by those benefiting as with computer searches, for example. Those with no interest in certain services need not pay for them.

Fees are not new to libraries. Charges are commonly made for photocopies, notification that reserved books are being held, rental of popular new books, use of typewriters, and so on. When the service is "consumed" by the individual or when the service provides an extra convenience, fees have long been accepted. They allow an enhancement or expansion of service without reducing the traditional services.

Fees may be a way to compensate for demands made by users not considered the primary clientele of a tax-supported library. The clearest instance of the value of such compensation is provided by the example of the university library that is relied upon by a multitude of businesses and even service professionals. Those doing marketing and tax research or preparing legal arguments for their own company's advantage and profit often dislodge the student, faculty member, or campus researcher for whom the collection was designed. When state budgets are cut, the university has no fiscal alternatives. The business can recover the cost of making alternate arrangements.

Entrepreneur librarians and researchers who use publicly funded collections as a basis for the services they sell are a particularly difficult problem. Certainly these freelance colleagues should contribute more directly to the institutions upon which their success depends.

Con: Tax-supported institutions or services are predicated on the concept of the public good. Taxes are paid for parole services as for schools, even if one has no expectation of ever using them. Even individuals who personally never use tax-supported libraries live a better life because others do use these services. The argument that public services should not be used by profit-making firms is specious. Business and industry are major taxpayers. It is in their interests to promote budget increases and institutional cooperation necessary to expand the public library's value to them. It is a matter of improving the return on money already invested and maximizing already present potential.

While the tax-supported "free" public library is subject to a full spectrum of political and social pressures, it can provide balance and moderation. A commercial, direct-fee service must be immediately responsive to particular, ephemeral pressures and interests. Fee services sap energies and attention from services responsive to other basic human values. The revenue-making services are glamorous, and their magic mists the fundamental democratic perspective of the free public library. Moreover, as tax-cutting and budget-trimming become fiercer, it will be hard to justify any nonfee services. Information will become the exclusive prerogative of the wealthy who will share only what it is in their immediate interest to share. A free public library that welcomes and encourages the individual as a human being, rather than as an element in an economic equation, is necessary to provide the background, breadth, and perspective required for human existence.

References and Suggested Readings

American Library Association. Free access to information. *ALA Policy Manual* 50.3. Chicago: American Library Association, 1980.

Blake, F. M., & Irby, J. The selling of the public library. *Drexel Library Quarterly,* 1976, *12* (January–April) 149–158.

Childers, T. The future of reference and information service in the public library. *Library Quarterly,* 1978, *48*(October), 463–475.

Gell, M. K. User fees I: The economic argument. *Library Journal,* 1979, *104*(January 1), 19–23.

Gell, M. K. User fees II: The library response. *Library Journal,* 1979, *104*(January 15) 170–173.

Waldhart, T. J., & Bellardo, T. User fees in publicly funded libraries. In *Advances in librarianship,* Vol. 9. New York: Academic Press, pp. 31–61.

HOURS OF SERVICE

Issue: There is no point in having the library open unless there is a reference librarian on duty.

Pro: Without reference service, the library is not truly open. Ideally libraries should be open and provide full reference service 24 hours every day. Soon electronic media may make 24-hour access possible. Meanwhile, during all hours that the library is open, at least one librarian should be scheduled to answer reference questions. Whether the collection is sophisticated, or the users unsophisticated, it is misleading and a disservice to have only a nonlibrarian or no one at the reference desk.

Con: Reference hours, like those for other professional services, should be carefully scheduled for maximum return on the librarian's time. After all, library services are not life-and-death services like fire and police protection. The number and category of staff assigned to the desk should be matched to both the volume and type of inquiries received. Many library users only want access to the materials, and do not require any staff assistance. Most questions are directional or very simple (see Chapter 5). Demanding reference questions are few and far between and are best handled in a calm interview situation. For such questions, users will be willing to make appointments in advance, as has been demonstrated by user acceptance of scheduling computer-search interviews. Prior scheduling increases the professional quality of the response, and provides the user with the best possible service, without reducing library hours to those when a reference librarian can be funded and scheduled.

Suggested Reading

California info line attracts calls from afar. *American Libraries,* 1980, *11*(March), 159.
(Also see discussion on "Assigning Nonlibrarians to the Reference Desk," in this chapter on p. 185.)

OPEN OR SECURE?

Issue: The reference room should be an open, beckoning environment that encourages use of its resources.

Pro: An attractive, open reference room with good signs can do much to overcome a user's reluctance and shyness. Major sources should be clearly visible, and simple guides should explain the arrangement of the room. Insofar as possible, the reader should be spared having to ask staff members for simple directions. The availability of special services can be announced in various ways. For example, having computer terminals in a public area readily visible from paths of routine traffic flow, can encourage requests for computerized searches. Awareness of other services can be promoted in similar ways. While making it easy as possible for the user to work independently, care must be taken not to discourage consultation with librarians. One simple way to reduce the distance between the user and the librarian is to provide nameplates introducing the librarian(s) on duty. But most important to encouraging use of the reference room is a friendly and approachable staff.

Con: A reference department that has proved itself by providing reliable efficient service will be besieged by people with all manner of questions. The level and extent of the service that can be provided is often undermined by (1) theft or mutilation of materials and (2) questions more properly addressed to other libraries or other agencies. All the encouragement in the world cannot provide information from material that cannot be found, and such heavily-used facilities may find that the best way to improve their service is to increase their security. This may mean controlling access to a larger percentage of the collection and requiring that books and information alike be dispensed by a librarian after consultation about the question. More likely, it will mean installing some sort of security system to monitor exit from the reference room. Similarly, the library may be foolish to leave any equipment, much less a computer terminal, in plain view to invite theft or vandalism. Unfortunately, in the impersonal, urban environment it is designed to counteract, indicating the names of librarians on duty may expose them to assorted varieties of harrassment, both on and off the job. Public libraries and university libraries alike are frequently used as lounges and social centers rather than as information services. Many of those present are not there for any reason directly related to the purpose of the library. All too often, these individuals not only cause crowding and disruption, but through their carelessness and lack of concern, also interfere with library service. They should not be encouraged and must be monitored for the sake of the serious user.

THE LIBRARIAN'S POSITION

STANDARDS OF COMPETENCE AND LICENSING

Issue: Only through formal certification or licensure will librarians achieve the consistently high level of performance necessary to command the confidence and respect accorded a profession.

Pro: The first step toward gaining the public confidence and recognition is to take ourselves seriously and place a proper value on the services librarians provide. Accurate and complete responses to questions asked at the reference desk are essential, and the reports of low success rates are reason to tighten-up on standards. Moreover, librarians increasingly will be held accountable for the information they supply as we reach out to provide services more directly involved with the life decisions of individuals or as we charge fees for particular services. The public deserves assurance of competent service, and acceptance of a Statement on Professional Ethics (see Appendix) is an empty gesture without some means of implementation. Such implementation should include requirements of basic education and training, monitoring to insure that skills have been maintained to reflect up-to-date knowledge, and even withdrawal of certification for good cause (''Professionalism'' 1977, pp. 1723–1724).

In addition to ensuring the competence of people who perform as librarians, certification provides the opportunity for those who have alternate education, backgrounds, personal qualities and interests that provide the necessary equivalent of the present formal education requirements of the master of library science (MLS). Social class and economic condition should not prevent career advancement. The public interest requires that those who are best suited for a job be allowed to fill it.

The only area for discussion is the proper means for assuring competency (Virgo, 1976). If the present system, relying on graduation from an accredited program, is not satisfactory, perhaps individually certifying graduates of such programs would meet the needs. Such certification presently exists for medical librarians (Schmidt, 1979) and for school media specialists. Both accreditation of programs *and* certification of individuals are established by a profession itself; state licensure or registration may be more effective in preventing professional insensitivity to public needs. However the basic competency is demonstrated, skills must be maintained and updated for continuance as a qualified professional.

Con: It is remarkable how, in an economy with diminishing job opportunities, librarians compensate for their inability to demonstrate the value of their skills by seeking the protection of educational and certification requirements. These formal requirements are expensive and time-consuming obstacles that do not ensure competency. Certification programs very often rely on inappropriate tests that measure only relatively unimportant skills rather than the qualities and complex competencies that are fundamental to true professionalism. Who can justify the expense of really stringent exams, perhaps equivalent to state bar examinations?

Librarians seek certification in a desperate attempt to validate librarianship as a profession. The public demands that professions be regulated when it is appropriate. As long as librarians insist on teaching patrons to find information for themselves, the public will not consider them professionals. Fine talk and formal requirements may comfort the incumbents, but they will not make librarianship a profession in which certification makes sense.

References and Suggested Readings

Asheim, L. Librarians as professionals. *Library Trends*, 1979, *27*(Winter), 225–257.

Berry, J. N. Certification debate—A preview. *Library Journal*, 1977, *102*(March 1), 527.

Cottam, K. Minimum qualifications and the law: The issue ticks away for librarians. *American Libraries*, 1980, *11*(May), 280–281.

Professionalism—An L.J. mini-symposium. *Library Journal*, 1977, *102*(September 1) 1715–1731. Especially Michael J. Reagan, Professionalism: Mandatory certification—A proposal that lost, pp. 1723–1724.

Schmidt, D. A. Certification of medical librarians, 1949–77: Statistical analysis. Medical Library Association *Bulletin*, 1979, *67* (January), 31–35.

Virgo, J. A. Degree or license. *Wilson Library Bulletin*, 1976, *51*(December), 341–345.

CONTINUING EDUCATION AND STAFF DEVELOPMENT

Issue: Library administrators have a responsibility to provide staff members with release-time and funds for continuing education activities.

Pro: Libraries must provide the best service possible. This requires properly trained and selected personnel with good morale. Proper training not only includes the maintenance of basic professional skills, but also the opportunities to increase effectiveness both within the library and the profession at large. Support staff may keep the library functioning, but librarians, and most especially reference librarians, must be aware of services and developments beyond their particular library. It is up to librarians to make the library a recognized and respected unit by their activities within the parent institution or jurisdiction.

Thus, the library must consider not only orientation for new staff members, but also the developmental needs of all staff members. Such needs may be met in a number of ways extending from on-site speakers to the provision of release-time and financing for participation in professional meetings, workshops, or formal courses. Such activities benefit the library and are a proper part of the librarian's professional work assignment. Even the most experienced of personnel can benefit from the stimulation of continuing education and should be prepared to implement the new ideas and skills presented.

Con: The library should no more pay for continuing education than reimburse individuals for basic professional education. It is the individual who reaps the major benefit and who should bear the major responsibility for such activities. Reading professional literature, attending meetings, and participating in professional associations are part of being a professional and of providing the best possible service to one's clientele. The money and time invested in workshops and courses earns one friends, professional contacts, recognition, and the personal satisfaction derived from top-notch performance on the job. A professional does not work merely a nine-to-five job.

Librarians have a primary responsibility to stay home and take care of the work they were hired to do. In reference departments, staff budgets usually are so tight that unless everyone is available during working hours, those who are at work have an extra burden. A good professional degree teaches not only the skills required for the job, but also the principles upon which to grow and develop on the job. All too many conferences, workshops, and courses are much ado about nothing, and when they are not merely opportunities for mutual self-congratulation, are devoted to providing the sponsors with extra revenue and participants with tax deductions. If libraries can be the "universities of the people," they can be the continuing education agencies of librarians. Any librarian worth a salary can learn what needs to be learned without traipsing across the country to do it while others are carrying the workload.

References and Suggested Readings

Buckland, M. K. Revisionist views on continuing education. *College & Research Libraries News,* 1980, *41*(April), 99.

Conroy, B. Introduction: In search of learning. In her *Library staff development and continuing education: Principles and practices.* Littleton, Colo.: Libraries Unlimited, 1978, pp. xi–xxi.

Neal, J. G. Continuing education: Attitudes and experiences of the academic librarian. *College & Research Libraries,* 1980, *41*(March), 128–133.

Stone, E. W. Responsibility for continuing education of librarians, pp. 271–314, of her Continuing education for librarians in the United States. In *Advances in librarianship,* Vol. 8. New York: Academic Press, 1978, pp. 241–331.

Wulff, L. Y. Keep CE decentralized. Letter. *Library Journal,* 1980, *105*(July), 1443.

ASSIGNING NONLIBRARIANS TO THE REFERENCE DESK

Issue: A master of library science degree is not required to perform well at the reference desk.

Pro: First of all, it should be recognized that there are three major categories of non-MLS library workers:
   (1) the untrained library clerk;
   (2) the library technician, a high school graduate with one or two years of course work in library procedures and policies; and
   (3) the library assistant, who may have many years of formal college-level education, but little or no formal education in librarianship.
In addition to levels and type of education, other factors, such as the amount of library experience, attitude, and the ability to get along with people on both sides of the desk, inevitably enter into the discussion. Not every library paraprofessional (any more than every librarian) wants to work at the desk or should be encouraged to do so. There are librarians lacking good general or subject educations, and ignorant of the necessary sources, who have poor attitudes and are unpleasant. Many nonholders of the MLS not only are fine workers, but also

have expertise and experience that should be available routinely at the reference desk. The mere lack of an MLS should not prevent their serving the public directly.

The contributions that nonholders of the MLS can make should be welcomed by competent librarians. Reference desk scheduling can be maintained or expanded without allocating the higher salary usually paid to librarians. Service can be improved because librarians can be freed from answering routine questions to tackle the more challenging ones, to conduct interviews prior to database searching, or to plan programs and lectures for special groups. These benefits are very real while the reasons given for disallowing desk duty to MLS holders can apply to many who happen to have the degree.

Con: The MLS makes an important difference to reference service, and it is a difference that goes beyond mere acquaintance with a few hundred standard reference works. A person with the MLS inevitably performs better than that same person would without the benefit of the fundamental values and skills learned during an MLS program. Confidence is an important quality in reference service, but it should not be based on lack of awareness of one's limitations. Years of experience or other education do not substitute for the systematic consideration of principles elucidated by mastery of selected examples. The context, policies, and ethics of the profession are best perceived through a formal program.

Routine, directional questions often are merely trial questions. Wittingly or unwittingly, they mask other questions that users do not know how to ask or are uncertain that they want to divulge to someone else. The implications of questions are easily overlooked from lack of general library education or unawareness of little-used sources. In many more instances opportunities are lost to expand the user's awareness of the potential information available.

At the reference desk there are social and temporal pressures that are more unrelenting than in other areas of the library. The response to the user cannot be put aside until a better time. It is difficult enough to provide consistently high-quality desk service with the MLS as a background, and the public should not be misled into accepting service from those handicapped by lack of training.

References and Suggested Readings

Astbury, E. C. Library technicians and the reference service. *Canadian Library Journal,* 1969, *26*(January), 54–57.

Bjorgo, M. Technicians in reference service—Another view. *Canadian Library Journal,* 1969, *26*(January), 58–60.

Coleman, K. L., & Margutti, E. Training non-professionals for reference service. *RQ,* 1977, *16*(Spring) 17–19.

Halldorsson, E. A., & Murfin, M. E. The performance of professionals and nonprofessionals in the reference interview. *College & Research Libraries,* 1977, *38*(September), 385–395.

Peele, D. Staffing the reference desk. *Library Journal,*1980, *105*(September 1), 1708–1711.

St. Clair, J. W., & Aluri, R. Staffing the reference desk: Professionals or nonprofessionals? With a response by Pastine, M. *Journal of Academic Librarianship,* 1977, *3*(July), 149–153.

PROFESSIONALS IN NONPROFESSIONAL POSITIONS

Issue: It makes good sense to hire the person most qualified for a job, and there is no such thing as being "overqualified" for reference work.

Pro: The reasons for not hiring a person with an MLS to fill a nonprofessional position are all artificial. It is a widespread practice to schedule nonlibrarians to answer questions at the reference desk, and often nonlibrarians are responsible for much of the public service provided in small libraries. It is a boon to the library and to the public when MLS holders are eager to fill these positions. Library school graduates will do excellent work, require less training and explanation, are sensitive to the broader, professional interests, and save the library money. Meanwhile, the individual can do enjoyable work, keep in touch with developments in the profession, and maintain awareness of professional openings as they become available. People who plan to go on for the MLS are particularly desirable employees; getting the MLS should not handicap them.

Con: It is poor practice to hire professionals into nonprofessional positions; both civil service regulations and union rules recognize that fact. Generally, when there are few professional positions available, the practice is particularly pernicious. Conscientious, well-prepared nonlibrarians are displaced by MLS holders, and the profession at large suffers from a devaluation of the skills presented by the MLS. The standing of all librarians as professionals is undercut. Even in normal circumstances, the lack of clear understanding of the distinction between professional and nonprofessional responsibilities prompts discontent. The librarian is trained to consider matters beyond what is immediately obvious, and to decide and act upon what is seen. Thus, the MLS holder in a nonprofessional job must develop the undesirable habit of overlooking problems, become inattentive to the job, impinge on the responsibilities of others, or work to have the job upgraded. Meanwhile, the position as designed is not being properly filled.

GENERALIST OR SPECIALIST?

Issue: Much time and much of the agony associated with the reference interview would be avoided if librarians were subject specialists and did not have to educate themselves about a question before starting to answer it.

Pro: Surely one of the reasons that people do not use the reference desk is that they know that the librarian will not understand their question, and a lengthy (and perhaps not gentle) interrogation will ensue. A subject specialist immediately recognizes the basis for a question and can quickly identify the important aspects without gathering extraneous background material. One major reason that librarians answer a question with a source or, worse, with another question is simply that they have no idea what the answer might be and are not even likely to recognize it should they find it. Persons asking librarians for help may be well-versed in the major sources for the subject; they are asking librarians to supply additional information based on in-depth subject knowledge.

Con: Librarians are not merely "bookish" subject specialists or subject specialists who have given up work in the field. The librarian's expertise derives from an understanding of how information is produced, tested, packaged, distributed, marketed, used, and stored. Given this expertise, reference librarians who are dedicated generalists with comprehensive and omnivorous interests and knowledge provide the best reference service. Unlike the subject specialist, they are not tempted to respond on the basis of their own knowledge without a formal review of the possibilities. It is the breadth, not the depth, of librarians' knowledge that enables them quickly to provide a productive context for even the most apparently arcane questions. The generalist's ability to range back and forth over several areas of knowledge is becoming increasingly rare. The ability to synthesize knowledge as a clear outline and to explain simply the connections in response to an inquiry are extremely valuable. The best librarians are guides to the whole forest, not connoisseurs of a particular tree.

Suggested Reading

Line, M. B. The case for information officers. In J. Lubans, Jr. (ed.), *Educating the library user.* New York: R. R. Bowker Company, 1974, pp. 383–391.

PROFESSIONAL OPINIONS

Issue: Librarians should no more recommend the purchase of a particular encylopedia than the purchase of a particular make or model of automobile.

Pro: Recommending that an individual buy an expensive reference work is not the same as selecting one for a library or recommending consultation of one work in preference to another. The choice that the individual makes is of relatively greater consequence. Usually libraries have similar or complementary materials, but few individuals will buy more than one encyclopedia. Moreover, in a library the librarian is operating according to established policies and within known priorities. These do not necessarily apply to the individual. Objective criteria considered in the evaluation may not be as important to the individual's satisfaction as more subjective considerations.

In any case, the librarian should refer the individual to published evaluations and encourage comparison and use of those in the library. The librarian also should be prepared to discuss the reasons the individual wants to buy the material. Is the anticipated use to be by young children or adults? Will it be used for recreation, school, or work? Alternative resources may seem more appropriate than those known to the individual. Indeed it can be argued that it is a waste for an individual to buy expensive reference materials. They take up space, actually are seldom used, and quickly become dated and unreliable. By making a recommendation, the librarian would be helping the person squander money.

Con: Nonsense; the librarian does not play the same role when recommending purchase of an encyclopedia as in advising on automobiles. Librarians know information sources, and they should be prepared to evaluate them. In fact, librarians routinely recommend consultation of one source in preference to another and the search of database ''A'' rather than database ''B.'' Daily, they spend other people's money adding material to the library and rightly so. Librarians have the training and the experience to test titles under a variety of circumstances. If they are professionals, then it is their role to provide individuals with recommendations. If an individual decides to buy a reference work, librarians should be prepared to recommend purchase of ''X'' over ''Y,'' as well as to show the reviews.

SOCIAL RESPONSIBILITIES

UNPOPULAR OPINIONS

Issue: Librarians have a special responsibility to safeguard the expression of unpopular and minority points of view.

Pro: Librarians have the best access to information about critical questions. It is their responsibility to seek out what has been produced on all sides of an issue and to promote awareness of that information. Today's sophisticated media provide clear advantages to wealthy, well-established interest groups. To achieve a full airing of concerns, librarians must work to overcome the unfavorable odds against the individual's access to unpopular or antiestablishment views. Moreover, librarians must encourage debate of issues that are being quietly handled without due discussion and to make known salient facts. When it is clear that material is biased or misrepresents a group or its interests, librarians should correct the situation, either by refusing the material or by giving equal representation to opposing points of view. While recognizing that it may be impossible to promote discussion while avoiding controversy, librarians must defend the interests of the information poor.

Con: Social activism is neither the library's role nor the librarian's professional role. When the library becomes an agent of propagandists, it usually offends someone else and jeopardizes the unique and singularly valuable contribution it makes as an impartial resource responsive to the particular individual. Social equity demands that there remain some refuge from the clamor of excited self-interest. The library's great social challenge lies in maintaining its viability and continuing to serve without subservience.

References and Suggested Readings

Fragasso, P. Getting angry at your local public library: Or, make way for the anti-reader's advisor. *Bay State Librarian,* 1977, *66*(October), 15-17.

Hauptman, R. Professionalism or culpability? An experiment in ethics. *Wilson Library Bulletin,* 1976, *50*(April), 626-627.

Smith, J. S. Book culture, counter culture. *New Library World,* 1977, *78*(June), 108-109.

PERSONAL VIEWS

Issue: Librarians must avoid any suggestion of partiality or support for a particular point of view, in order to safeguard the library's most important characteristics—neutrality and fairness.

Pro: Libraries exist to encourage inquiry and to promote knowledge. Any indication that individual staff members favor one cause over another raises doubts about their willingness to extend their best efforts on behalf of those with differing opinions. The mere indication of support through the wearing of a button or the posting of a slogan may deter persons with questions unrelated to the issue being aired. Furthermore, the librarian's convictions may run counter to those held by the parent institution or those considered in the library's best interest. The library is a governmentally funded service and politically vulnerable. Librarians are free to express their opinions and to exercise their rights, but only to the extent that other individuals are, and not on the job or as librarians as such.

Con: A citizen has the basic right to free speech and personal expression. How can librarians relinquish a liberty they have supported so strongly on behalf of others? Librarians must resist efforts to exclude them from the political process whether by application of the Hatch Act or by institutional censure (see Readings). But even more dangerous is the genteel tradition of self-imposed, prior restraint. Such restraint creates a ridiculous and pathetic situation in which librarians refuse to speak out against, or work to defeat legislation destructive to libraries such as California's Propositions 13 (1979) and 9 (1980). Groups are politically more effective than individuals, and librarians must join together to combat undesirable legislation and to support desirable measures such as the Equal Rights Amendment.

On the job, librarians holding strong views on political issues should be open about them. The library user should have the opportunity to avoid an individual committed to an opposing viewpoint and should not be deceived into considering that the librarian is personally impartial. The face-to-face exchange that may evolve is in the spirit of inquiry and open discussion that libraries aim to promote.

References and Suggested Readings

Hatch Act keeps librarian off ballot. *Wilson Library Bulletin,* 1977, *52*(September), 16.

Maoist law librarian faces censure by University of British Columbia. *Library Journal,* 1977, *102* (April 15), 858.

Wayne, J. P. Head not heart: Why I am *against Library Workers Against Uranium Mining. Australian Library Journal,* 1977, *26*(November 18), 326–328.

Mack, V. See no evil, hear no evil, speak no evil: Why I am *for* Library Workers Against Uranium Mining. *Australian Library Journal,* 1977, *26*(November 18), 329–331.

CENSORSHIP

Issue: Can we avoid racism, sexism, and the crippling effects of other forms of prejudicial stereotyping without recourse to censorship?

The authors fully support the *Freedom to Read* statement jointly issued by the American Library Association and the Association of American Publishers and subsequently widely endorsed by concerned organizations. However offensive the view being expressed, all forms of censorship must be resisted. If actions are illegal or liable to civil action, they, but not the words, should be prosecuted. Words and ideas must be countered by other words, ideas, and the compulsion exerted by the example of a better way of doing things. Surrender to pressure from a particular group means both subservience of the library and abandonment of the principle of intellectual freedom, a freedom that must be safeguarded for others as well as for librarians. Whether making book purchases, scheduling facility use, mounting exhibits, or hosting programs, library policy should be scrupulously and impartially followed. The library must never yield to demands to abort that policy.

The terrible difficulties raised when a particular group is offended is painfully evident in the controversy created within the American Library Association upon its release of the film *The Speaker* in 1978. That controversy is well-documented in the professional press. The intricacies and the nuances of the situation merit the attention of every student and librarian.

References and Suggested Readings

American Library Association. Combating prejudice, stereotyping, and discrimination. *ALA Policy Manual* 52.1.1. Chicago: American Library Association, 1980.
American Library Association *Freedom to Read*. Chicago: American Library Association, 1953.
Berninghausen, D. K. The speaker, pp. 17–23 of his Intellectual freedom in librarianship: Advances and retreats. In *Advances in librarianship*, Vol. 9. New York: Academic Press, 1979, pp. 1–29.
Take 2: The speaker, highlights/spotlight. *American Libraries,* 1978, 9(March), 150–154.

TECHNICAL SERVICES ISSUES CRITICAL FOR PUBLIC SERVICES

The future of the catalog is too important to be entrusted only to technical services librarians and administrators.

A longstanding but unfortunate tradition plays up antagonism between those librarians who become catalogers and those who opt for reference or public service. It should be clear that cataloging requires mastery over reference sources and that reference work requires a thorough understanding of both past and current cataloging principles and practices. Less than ever before, it is a matter of reference librarians simply ''knowing enough about cataloging'' to make their way through the catalog of the local collection or the published catalogs of major institutions. Today, the pressures of efficiently acquiring, describing, and housing library materials are juxtaposed with promising electronic capabilities as manifested in bibliographic utilities such as OCLC, Inc.; RLIN; WLN; and a profusion of networking possibilities. Changes will continue to be made, and the effect on reference and public service will be direct—perhaps drastic. Reference librarians have responsibilities in helping to determine how the library can best make the necessary, difficult adjustments. Teamwork between technical and public service librarians is essential.

The appearance of a new code (AACR 2) has become the occasion for a reexamination of procedures and priorities as well as policies. Reference personnel who clearly recognize the implications of the proposed changes will go along with unimportant ones while being prepared to explain the undesirable local ramifications of accepting national or network decisions in other specific instances. For example, when reference works are reclassified, the department should be consulted about whether the run should be split or reclassified. Similarly, reference librarians should advise about when not to accept L.C.'s choice of Cutter–Sanborn numbers. Such recommendations are made on the basis of local conditions and specific local needs.

The reference staff's awareness of how the public uses the library's materials and approaches its catalog and the difficulties encountered also provides the basis for recommending cataloging priorities. These priorities encompass decisions as to what materials should be cataloged most promptly, as well as the appropriate type and extent of record to be made. It is particularly important to consider when locally produced analytics are required for addition to the catalog and when references most sensibly can be made to complementary bibliographic tools. When there is inadequate involvement of reference librarians in the preparation of in-house records, the additional staff time consumed in repetitious explanations to the public can be enormous and difficult to account for in the budget. It is truly astonishing and annoying, for example, how often cooperating libraries will devise new location symbols when the National Union Catalog has a comprehensive and widely published set with which reference librarians and many library users already are partially familiar.

Materials not housed on the library's immediate premises pose other problems. The additional delay, trouble, and expense involved in calling for material from another location—whether a cooperating library or a storage facility—can be reduced by bibliographic records sufficiently detailed to allow a majority of inappropriate works to be dismissed without actual examination. The increased pooling of resources and records also makes shared authority records more important. We are assured that there are few cases of conflict and that those can be resolved if, and when, the need arises. In fact, this means that the burden of deciding whether Francisco Martínez Fernández is Francisco Martínez or Francisco Fernández or indeed a third person, is left to the reader or to the reference librarian to resolve—on the run, without the book(s) in hand, and without a record of previous work done on the problem. This is false economy and saves the technical services budget at the expense of the library public.

A feature of North American libraries widely appreciated by library users has been classified shelf arrangement and open stacks. It will become obvious that, as more and more material is dispersed for storage or other reasons, this feature is vitiated. Public access to a classified or "shelf" list is essential to maintain previous levels of access. Having secured such a listing, the reference librarian will have to train the North American public to appreciate its usefulness.

Any crisis in cataloging and technical services is of immediate concern to reference librarians. By expending their energy and sharing their perspective with their colleagues, reference librarians can do their part to control library costs while taking maximum advantage of new possibilities to improve, not merely change, access to information and materials.

Responsibilities and Ethics: The Profession's View

The statements reproduced in this section are the closest approximation to a code of ethics or conduct designed to guide librarians in the United States. The result of lengthy and careful debate, they represent the ideals of librarianship as endorsed by the professional groups indicated, and are subject to occasional reexamination and amendment. The work of each librarian should be informed by these principles.

A. STATEMENT ON PROFESSIONAL ETHICS, 1975

Statement on Professional Ethics, 1975

Introduction

The American Library Association has a special concern for the free flow of information and ideas. Its views have been set forth in such policy statements as the *Library Bill of Rights* and the *Freedom to Read Statement* where it has said clearly that in addition to the generally accepted legal and ethical principles and the respect for intellectual freedom which should guide the action of every citizen, membership in the library profession carries with it special obligations and responsibilities.

Every citizen has the right as an individual to take part in public debate or to engage in social and political activity. The only restrictions on these activities are those imposed by specific and well-publicized laws and regulations which are generally applicable. However, since personal views and activities may be interpreted as representative of the institution in which a librarian is employed, proper precaution should be taken to distinguish between private actions and those one is authorized to take in the name of an institution.

The statement which follows sets forth certain ethical norms, which, while not exclusive to, are basic to librarianship. It will be augmented by explanatory interpretations and additional statements as they may be needed.

The Statement

A Librarian

•Has a special responsibility to maintain the principles of the *Library Bill of Rights.*

•Should learn and faithfully execute the policies of the institution of which one is a part and should endeavor to change those which conflict with the spirit of the *Library Bill of Rights.*

•Must protect the essential confidential relationship which exists between a library user and the library.

•Must avoid any possibility of personal financial gain at the expense of the employing institution.

•Has an obligation to insure equality of opportunity and fair judgment of competence in actions dealing with staff appointments, retentions, and promotions.

•Has an obligation when making appraisals of the qualifications of any individual to report the facts clearly, accurately, and without prejudice, according to generally accepted guidelines concerning the disclosing of personal information.

Reprinted from *American Libraries,* 1975, 6 (April), 231; reprinted by permission of the American Library Association.

RASD

A COMMITMENT TO INFORMATION SERVICES:

Developmental Guidelines

1979

Prepared by

Standards Committee
Reference and Adult Services Division
American Library Association

Adopted January, 1976, and revised January, 1979, by
Reference and Adult Services Division, American Library
Association, 50 East Huron Street, Chicago, Illinois 60611

A Commitment to Information Services: Developmental Guidelines

INTRODUCTION

The emergence of entirely new and sophisticated information retrieval systems has required rethinking of established concepts and methods of reference and information services. The institutional framework for those services becomes less important than the delivery of services of high quality. In addition, the increasing diversity of the user populations requires a change in the traditional modes of the delivery of information services, particularly in relation to cooperative endeavors and networking arrangements where back-up levels of information resource capability are provided.

The librarian/information specialist must be the intermediary or the negotiator for unlocking these multifarious information resources. This responsibility places the concept of good service on the ability of the librarian/information specialist to be an effective facilitator in this transaction. In all transactions the librarian/information specialist must be impartial and non-judgmental.

It is recognized that service strategies need to be designed that are more sophisticated and sensitive to the complex user patterns never known to our profession before. The guidelines for services reflect a suggested level of performance in meeting the needs of users in those institutions and agencies which need practical methods of procedure and self-evaluation for the delivery of information services.

The guidelines are directed to all those who have any responsibility for providing reference and information services, including the reference or information specialist, supervisors or department heads, administrators, educators, and trustees. In providing services, they shall consider the needs and interests of all users, including children, young adults, adults, people who do not come to a library information center, and potential clients.

SCOPE

Providing reference services in a library or information center should be recognized as a critical responsibility in meeting the information needs of users and prospective users.[1] It should be organized to provide, as appropriate, for the coordinated access to the information resources existing within an area or a given field of endeavor.

Since all functions of a library or information center should be viewed, in ultimate terms, as facilitating the transfer of information, the distinguishing feature of reference services is that it specifically ensures the optimum uses of information resources through substantive interaction with the users on direct and indirect levels cited below:

A. *Reference or information services* consist of personal assistance provided to users in pursuit of information. The character and extent of such services will vary with the kind of library or information center; with the user the institution is designed to serve; with the skill, competence, and professional training of the librarian/information specialist providing the service; and with the resources available both inside and outside the institutional framework to which the user has come. This service may range from answering an apparently simple query to supplying information based on a bibliographical search combining the library/information specialist's competence in information-handling techniques with competence in the subject of inquiry. The feature of information service, irrespective of its level or its intensity, is to provide an end-product in terms of information sought by the user.

B. *Formal and informal instruction in the use of the library or information center and its resources* may range

[1]The term information center in this document includes any service point from which a user or prospective user may seek information of any level or type through direct or electronic means. Information services is a term used in the guidelines to include all traditional reference and information services and to be the broadest term possible.

from the explanation of the use of the bibliographical aids (e.g., catalogs, information data bases, traditional reference works) to more formal assistance through interpretative tours and lectures designed to provide guidance and direction in the pursuit of information, rather than providing the information itself to users.

C. *Indirect reference service* reflects user access to a wide range of informational sources (e.g., bibliographies, indexes, information data bases) and may be the extension of the library's information service potential through cooperation with other library or information centers. This type of service recognizes the key role of interlibrary and interagency cooperation to provide adequate information service to users.

DEVELOPMENTAL GUIDELINES

1.0 *Services*

1.1 Reference or information services are to be developed not only to meet user needs and to improve present services but to anticipate user needs and demands.

1.2 A published service code with stated objectives is to be used to carry out information services and is to be available to all users. The code is to detail the circumstances under which services and resources are to be offered, the extent to which they are to be provided, any limitation on their provision, and to whom and by whom such services are to be provided. (See Appendix A for a sample draft outline)

1.3 Reference or information services are to be reviewed at regular intervals to identify those individuals who are and are not being served and to determine how individuals not utilizing such services can be reached.

1.4 Provision is to be made for continuous feedback from users concerning their satisfaction with services and success in locating information.

1.5 A specific plan for the instruction of individuals in the use of information aids is to be developed and coordi-

nated among all types of libraries, information centers, or units of library activity.

1.6 Bibliographical and other informational access guides are to be developed by librarians/information specialists as an active "alert" service signifying the potential of the information resource base available to users.

1.7 Access to reference or information services is to be promoted and provided in adaptable settings, including person-to-person contact, correspondence, and/or through other communication media.

1.8 Formal cooperation among other information handling units, centers, or agencies at local, regional, state, and national levels is essential to provide for the needs of all users and potential users.

1.9 Referrals to other sources and agencies are to be a standard level of information service operation. The effectiveness of these referrals should be evaluated at selected intervals to determine the effectiveness of the delivery service and the quality of the response to the user.

2.0 *Resources*

2.1 A selection policy is to be developed which addresses the needs and anticipated needs of the user and reflects the available resources to the user within an accessible area. Consideration should be given to a cooperative selection policy within a given service area.

2.2 Materials are to be added which reflect a diversity in format, levels of information service activity (e.g., general information service, resource back-up and research capability), and known user patterns of the past.

2.3 Frequently used materials are to be available in multiple copies in order to address user demands more quickly.

2.4 All information materials are to be examined regularly for condition, usefulness and currency, and either retained, discarded, or replaced.

3.0 *Environment*

3.1 The importance of information services requires that service points be as near as possible to the main focal point of activity in the library or information center. In some instances, this will be near the main entrance.

3.2 The reference or information collection should be situated so that it is near an open area where access allows for quick and effective service.

3.3 Individual carrels or other provisions for quiet concentrated study are to be available for users of the reference or information collection.

3.4 The main reference or information area is to be situated so that the necessary conversation between library users and librarians/information specialists is not disturbing to others.

3.5 Additional service points are to be located so that access to librarians/information specialists is available throughout the library with communication equipment and techniques provided when appropriate.

4.0 *Personnel*

4.1 Staffing patterns and hours open are to reflect directly the needs of the users.

4.2 A professional librarian/information specialist should be available to users during all hours the library is open.

4.3 The reference or information staff is to promote actively the use of all library services. This should be done by whatever means are appropriate to the institutional setting, e.g., canvassing a public library area to offer assistance.

4.4 When staff size permits, individual librarians/information specialists should have training in specific subject fields.

4.5 Staff members are to be chosen with consideration given not only to their academic background and knowledge, but also to their ability to communicate easily with people.

4.6 Continuing education of the librarian/information specialist is basic to professional growth and is the responsibility of the individual, the institution, and the policymaking body of the institution.

5.0 *Evaluation*

5.1 User data are to be collected on a regular basis to determine effectiveness of information service patterns. This implies the budgeting for such analysis through user surveys and other analytic measures.

5.2 The measurement and evaluation of reference or information services should be the responsibility of one or more staff members with some skills in this field.

5.3 Statistics are to be collected on a systematic basis for use in evaluation, policy decision, reports, and in budget preparation.

6.0 *Ethics of Service*

6.1 Information provided the user in response to any inquiry must be the most accurate possible. Type of question or status of user is not to be considered. Eligibility of users will be determined by the role, scope, and mission of individual institutions.

6.2 Personal philosophies and attitudes should not be reflected in the execution of service or in the extent and accuracy of information provided.

6.3 Information contacts with users, whether reference or directional, are to be treated with complete confidentiality.

6.4 All rules and practices regarding availability and use of information or resources must be administered impartially. Rules and practices must be codified (i.e., reference policy statement) and made available to the user in written form.

6.5 No personal financial gain should result because of the librarian/information specialist role as a representative of the library in dealing with the user.

APPENDIX A

Draft Outline of Information Service Policy Manual

I.   Introduction
   A. Nature of Information Service
   B. Statement of Objectives
   C. Purpose of the Policy Manual
     1. Guidance
     2. Standards

II. Types of Service
   A. General Statement
   B. List of Services

1. Information Service at Desk
   a. Information service—answers to specific questions, statistics, biographies, etc.
   b. Instruction in the use of the library—how to use the card catalog, periodical indexes, bibliographies, services, etc.
   c. Bibliographic verification of items in the library or not in the library—including assistance in obtaining items by purchase, copy, or loan of items not in the collection.
   d. Instruction in methodology and bibliography—how to do a literature search, how to bibliographically cite a publication or article.
   e. Assistance in locating library material.
  2. Interlibrary Service
   a. Borrowing
   b. Lending
   c. Answering inquiries from other libraries
  3. Bibliographic Service
   a. Bibliographies
   b. Demand bibliographies
   c. Current awareness services
  4. Correspondence—answering inquires from individuals
  5. Document Service
  6. Orientation and Instructional Services
III. Library Users
  A. General Statement
  B. Categories of Users
IV. Priorities
V. Desk Service Policies and Instructions
  A. General Guidelines for Desk Duty
   1. Nature and extent of responsibilities
   2. Guidelines for handling inquiries
    a. General inquiries
    b. Problem inquiries
   3. Behavior and attitudes
    a. Approachability
    b. Mobility
   4. Recording statistics and questions
   5. Reporting problems
  B. General instructions for information assistants on desk duty (Limitations concerning responsibilities outlined in Section I).
  C. Telephone
   1. Incoming Calls
    a. General guidelines (Time involved in answering phone, priority to user in building, etc.)
    b. Paging patrons
    c. Checking public catalog
    d. Circulation inquires (checking shelf for material)
    e. General library information (switchboard function)
    f. Personal calls

    g. Emergency and nuisance calls
   2. Outgoing calls
    a. General guidelines for making calls
    b. Patron use of phone
    c. Personal calls
  D. Circulation Functions of Information Staff
   1. Reference books and other restricted materials
    a. Reference collection
    b. Stack Reference
    c. Archives
   2. Authorizing extended loans of periodicals
   3. Documents
   4. Vertical file
   5. Microforms
   6. Unprocessed materials
  E. Responsibility for service at nights, on weekends, and during skeleton coverage
   1. Public service areas
   2. Closed area
  F. Inquiries for "In Process" materials
  G. Referrals
   1. Information
   2. Other libraries and services
  H. "Special Information Collections"
   1. Documents
   2. Microforms
   3. Archives
   4. Vertical file
  I. Card catalog service
   1. Inquiries
   2. Surveillance of user at catalog
  J. Questions for exams, quizzes, puzzles
  K. Genealogical questions
VI. Interlibrary Loan Service
VII. Bibliographic Services
  A. Reference initiated
  B. Users' requests
   1. Individuals
   2. Courses
   3. Administrative staff
  C. Current awareness services
VIII. Information Correspondence
  A. Incoming
   1. General information
   2. Bibliographical information (holdings)
   3. Surveys
  B. Outgoing
   1. Preparation and review of replies
   2. Letters of introduction
IX. Document Services
X. Orientation and Instructional Services

Prepared by the Standards Committee, Reference and Adult Services Division, American Library Association. Adopted by the Reference and Adult Services Division in January 1976. The section on "Ethics of Service" was adopted in January 1979.

𝕷𝖎𝖇𝖗𝖆𝖗𝖞 𝕭𝖎𝖑𝖑 𝖔𝖋 𝕽𝖎𝖌𝖍𝖙𝖘

The American Library Association affirms that all libraries are forums for information and ideas, and that the following basic policies should guide their services.

1. Books and other library resources should be provided for the interest, information, and enlightenment of all people of the community the library serves. Materials should not be excluded because of the origin, background, or views of those contributing to their creation.

2. Libraries should provide materials and information presenting all points of view on current and historical issues. Materials should not be proscribed or removed because of partisan or doctrinal disapproval.

3. Libraries should challenge censorship in the fulfillment of their responsibility to provide information and enlightenment.

4. Libraries should cooperate with all persons and groups concerned with resisting abridgment of free expression and free access to ideas.

5. A person's right to use a library should not be denied or abridged because of origin, age, background, or views.

6. Libraries which make exhibit spaces and meeting rooms available to the public they serve should make such facilities available on an equitable basis, regardless of the beliefs or affiliations of individuals or groups requesting their use.

Adopted June 18, 1948.
Amended February 2, 1961, June 27, 1967, and January 23, 1980,
by the ALA Council.

Reprinted by permission of the American Library Association.

D. RESOLUTION ON CHALLENGED MATERIALS: AN INTERPRETATION OF THE LIBRARY BILL OF RIGHTS

Resolution on Challenged Materials: An Interpretation of the Library Bill of Rights

WHEREAS, The LIBRARY BILL OF RIGHTS states that no library materials should be proscribed or removed because of partisan or doctrinal disapproval, and

WHEREAS, Constitutionally protected expression is often separated from unprotected expression only by a dim and uncertain line, and

WHEREAS, Any attempt, be it legal or extra-legal, to regulate or suppress material must be closely scrutinized to the end that protected expression is not abridged in the process, and

WHEREAS, The Constitution requires a procedure designed to focus searchingly on the question before speech can be suppressed, and

WHEREAS, The dissemination of a particular work which is alleged to be unprotected should be completely undisturbed until an independent determination has been made by a judicial officer, including an adversary hearing,

THEREFORE, THE PREMISES CONSIDERED, BE IT RESOLVED, That the American Library Association declares as a matter of firm principle that no challenged library material should be removed from any library under any legal or extra-legal pressure, save after an independent determination by a judicial officer in a court of competent jurisdiction and only after an adversary hearing, in accordance with well-established principles of law.

Adopted by the ALA Council, June 25, 1971.

Name and Title Index

A

ABC-Clio, Inc., 42
ARBA, see American Reference Books Annual
ARLIS, 52
Abstracting Services, 75
American Book Publishing Record (BPR), 84, 86, 87–88
American Library Association Ad Hoc Reference Books Review Committee, 66–67
American Reference Books Annual (ARBA), 44, 55–56, 81, 89–90
Audiovisual Market Place: A Multimedia Guide, 33

B

BLAISE, *see* British Library Automated Information Service
BNB, see British National Bibliography
BPR, see American Book Publishing Record
Bates, M., 101
Best Buys in Print, 45
Best Reference Books: Titles of Lasting Value, 56
Besterman, Theodore, 45, 52, 70
Bibliographic Index, 70
Bibliographie der Rezensionen, see Internationale Bibliographie der Rezensionen wissenschaftlicher Literatur
Bibliography, Documentation, Terminology (BDT), 59, 89–90
Bibliography of Discographies, 34
A Bibliography of United States Government Bibliographies, 62, 92
Biographical Dictionaries and Related Works, 70–71
Book Review Digest, 36, 53, 54

Book Review Index, 53
Booklist, 58, 59–61
Books for College Libraries, 78–79, 93
Books for Junior College Libraries, 79, 93
Books in Other Languages: How to Select and Where to Order Them, 90
Books in Print, 82, 86, 88
Books in Print Supplement, 83, 86, 88
Books in Series in the United States, 82
Books of the Month and Books to Come, 84, 86, 89
Books on Demand, 82
Bookseller, 83, 85–86
R. R. Bowker Company, 42–43, 87–88
Brewer, Annie, 72
British Books in Print, 86, 89
British Library Automated Information Service (BLAISE), 89
British Library Catalogue, 45, 89
British Museum Catalogue, see British Library Catalogue
British National Bibliography (BNB), 86, 88–89, 92
Bulletin, 52
Bulletin of Bibliography, 43, 89
Bulletin of Reprints, 82
Business Books in Print, 88

C

CBI, see Cumulative Book Index
Canadian Library Association, 90
Canadian Reference Sources: A Selective Guide, 67
Carlson, G., 101
Catalog of Reprints in Series, 82
Catalog of United States Census Publications, 38, 76

Chen, Ching-chih, 77
Chicorel Index to Abstracting and Indexing Services, 75
Children's Books in Print, 88
Children's Catalog, 79
Children's Literature: A Guide to Reference Sources, 79
Chisholm, Margaret, 33
Choice, 54, 55, 56-57, 81, 89
Classified List of Periodicals for the College Library, 56, 81
College and Research Libraries, 57-58, 89
Combined Retrospective Index to Book Reviews in Humanities Journals, 54
Combined Retrospective Index to Book Reviews in Scholarly Journals, 54
Computer-Readable Data Bases: A Directory and Data Sourcebook, 37
Cooper, David, 34
Crowell-Collier Publishing Company, 49
Cumulative Book Index (CBI), 46, 86, 88-89
Cumulative Subject Guide to United States Government Bibliographies, 92
Cumulative Subject Index to the Monthly Catalog of U.S. Government Publications, 1900-1971, 91
Current Book Review Citations, 53

D

Dictionaries, Encyclopedias, and Other Word-Related Books, 72
Dictionary Buying Guide, 71
Directory Information Service, 73
The Directory of Directories, 72-73
Directory of Online Databases, 37
Dumaux, Sally, 31

E

Education Index, 91
El-Hi Textbooks in Print, 88
Encyclopaedia Britannica, Inc., 48
Encyclopedia Buying Guide: A Consumer Guide to General Encyclopedias in Print, 74

F

Fachwörterbücher und Lexica: ein internationales Verzeichnis, 72

Farber, Evan, 56, 81
F. W. Faxon Company, 43
Field Enterprises Educational Corporation, 48
Forthcoming Books and New Books in Print, 83, 86, 88
Freedom to Read Statement, 191-192

G

The GPO Sales Publication Reference File, 91
Gale Research Company, 72
General World Atlases in Print, 69-70
Government Publications: A Guide to Bibliographic Tools, 92
Government Reference Books: A Biennial Guide to U.S. Government Publications, 56, 92
Gray, Michael, 34
Grolier Incorporated, 48-49
Guide to American Directories, 73
Guide to Current British Journals, 81
Guide to Educational Media, 33
A Guide to Foreign Language Courses and Dictionaries, 71-72
Guide to Microforms in Print, 35
Guide to Reference Books, 57, 65-68, 77
Guide to Reference Books for School Media Centers, 33, 79-80
Guide to Reference Material, 66, 68-69, 82
A Guide to Sources in Educational Media and Technology, 33
Guide to Theses and Dissertations, 90

H

G. K. Hall & Company, 43-44
Harvard Guide to American History, 77
Harvey, Jovan M., 76
Haviland, Virginia, 79
Herman, Esther, 31
Hernon, Peter, 92
The Humanities: A Selective Guide to Information Sources, 77

I

Index Omnibus, 31
Index to Book Reviews in Historical Periodicals, 55
Index to Book Reviews in the Humanities, 53, 57
Index to Government Periodicals, 91

Index to Instructional Media Catalogs, 33
Index to Reviews of Bibliographical Publications, 44, 54
Index to Scientific Reviews, 55
Information Market Place: An International Directory of Information Products and Services, 37
Information Sources in Children's Literature, 79
International Bibliography of Directories, 73
International Bibliography of Discographies: Classical Music and Jazz and Blues, 1962–1972, 34
International Bibliography of Reprints, 82
Internationale Bibliographie der Rezensionen wissenschaftlicher Literatur, 54, 57
Irregular Serials and Annuals, 81

J

Jahoda, G., 101
Jennerich, E. J., 115
Jennerich, E. Z., 115
Josel, N., 101
Junior High School Catalog, 79

K

Katz, Bill, 58, 75, 81
Keys to Music Bibliography, 34
Kister, Kenneth, 71, 74–75
Klein, Bernard, 73

L

Lancaster, F. W., 101, 123
Libraries Unlimited, Inc., 44
Library Bibliographies and Indexes, 31
Library Bill of Rights, 202–203
Library Journal, 42, 54, 55, 56, 58–59, 81, 83, 89
The Library Journal Book Review, 58
Library Literature, 57
Library of Congress, 87
Library of Congress Catalogs: Monographic Series, 87
Library of Congress Catalogs: National Union Catalog, see National Union Catalog
Library of Congress Catalogs: Subject Catalog, 86–87

Library of Congress Main Reading Room Reference Collection Subject Catalog, 28, 68
Library of Congress Subject Headings, 77, 88
Limbacher, James L., 33
List of Periodicals for the College Library, see Classified List of Periodicals for the College Library
López Muñoz, J., 115
Lynch, M. J., 98, 99

M

MTLA, see Micropublishers Trade List Annual
Magazines for Libraries, 59, 81
Malclès, Louise-Noelle, 66–68
Malinowsky, H. Robert, 77
"Mansell", 87; *see also National Union Catalog*
Manuel de Bibliographie, 67–68
Marquis Who's Who, Inc., 44
Marshall, Joan K., 81
Meacham, Mary, 79
Media Indexes and Review Sources, 33
Medical Books in Print, 88
Microform Review, 35
Micropublishers Trade List Annual (MTLA), 35
Miller, W., 99
Monthly Catalog, 91
Municipal Government Reference Sources: Publications and Collections, 92

N

National Library Service Cumulative Book Review Index, 54
National Register of Microform Masters, 36
National Union Catalog, 86–87, 91
New Serial Titles, 89
New Serial Titles Classed Subject Arrangements, 89
New York Review of Books, 63
New York Times Book Review, 63, 73
New York Times Book Review Index, 54–55
Notes, 52

O

O'Brien, Jacqueline, 76
Olson, P. E., 101
Orton, Robert, 82
Owen, Dolores, 75

P

PAIS, see Public Affairs Information Service Bulletin
PTLA, see Publishers Trade List Annual
Palic, Vladimir, 92
Paperbacks in Print, 86, 89
Paperbound Books in Print, 86, 88
Parish, David, 92
Periodicals for School Libraries, 81
Peterson, Carolyn Sue, 79
Pierian Press, 44–45
Pirie, James, 79
Public Affairs Information Service Foreign Language Index, 73
Public Affairs Information Services Bulletin (PAIS), 73, 91
Public Library Catalog, 78, 93
Publishers Trade List Annual (PTLA), 41–42, 47, 83
Publishers Weekly, 36, 38, 42, 66, 84–87
Purchasing an Encyclopedia: 12 Points to Consider, 74–75

R

RQ, 59, 83
RSR, see Reference Services Review
Reader's Adviser: A Layman's Guide to Literature, 78
Reference and Subscription Books Reviews, 53, 55, 59–61
Reference Book Review Index, 55
Reference Books for Small and Medium-Sized Libraries, 28, 66–67, 93
Reference Books in Paperback: An Annotated Guide, 67, 69
A Reference Guide to Audio Visual Information, 33
Reference Serials, 75
Reference Services Review (RSR), 45, 61–62, 75
Reference Sources, 55, 62
Reynolds, Michael M., 90
Richards, Berry Gargal, 81
Richardson, John, 92
Rogers, Robert, 77
Rowman & Littlefield, 45
Rufsvold, Margaret I., 33
Ryder, Dorothy, 67

S

Saturday Review, 54
K. G. Saur Publishing, Inc., 45
Scarecrow Press, Inc., 45
Schiller, A. R., 174
Science and Engineering Literature: A Guide to Reference Sources, 77
Scientific and Technical Information Sources, 77
Scott, Marion, 81
Screen, J. E. O., 71–72
Selected U.S. Government Serials: A Guide for Public and Academic Libraries, 91
Selecting Instructional Media, 33
Senior High School Library Catalog, 79
Serials for Libraries, 81
Serials Review, 45, 61, 62, 81, 89, 90
Sheehy, Eugene P., 57, 65–67, 68, 77, 90
The Shoe String Press, Inc., 46
Sive, Mary Robinson, 33
Slocum, Robert B., 70–71
Les Sources du Travail Bibliographique, 66–67
Sources of Information in the Social Sciences, 77
Special Libraries Association Geography and Map Division *Bulletin*, 52
Standard Periodical Directory, 81
State Government Publications: An Annotated Bibliography, 92
Statistical Abstract, 76
Statistics—Africa, 76
Statistics—America, 76
Statistics—Asia and Australasia, 76
Statistics—Europe, 76
Statistics Sources, 76
Subject Guide to Books in Print, 88
Subject Guide to Children's Books in Print, 36, 88
Subject Guide to Forthcoming Books, 83–84, 86
Subject Guide to Government Reference Books, 92
Subject Guide to Microforms in Print, 35
Subject Guide to Reference Books, 55
Subscription Books Bulletin, see Reference and Subscription Books Reviews

T

TLS, see Times Literary Supplement
Taggart, Dorothy T., 33
Taylor, R. S., 101

Technical Book Review Index, 55
Technical Books in Print, 88
Times Literary Supplement (TLS), 63, 73
Toomey, Alice M., 70
Tudor, Dean, 77

U

Ulrich's International Periodicals Directory,
    75, 80–81
Ulrich's Quarterly, 81, 90
United States of America Bibliographical and
    Abstracting Services and Related Activi-
    ties, 59
United States Bureau of Census Catalog of Pub-
    lications, 1790–1972, 76
United States Superintendent of Documents, 91

V

Van Zant, Nancy Patton, 91

W

Walford, Albert, 66, 68–69, 71–72, 90
Walsh, S. Padraig, 69–70
Wasserman, Paul, 31, 76
Weekly Record, 84, 86–87
I. W. Whitaker and Sons, 89
Whitaker's Cumulative Book List, 85–86
White, Carl, 77
Wilkinson, J. P., 99
The H. W. Wilson Company, 46
Wilson Library Bulletin, 46–47, 56, 61, 62–63,
    83, 89
Wine, Beer, and Spirits, 77
Woodworth, David, 81
A World Bibliography of Bibliographies, 45, 52,
    70
A World Bibliography of Bibliographies Sup-
    plement, 1964–74, 70
Wynar, Bohdan, 67, 69
Wynar, Christine E., 33, 79–80
Wynkoop, Sally, 92

Subject Index

A

Acquisitions work, 23
Administration, 137–169
  decision-making, 145–147
  goals and objectives, 151–152
  importance of personal attributes, 139–141
  legal sanctions, 153–154
  policy statements, 152–153
  publicity, 154–155
  responsibility and authority, 144–147
Advising patrons on book purchases, 188–189
Appraisal of books or property, 128
Assignments, dual, *see* Split positions
Associations as publishers, 48
Atlases, selection aids, 69–76

B

Bibliographic guides
  general, 65–69
  special, 76–77
Bibliographic instruction, 11–12, 175–176
Biographical dictionaries, selection aids, 70–71
Bibliographies
  compilation, 15–19
  computer-produced, 16–19
    online and offline, 17–18
    SDI (Selective Dissemination of Information), 18
Bibliotherapy, 178
Body language, 115
Book trade journals, 84–85
Books for children, selection aids, 79–80
Books for college students, selection aids, 78–79
Books for young adults, selection aids, 79–80
Books, selection aids, 65–89
Books, evaluation, 83
Books, selective lists, 77–80
Boolean logic, 112–113
Budget preparation, 158–161
Business community, service to, 177

C

Cataloging and reference service, 192–193
Cataloging work, 23
Censorship, 132, 191–192, 202–203
Certification, 182–184
Clipping files, 21
Collection development policy, 28
College catalogs, 32
Complaints, 132
Computer-assisted search, 113
  costs, 114
  participation of requestor, 113
  searcher qualifications, 18
Computer-produced bibliographies, *see* Bibliographies, computer-produced
Continuing education, 168, 184–185
Correspondence inquiries, 9–10
Counseling services, 12–15
  special subject counseling, 15
Crises, *see* Emergencies
Current awareness, 82–83; *see also* Bibliographies, computer-produced

D

Databases, 36–38
  selection aids, 37–38
Dictionaries, selection aids, 71–73
Directional assistance, 8–9; *see also* Questions, directional
Directional questions, *see* Questions, directional

Directories
  selection aids, 72–73
  updating, 21
Discographies, selection aids, 34
Documents work, 23–24

E

Emergencies, 132–133
Encyclopedias, 73–75
  selection aids, 74–75
Ethics, 190–191, 195–196

F

Fees, 160–161, 179–182
Foreign language reference material
  reviews, 57
  selection aids, 90
Funding, extramural, 159–160

G

Government publications, selection aids,
  91–92
Guides to literature, *see* Bibliographic guides
Guides to reference books, *see* Bibliographic
  guides

H

Handicapped, service to, 154, 177–179
Hours of service, 181

I

I & R (Information and Referral), 13–14
Indexes and abstracts, 75, 80–81
  selection aids, 75
Indexes to library collections, *see* Library
  catalogs and indexes
Indexing, in-house, 19–21; *see also* Library
  catalogs and indexes
Information and referral, *see* I & R
Information desks, *see* Directional assistance
Information files, 19–20, 30–32
Interlibrary loan, 21–23 .
Interview, 114–123
  levels of information need, 118–119
  opening response, 118–119
  style, 96, 115

J

Joint appointments, *see* Split positions

L

Legal questions, *see* Questions, legal
Library catalogs and indexes, 30–32
Library instruction, 10–12
  guides and finding aids, 11
  orientation/tours, 10–11
  training of library staff, 12
Literature search, 101–114
  evaluation of, 123–124

M

Management systems, 141–144
  hierarchical, 141–142
  participative, 142–144
Measurements of activity, 155–157
Media, 32–34
  selection aids, 33–34
Medical questions, *see* Questions, medical
Microform, 34–36
  selection aids, 35–36
Minority views, protecting, 189–190

N

National and trade bibliography, 83–89
Nonbook reference resources, 30–38
Nonprofessionals, *see* Paraprofessionals

O

Opening day collections, 92–93
Organization of reference department, 147–151
Out-of-print material, selection aids, 81–82

P

Paraprofessionals, at the reference desk, 163–
  164, 185–187
Personal interaction, *see* Interview
Personnel, 162–169
  education and expertise, 163–164
  evaluation, 168–169
  full time versus part time, 164–165
  recruitment and selection, 165–166

Policy manual, 134; *see also* Collection development policy
Post-coordinate searching, 112
Pre-coordinate indexing, 112
Problem patrons, 128–131
Professional courtesy, 133–134
Professionals in nonprofessional positions, 187
Propaganda, 189–190
Public relations, 25
Publishers, 41–50
Publishers' catalogs and announcements, 72, 83

Q

Questions
    categories, 98–100
    clarifying, 117–122
    directional, 98–99, 186
    legal, 128
    medical, 128
    open-ended, 119
    problem, 126–128
    referral, 125–126
    success in answering, 99, 123
    unanswered, 124–125

R

Reader's advisory service, 13, 36, 178
Reference book selection, *see* Reference books and serials, evaluation and selection
Reference books and serials
    evaluation and selection, 28–29, 50–52
    publishing, 41–50
    reviews, 52–63
    indexes to, 53–55
Reference collection policy, *see* Collection development policy
Reference desk
    location, 97
    resources, 30–32
    responsibilities at, 131–133
Reference librarians, skills and attributes, 1–5, 162–165
Reference serials, *see* Reference books and serials
Reference service
    guidelines, 197–201
    philosophy, 174–175

Reference transaction, 98–126; *see also* Questions
    evaluation, 123–124
    level of service, 117
Reprints, selection aids, 81–82
Reviews, *see* Reference books and serials, reviews
Rights, librarian's political, 190–191; *see also* Censorship

S

SDI, *see* Bibliographies, computer-produced
Search results, reporting, 114
Search strategy, 101–114
Security of facilities, 181–182
Selection aids, *see specific formats and materials such as* Databases, Encyclopedias, Microforms, Serials
Serials, selection aids, 80–81, 89–90
Serials, selective lists, 81
Serials work, 24
Service desks, 8–9; *see also* Reference desks
Social responsibilities, 189–191
Societies as publishers, 48
Sources for answering questions
    arrangement and access, 104–105, 111–112, 121
    basis for choosing, 105–107
    identifying, 103–104
    vocabulary control, 107–111
Space and facilities, 157–158, 181–182
Specialists, 164, 187–188
Split positions, 23–24
Stack collection, 38
Staff development, 166–168, 184–185
Staffing
    split positions, 23–24
    supplementary, 161–162
        other library staff, 162
        volunteers, 161–162
Statistical sources, selection aids, 75–76
Statistics, *see* Measurements of activity
Subscription books publishing, 48–49

T

Technical services issues, 192–193
Telephone directories, 32

Telephone service, 9, 32, 127–128
Term paper clinics, 14
Theses and dissertations, selection aids, 90
Thesis advising, 14–15
Trade bibliography, *see* National and trade bib-
    liography
Training, 166–168
Troubleshooter, 24–25

U

University presses, 47

V

Vocabulary control, *see* Sources for answering
    questions
Volunteers, *see* Staffing, supplementary